C000276951

EGYPTIAN
MYTHOLOGY

EGYPTIAN MYTHOLOGY

A Traveller's Guide from Aswan to Alexandria

with 58 illustrations

GARRY J. SHAW

CONTENTS

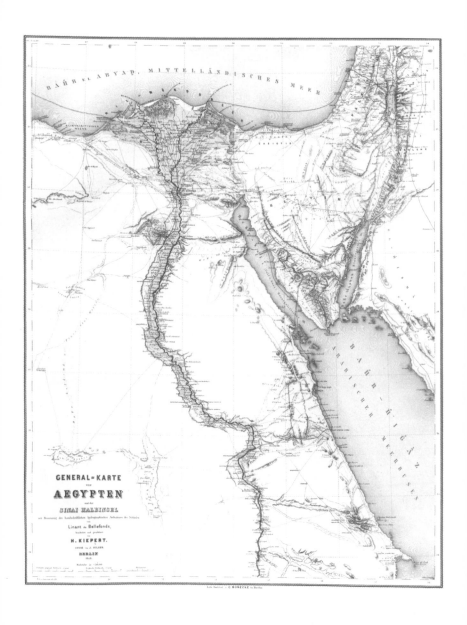

A map of Egypt made after the Prussian expedition of the 1840s, led by German Egyptologist Karl Richard Lepsius. Our journey will take us from Aswan, near the bottom of the map, to Alexandria in the north-west Delta.

INTRODUCTION

∿∿∿∿∿∿∿∿∿

Preparing for a Journey
Along the Nile

You close your eyes and imagine the journey ahead. All of Egypt – with its ancient myths and legends, gods, temples and tombs – lies between you, newly arrived in Aswan, and Alexandria, 850 kilometres (530 miles) to the north. In your mind, you become the falcon god Horus, flying high over the Nile. Your wings catch the wind. You can see far. Look! Over in the distance. That hill is where the sun god defeated the followers of the chaos snake Apophis. The blood of Bastet created that peculiarly coloured rock. Those mounds are the tombs of the most ancient gods. Every stone, hill, temple and town that you pass as you fly over the land has a meaning, tied to the actions of divine forces. The Nile's eternal journey north, cutting its channel through the harsh desert over millions of years, created this landscape. Its water feeds the fields that flank its route. From the rocky bends of the great river in the south, where the Nile flood was believed to erupt into the world from the infinite waters surrounding creation, northwards to Memphis, where it fans out to create the marshy Delta, Egypt is a land of mythology.

Starring in these myths were the hundreds of divinities that comprised Egypt's pantheon, beings that the Egyptians called *netjeru*. On the whole, these were gods with jobs, important roles in the cosmos: Osiris was responsible for processes of regeneration; Re was the sun at its most powerful; Ptah was the creative mind; and so on. These gods had many manifestations, but they weren't everywhere at once. They were powerful, but only within their own areas of influence. They could travel freely throughout creation, but not beyond its limits. They were long-lived, but not immortal. They knew more than you and me, but they didn't know everything. They had human emotions, and human flaws. These powerful forces at work in the Egyptian world could be dangerous or helpful. They were ever changing, ever present and, to the Egyptians, very real.

Egypt's temples were called 'mansions of the gods'. These were exclusive places, where priests, literally the 'god's servants', made offerings to please those divinities who had cosmic responsibilities. These gods lived in the sky, their true forms – like blinding, earth-shaking light – always distant. But they sent down their manifestations to inhabit the statues crafted in their names. In this way, they could smell the sweet incense burning before them; suck the energy from food and drink left in their sanctuaries; feel the freshly washed linens wrapped around their bodies each day. This is what kept them happy. The priests' actions kept the world turning, ensuring the annual flood and harvest and keeping Egypt in the gods' favour. In order to do this successfully, they had to perform the correct rituals, the correct way, every day. To the Egyptians, this was not a belief system, for belief implies the existence of options. This was simply the way the world worked. The gods were a demanding bunch.

But to most people, in their day-to-day lives, the most influential deity wasn't the most important or powerful god in the pantheon. Re had a key role in creation, and was involved in running the cosmos, but when it came to your crops or illness, he had little interest. You wouldn't call the local mayor if your fridge broke down; they might have a lot of power, but their interest in your fridge is limited. It's the same with the Egyptian gods. Yes, Re might be able to help you with your field or your ailments, but realistically, he has better things to do. The oldest or most powerful god is not always the first port of call.

Rather than worrying about Re's opinion of them while he went about his business in the cosmos, most people were more concerned about demons and ghosts. Demons inhabited the dark realm of the Duat, a place that was sometimes beneath the ground, sometimes in the sky. Such beings could escape this place through caves and bodies of water to terrorize the living, bringing sickness and disease. Ghosts, too, walked the earth, and could enter people's homes, in a threatening or helpful capacity, depending on their mood. But it wasn't all bleak. Popular household gods also had a particular influence on daily life, such as Bes and Taweret, who looked after women and children, or Renenutet, who was responsible for the harvest. And the ancestors were never far from people's minds, because they had a direct line to the gods.

All of these beings – great or small – were as much a part of Egypt's environment as the desert, fields, cities, towns, villages and temples.

The Egyptians knew they were all around us, all the time. The supernatural permeated every aspect of life and death. Myths, told around campfires, spread through literature or kept in temple libraries, explained this world through the actions of gods and the invisible. They brought order and understanding to the chaos of life, and comfort in hard times. Myths are more than stories; they are a reflection of us, representing a universal human need to make sense of reality.

Assembling Egyptian myths: our sources

How do we know any of this, you might be asking? The short answer is: with difficulty. Many problems face anyone attempting to reassemble the myths of ancient Egypt. There was no single source that gathered all the myths together – no holy book of Egyptian religion. Myths are found in a variety of places, from temple and tomb walls to magic spells, but these often don't include all the details we'd need to reconstruct the myth. Rather, we tend to find allusions to the myths, their meaning clear to readers or listeners who were already aware of the broader story. Episodes in the myths were also omitted for religious reasons. Art and texts were believed to have the power to magically bring whatever was represented or described into being. So, because temples and tombs were sacred spaces, requiring any inscription or carving to exhibit the perfection of divine order (*maat*), the Egyptians avoided directly mentioning ritually dangerous aspects of myths, or parts that would introduce disorder to the environment – so, the death of Osiris, a fundamental mythic event in Egyptian afterlife belief (see Chapter 6), is never mentioned directly.

Mythological snippets can most often be found on temple walls, in carved scenes that show – and so recreate for eternity – the rituals and festivals performed before the gods; or in funerary texts, magical inscriptions meant to assist the dead in the afterlife by describing key locations, divinities, dangerous beings and helpful rituals and spells. At different times, such texts were inscribed on the interior walls of royal pyramids, in the tombs in the Valley of the Kings, on the sides of nobles' coffins or written on papyrus rolls, placed near the deceased – a collection of spells today known as 'The Book of the Dead'. Other abbreviated myths are found in sources from daily life: for example, at the start of magic spells, often used to cure illnesses, giving them a divine precedent when the gods used the same magic. This reassured the user that the spell had worked in the mythological past, so it would work again. The writings of Greek and Roman authors are important sources too, though these were sometimes adapted for their non-Egyptian audience.

Egypt's priests also kept 'mythological manuals' in their libraries, accounts of local traditions, written on papyrus rolls, some of which survive in a fragmentary state. These same myths can sometimes be found inscribed in stone on temple walls – a clever way of ensuring their survival for future generations of priests. As guides to the myths of Egypt's various regions – called 'nomes' by Egyptologists, using the Greek term – they are an excellent resource for understanding local myths, and often feature the nome's god in a prominent role, promoted to the prime god in mythology. These myths tend to be aetiological, explaining how a local topographical feature – a hill, a lake, the colour of certain rocks – came to be, or the reason for the location of a temple. Indeed, the need to explain is one of the prime reasons for Egyptian myths; even myths recorded on temple walls tend to be inscribed only to provide a reason why certain rituals were performed, or why certain festivals were celebrated in that location.

So, although we know the major cult centres of Egypt's gods and goddesses – the places we visit in this book – their mythology must be reassembled using all the evidence at our disposal, not just that found in the local area from a particular phase of history. With such varied sources, spread over time and space, each providing limited information in an ancient language, any attempt at reconstructing a myth is somewhat artificial, and must include a degree of interpretation. This is somewhat fitting, given that there was no fixed, correct version of any of Egypt's myths anyway. All the best tales are fluid, reshaped again and again by storytellers for their readers or listeners. This book is my attempt to shape Egypt's myths for you.

Egyptian chronology and history

You're almost ready to leave. But before you go, let's first get to grips with Egypt's history and chronology. The time frame covered by 'ancient Egypt' is around 3,000 years, from *c.* 3150 BC, when we find the first kings of a unified country, through to the death of Cleopatra VII in 30 BC (and even longer if you include the Roman phase). During the 3rd century BC, a priest named Manetho looked back over history and organized Egypt's kings into thirty royal dynasties. He presented each as an individual family line, ruling one after the other, and wrote down the lengths of the king's reigns, creating an early chronological framework. But it is now clear that some of his dynasties include unrelated rulers, while at other times, families are split across dynasties. Some family lines, presented as successive by Manetho, actually ruled simultaneously in different locations. An additional problem is that Manetho's text, called the *Aegyptiaca*, has only survived in the writings of later authors, so there is no complete and original version for us to read.

Nonetheless, today, after two centuries of excavation and textual analysis, and with the help of scientific techniques, Egyptologists have built on Manetho's framework, clarifying the lengths and order of kings' reigns to roughly establish when in time they ruled. In turn, events that occurred under these kings can now be assigned dates. They've also placed his dynasties into longer phases, divided according to whether they were 'kingdoms' – periods of political unity in which a single king reigned at any given time – or times of division known as intermediate periods, when the rulers of separate (sometimes competing) dynasties overlapped in different parts of the country. This time span, covering Egypt's thirty dynasties, can, as a whole, be called the Pharaonic Period or the Dynastic Period. In addition, before the 1st Dynasty and the unification of Egypt, there was the Predynastic Period, while at the other end of the chronological line, after a phase of renewed Persian rule (sometimes referred to as the 31st Dynasty) and the brief reign of Alexander the Great and his family, there was the Ptolemaic Period, ending with Cleopatra VII, and then the Roman Period. This phase of Greek and Roman rule can be referred to jointly as the Graeco-Roman Period.

Egyptologists are still refining the chronology of ancient Egypt, particularly its earliest phases. Dates after 664 BC are accurate, but the

The chronology of ancient Egypt

Predynastic Period			*c.* 5000–3150 BC	
Dynastic Period		Early Dynastic Period	*c.* 3150–2584 BC	Dynasties 1–2
		Old Kingdom	*c.* 2584–2117 BC	Dynasties 3–6
		First Intermediate Period	*c.* 2117–2066 BC	Dynasties 7–11
		Middle Kingdom	*c.* 2066–1781 BC	Dynasties 11–12
		Second Intermediate Period	*c.* 1781–1549 BC	Dynasties 13–17
		New Kingdom	*c.* 1549–1069 BC	Dynasties 18–20
		Third Intermediate Period	*c.* 1069–664 BC	Dynasties 21–25
		Late Period	664–332 BC	Dynasties 26–31
Ptolemaic Period			332–30 BC	
Roman Period			30 BC–AD 395	

further back in time we go, the greater the margin of error. By the time we reach the Early Dynastic Period, our date estimates could be off by about a century. New discoveries can also alter our knowledge of the lengths of kings' reigns. For these reasons, you'll find that books offer slightly different chronologies. It also means that if you invent a time machine, I, and other Egyptologists, can't be blamed for you missing the construction of the Great Pyramid by several decades. We're trying our best. In this book, the chronology used follows Dodson and Hilton's *The Complete Royal Families of Ancient Egypt* (2004).

Bon voyage!
I think you're now ready to begin your journey. Whether this is your first visit to Egypt or your thousandth, my hope is that this book will shine a new light on your experiences in this ancient country. As you turn the pages, you'll become a modern-day Herodotus, travelling along the Nile from city to city, town to town, village to village, hearing about the ancient Egyptians' myths, legends and stories. Whether you're an armchair traveller, picturing the journey in your mind; on a Nile cruise, exploring new sites every day as you drift along the river; or backpacking the length of the country on a shoestring, this book will help you to get a feel for the monuments you see, and more importantly, the beliefs held by the ancient Egyptians who built them.

Places can go by many names in Egypt, ranging from their transcribed names from ancient Egyptian, their Greek or Roman names, and their modern Arabic names. In this book, I've decided to use whichever name a given location is most popularly known by; thus you will find the Egyptian Pi-Ramesses, the Greek Hermopolis and the Arabic Dendera all sharing these pages. The same goes for the names of people and divinities: if a god or goddess is best known by their Greek name, that's the one I use. So, here it is Thoth rather than Djehuty; Osiris not Asir; Isis not Iset. For names transcribed from the ancient Egyptian language, there are also a great many variations, because the Egyptians didn't write down vowels. In the end, the spelling used tends to depend on personal preference. I prefer Re to Ra, for example, and Amun to Amen. Just to confuse things though, I write Amenhotep rather than Amunhotep.

This book takes a different approach to Egyptian mythology from many others. By presenting the myths location by location, we get a feel for how varied Egyptian mythology was; how each location had its primary family of deities and local beliefs, while still guest-starring gods and goddesses from other parts of the country. Many locations had their own mythic explanation for the creation of the world, or of local geography, but still fitted into the same wider system of beliefs about the workings of the cosmos and the afterlife. What emerges from this new approach is the freedom to tell different stories – ones that go beyond a narrative history of the gods and their experiences to show what people in different parts of the country believed.

So, here we go.

It's time to board the boat, cast off the mooring rope and set sail. Remember, if the past is another country, mythology is another world. There's as much you'll find confusing as you'll find fascinating. But in the end, isn't that all part of the fun of travel? Whatever your feelings are on the journey, when you get back, you'll definitely have a story to tell.

Enjoy the ride.

The ruins of the Temple of Isis on Philae Island, before its removal to Agilkia Island.
In ancient times, pilgrims travelled great distances to visit this temple.

1

ASWAN

~~~~~~~~~~~~~~~~~~~~~

At the Edge of the World

'Isis, the great one, mother of the god, lady of Philae,
wife of the god, who praises the god.... She is the lady of the sky,
the land, and Duat [the afterlife realm], who caused them to come into
being through what her heart created and what her arms made.'

From two hymns in the sanctuary of the Temple of Isis at Philae, c. 250 BC.

The River Nile gently splashes against the boulders clinging to its banks
and islands. Their grey granite surfaces have been smoothed and
rounded by millennia of relentlessly flowing water. Feluccas – small
wooden sail boats, painted red, white and green – bob up and down
on the shores. They share the river with larger sail boats called dahabi-
yas, the preferred luxury vessels of Victorian travellers. Today, mammoth
cruise ships are more popular. They dock along the east bank's riverfront, and the city of Aswan stretches off behind them. Hotels and
restaurants await their guests. Vendors in souqs sell fruits, meat, spices,
cloth and souvenirs. Minarets, apartment blocks and the dome and
spires of a Coptic cathedral rise above the trees that line the river's
edge. On the opposite side of the Nile, along its west bank, sandy hills
slope upwards to the desert plateau, forming a natural border to the
living world. The tombs of ancient nobles are cut into this escarpment,
beside the domed Mausoleum of Aga Khan, built in the 1950s for the
burial of the spiritual leader of the Nizari Ismailis Sir Sultan Mahomed
Shah, Aga Khan III. Several kilometres to the south is Philae, the sacred
island of the goddess Isis. Two thousand years ago, this was the destination of pilgrims from across the known world, drawn by the goddess's
fame as a healer. This region has always been a tourist magnet.

Meanwhile, I'm sitting on Elephantine, a relaxed island in the
middle of the Nile, a short ferry ride from Aswan's riverfront. Around

me, the foundations of mud-brick houses that were long ago abandoned and reclaimed by the sand have been exhumed by archaeologists. The remains of a temple to the god Khnum are scattered to my side. Two jambs of a gateway, decorated with images of the king and local gods, represent the only part still standing. Khnum's granite shrine lies tipped on its back – he can't be pleased. A short distance away is a temple dedicated to the goddess Satet, its angular shape reconstructed from excavated blocks. Smaller temples have been moved and reconstructed near the Nile shore. There was even once a temple to Yahweh, representing the island's ancient Jewish population. Everywhere you look, there are ruins from across Egyptian history. Elephantine's romantic jumble of time-worn walls and rubble gives the impression that long ago, everyone decided to just pick up and move, rather than tidy up the mess they'd made.

Aswan, with the island of Elephantine as its ancient heart, marks the beginning of the first cataract of the Nile, a rocky zone full of rapids and swirling pools that served as a natural barrier between Egypt and Nubia, a region to its south that at times belonged to the powerful Kingdom of Kush in Sudan. Aswan was a border, a trading centre, a home to military garrisons. And its ruins were left by a diverse population: settlers, traders, soldiers, foreign mercenaries, tourists, priests and pilgrims – people who had moved from across Egypt and beyond to make a living on the edge of the world. Storytelling thrives in such conditions. Before pilgrims' stories brought international fame to the Temple of Isis on Philae Island, the people of Aswan were already known throughout Egypt for their myths and legends about the river, its deities and its power. After all, this wasn't just a place of commerce and border controls, it was where the Egyptians believed the Nile began.

The waters of creation and the Nile flood

Where does the water of the Nile come from? This is a question that many ancient Egyptians pondered. They never reached a consensus. It was answered in a variety of ways depending on the time period or the city. Sometimes the Nile was the sweat of the crocodile god Sobek, or the efflux of Osiris, king of the blessed dead. Sometimes it was the tears of Osiris' sisters, the goddesses Isis and Nephthys, shed after the murder of their brother. In other myths, the waters entered Egypt from outside the great disc on which we all live. Beyond our bubble of creation was an infinite, inert and dark water – the Egyptians' equivalent of outer space, which they believed to be a manifestation of the god Nun. Nun existed before the first mound of land, before the first gods, and the first sunrise. But once the world had come into being – a process that we'll see took many forms – Nun flowed through it as water, most dramatically as the Nile.

According to the Egyptians, the Nile entered Egypt in the Aswan region, erupting from two caverns at Elephantine Island, or from the nearby rocky island of Biga, just south of Aswan beside the island of Philae. A temple scribe at Sais repeated a similar story to the Greek historian Herodotus during the 5th century BC. The scribe told Herodotus that between Aswan and Elephantine were two sharp-peaked hills, and between them were the springs of the Nile. From there, one half of the water went north and the other half flowed south. King Psamtik I (r. *c.* 664–610 BC) of the 26th Dynasty plunged an extremely long rope into the water there, only to discover that it was bottomless, Herodotus adds.

A map of Aswan made by the Napoleonic mission around 1800.
The Egyptians believed that the source of the Nile was in the Aswan region.

The Egyptians saw the waters of Nun above and below them, too. The sky is blue because it's the underside of the infinite Nun, held back by the magical force of the goddess Nut. The gods sail in boats on this water, manifesting as heavenly bodies, explaining the movement and path of the sun, the moon, the planets and stars. And sometimes – though not frequently in a country as hot as Egypt – this water falls into our world as rain. You can see Nun emerging from the earth, too. If you dig deep enough, you reach water. It gurgles up from caverns, or from the underworld that the Egyptians called the Duat.

Because the Egyptians believed the Nile to be part of the infinite Nun, they never worshipped it as a distinct deity in itself. But the Nile flood was a different matter. Between June and September each year, like clockwork, the Nile rose and burst its banks for a few months. This phenomenon was key to Egypt's success: the floodwater washed away the old, used soil and replaced it with new, fertile silt, perfect for agriculture. One of the gods believed responsible for the annual inundation, or who at least personified it, was Hapy, who lived in a cave at Elephantine (or sometimes more generally in the cataract region). He was a god of fertility and rejuvenation, shown in human form, often with blue skin, a swollen stomach, and breasts. And because the goddess Isis was associated with Sirius, a star that rose just before the sun at dawn after seventy days of disappearance, heralding the start of the flood season, she was believed to pour Hapy from his cave. As a daughter of Nun, the goddess Hathor – more usually a deity of sex, music and love – also had influence over the annual inundation. One of her titles was 'Lady of the Caverns' – a reference to the waters erupting from the caves in the Aswan region.

To other Egyptians, the floodwaters emerged from the wounded leg of Osiris, kept at Elephantine after his brother Seth murdered him and cut his body into pieces. Indeed, the Greek author Plutarch wrote that the Egyptians believed all water to be discharge from Osiris' corpse. Osiris had a tomb on the island of Biga (not the only Osiris tomb in Egypt), south of Aswan. His body was carried there by a crocodile – probably a manifestation of Horus. Osiris' feet were kept as relics on Biga, and each foot was regarded as a source of the Nile. Every ten days, a statue of Isis travelled from her temple on the island of Philae to the tomb of Osiris on Biga, watched and celebrated by pilgrims.

The divine family of Aswan: Khnum, Satet and Anuket

Despite the importance of Nun, Hapy, Hathor and Isis at Aswan, it was the ram-headed god Khnum who was most celebrated in the region.

Typically shown wearing an *atef*-crown – a tall and bulbous crown with horns, most often associated with Osiris – Khnum had an important temple complex on Elephantine Island, now ruined but open to the public, which he shared with his wife Satet and daughter Anuket. A second major temple to Khnum stands further north, along the Nile at Esna (though here he has a different family – scandal!). Khnum was another god believed to control the Nile inundation, and the Egyptians worshipped him as a creator, particularly of humans and especially of the king. For this reason, in art they showed him shaping people on a potter's wheel, sometimes along with the person's *ka*-spirit – a form of life-force, or their spiritual double.

The Great Hymn to Khnum, inscribed on the walls of his temple in Esna, describes the god's creative role in detail. To his followers, Khnum created all things, from people (both Egyptian and foreign) and deities, to birds, fish and cattle. When it was time for a woman to give birth, Khnum made it happen. And unlike other gods, who completed their acts of creation at the beginning of time and then went off to take up other pursuits, Khnum's creative process was ongoing, symbolized by his ever-turning potter's wheel. On this wheel, he created every living thing. He made hair grow, formed bones, placed skin on limbs, built the head and fashioned the face. He made the mouth and tongue, the eyes, ears, throat, heart, spine, bladder and every other part of the body. The Egyptians celebrated Khnum's creative role during an annual festival at Esna, when the temple priests, acting as gods, explained how they helped to create the first royal child on Khnum's potter's wheel. Following various rituals, including lighting torches and making purifications, the priests performed a rite in which the power of Khnum was transferred into women. This was called 'the placing of the (potter's) wheel in the belly of all female beings'.

Khnum's wife, Satet, was a goddess of the waters that purified and brought fertility and new life to Egypt's fields. She wears the White Crown of Upper (southern) Egypt adorned with antelope horns, and like other powerful goddesses, could manifest as the dangerous Eye of Re (more on this in Chapter 5). A Satet shrine existed on Elephantine from at least the Early Dynastic Period, long before the Egyptians raised any temples to Khnum in the region. It consisted of little more than simple mud-brick walls built against three boulders, which stood on the spot where the Egyptians believed they could hear the floodwaters gurgle before the inundation. When it came time to construct a more elaborate temple to Satet, the Egyptians built above this early shrine, burying it beneath the floor. Over centuries, they did the same for every subsequent iteration of the temple, leaving a series of Satet temples for archaeologists to discover millennia later.

Khnum and Satet's daughter was Anuket, who wears a headdress of tall feathers. She personified Egypt's southern border, the land of Nubia beyond, and the Nile flood. The Egyptians dedicated a temple to Anuket on Sehel Island, just south of Aswan, and carved inscriptions for her on the surrounding rocks. Many of these inscriptions were left by expedition teams to thank the goddess for their safe return from Nubia, or to ask her in advance for a successful journey. The most famous inscription on the island is that on the Famine Stele, composed in the Ptolemaic Era, but pretending to be of 3rd Dynasty date to give it some 'ancient authority'. Dedicated to Khnum, Satet and Anuket, it is carved on a boulder with a huge mouth-like horizontal fracture, giving the impression that the stone itself might narrate the inscription to visitors. The tale goes as follows: It was a time of famine. The Nile hadn't flooded properly for seven years. Grain was in short supply. The people were miserable. And even temples had closed. Searching for a solution, King Djoser (r. *c.* 2584–2565 BC) asked his chief lector-priest, Imhotep – better known today as the architect behind Djoser's Step Pyramid at Saqqara – to find the source of the inundation. Imhotep duly visited the sanctuary of Thoth at Hermopolis to consult the sacred scrolls, and there found his answer: Elephantine. He reported his findings to the king, telling him that Khnum was the region's god, and that it was this divinity who, when he so desired, opened the floodgates. Djoser listened carefully to Imhotep's words, and before going to sleep that night, made an offering to Khnum. The god must have been pleased, for he appeared to Djoser in a dream, telling him that he had released the waters. In thanks, Djoser made a royal decree, giving the cult of Khnum at Elephantine the right to a share of the taxation from local produce and imports from Nubia.

Imprisoned on Elephantine: the unfinished tale of the magician Hihor

The short tale of the magician Hihor, written during the 1st century BC, features the island of Elephantine. It's incomplete in places, but begins with a letter from a man to the pharaoh, in which he says that he will tell a story of birds and Hihor the magician. After a break in the text, we learn that Hihor had been incarcerated in Pharaoh's prison on the island of Elephantine (perhaps a bit like an ancient Alcatraz). Luckily, help arrived in an unusual form. A hen and a duck, each given life by Hihor when still in their eggs, had travelled to Egypt in search of the magician. They quickly learned of Hihor's predicament and visited the prison. Sat at its entrance, they said: 'O Hihor, if you write your story on two papyrus rolls, we'll drop them into the palace's hall before Pharaoh.' Not one to turn down advice from helpful poultry, Hihor did as suggested. He gave one scroll to the duck and the other to the hen, and made a third copy for good measure. The birds left to complete their mission. Sadly, the story breaks off here, but we must assume that it ended with the king releasing the unfortunate Hihor. The use of wise words to win the king's favour was a common theme in Egyptian literature.

Sailing past Biga Island: the 'Tale of the Shipwrecked Sailor'

Because of Aswan's importance as a trading centre, the town was the start and end point for many expeditions south into Nubia, a source of many luxury goods, such as animal skins, ebony, ivory and incense, and, most importantly, gold. The 'Tale of the Shipwrecked Sailor', a classic of Egyptian literature, tells the story of one such mission. The story opens with a boat sailing north, returning from Nubia to Egypt. When the boat was passing the island of Biga, just south of Aswan, a member of the crew approached his captain, who was in a despondent state. 'Although our expedition to Nubia was a failure,' the sailor said, 'at least the crew have returned home safely – surely that's something?' The ship's captain wasn't swayed from his depression. He worried about meeting the king, fearing the royal response. The sailor urged the captain to purify himself before entering the royal presence, and to answer the king's questions clearly. 'Don't stammer. Speak smartly,' the sailor advised. 'What a man says can save him.' The captain continued to ignore the sailor. Nothing, it seemed, would help. In one final endeavour to inspire his superior, the sailor told his own story.

The sailor had once travelled on an expedition to the sovereign's mines, crossing the great green sea with a crew of 120 men. But the ship sailed into a storm. A huge wave rose from the waters and tore the ship apart. None survived except the sailor, who clung to the broken mast with all his strength. Alone now, he drifted to an island. He spent three days unconscious on its shore. When he came to, he picked himself up and built a shelter. Then, he searched for food. Luckily for him, the island was a land of plenty: there were figs, grapes, vegetables, fish, birds. More than he could eat. In thanks, the sailor made a burnt offering for the gods.

Thunder crashed through the air. Trees tumbled. The ground quaked. The sailor hid his face. When he finally removed his fingers from his eyes, a snake reared before him. It stretched 15 metres (50 feet) long; its body was gold, its eyebrows lapis lazuli. Its beard alone was a metre (3 feet) in length. These were the features of a divinity. The sailor threw himself on his belly, supplicating himself before the giant snake. 'Who brought you to this island?' the snake said. 'I will burn you to ashes if you don't reply quickly.' The sailor, in shock, could only utter two sentences: 'You speak, but I can't hear it. You stand in front of me, but I don't know myself.' The snake – perhaps confused – gripped the sailor in his mouth and slithered to his resting place. There, again, the snake asked the sailor who had brought him to the island. Bending his arms in adoration, the sailor explained that he had been on a mission for the king, en route to the mines, when his ship had been destroyed and his crew killed. The snake listened carefully and relaxed. 'Don't be afraid,' he said. 'God let you live. He brought you here, to this magical island, where there is an abundance of every good thing.' The sailor would spend four months on the island, the snake told him, and then be rescued by a boat manned by sailors that he knew. The sailor would return to the royal residence and one day be buried in Egypt.

The snake was touched by the sailor's plight, because he himself had once experienced similar suffering. A long time ago, the snake told the sailor, he had lived on this island with seventy-four other snakes. One day, while the snake was away, a star fell to earth. When it crashed into the ground, its flames burned his family to death, and the snake returned to find only a pile of corpses. He died for them that day. So, just like the sailor, he had survived disaster alone. The snake urged the sailor to be brave. To have self-control. If he did, the sailor would embrace his children once again, kiss his wife and see his home. The sailor lay on his belly, touching the ground in adoration of the snake. He told the snake that he would relate his story to the king, and ensure that offerings, including burning incense from myrrh, would be made to him in Egypt's temples. The snake laughed: 'You don't have a great deal of myrrh,' he said. 'I am the Ruler of Punt, and myrrh belongs to me. Once you leave this island, you'll never see it again. It will vanish beneath the waves.'

These words must have been on the sailor's mind when, finally, a boat arrived. From the top of a tall tree, the sailor watched the crew. He recognized them, just as the snake had predicted. He went to tell the snake, but he already knew. The snake told the sailor that he would see his children. His only request was that the sailor make a good name for him in his city. The boat reached the shore, and thanks to the snake's kindness, the Egyptians filled its hull with precious items, incense and ivory, monkeys, myrrh and galena (eye paint). The sailor praised the snake one final time. The snake told him that he would reach the royal residence after two months of sailing – another prediction that came true. The sailor brought the island's exotic goods to the king, who rewarded him with a promotion and 200 servants.

The sailor's tale ended. By now, he hoped to have convinced his captain that some good can come from even the worst situations. But the captain dismissed the sailor's advice. 'Who gives water to a bird on the morning that it will be slaughtered?' he said. What's the point of offering hope to the doomed? It's a twist ending, and a cliffhanger – perhaps, somewhere out in the desert, a lost papyrus bears the sequel.

The goddess Isis and her temple on Philae Island

Let's now leave Aswan and Elephantine behind, and travel the short distance south to Philae, sacred island of the goddess Isis. The Temple of Isis on Philae was built and decorated under Kings Ptolemy II and III during the 3rd century BC, though other monuments on the island date as early as the 4th century BC. What had perhaps begun life as a small outpost where soldiers worshipped Isis soon transformed into an important place of pilgrimage for people from across the Mediterranean and North Africa. Kushites, Greeks and Romans all visited the island, many leaving graffiti in their own languages on its monuments. The island was so popular that it remained a place of pilgrimage for 700 years,

View of the Temple of Isis on Philae Island from Biga,
an island associated with Osiris.

Carving from the Temple of Isis at Philae. The goddesses Isis (right) and Nephthys (left) protect the resurrected Osiris after his murder by their brother, Seth. The god Hapy kneels at bottom right.

right up to the 6th century AD. But why did these pilgrims make this long journey to southern Egypt? Who was Isis? And what did she mean to them?

Although the Temple of Isis on Philae was constructed late in Egyptian history, the earliest evidence for the goddess herself dates back to the 5th Dynasty, 2,000 years earlier. Isis was powerful in magic, a mother goddess, a protector of the dead and ensurer of the harvest. Like other goddesses, she could be the uraeus (rearing cobra) that defended the sun god and the king. Isis was also the star Sirius (Sopdet to the Egyptians, Sothis to the Greeks), whose rising marked the coming Nile inundation and the start of the solar new year. In art, Isis usually takes human form, wearing a throne hieroglyph on her head – the symbol that spells out her name. Sometimes, she wears horns, in the same manner as the goddess Hathor, making it difficult to differentiate between the two. Her family is the most important in Egyptian religion; to say that they had a complex relationship would be an understatement. A daughter of the sky goddess Nut and the earth god Geb, Isis was sister to Nephthys, Seth and Osiris, who was also her husband. With Osiris, she conceived Horus. Much mythology centres on the interactions between these gods.

After Isis' husband Osiris came to the throne, he was murdered by their brother Seth. Her mourning for Osiris became a symbol of grief in Egypt, painted on tomb walls and coffins, and the subject of funerary hymns. One hymn presents Isis calling out to her husband and weeping because he cannot hear her. Nephthys proclaims that Osiris' enemy (Seth) has fallen, and that she will be Osiris' bodyguard for eternity.

As well as symbolizing grief, Isis also represented motherhood. When Isis discovered Osiris' body, she used her magic to become pregnant with Horus, the child that would avenge his father's murder and take the throne of Egypt. The story of her pregnancy, and how she protected the infant Horus from Seth, was another popular topic that endured in mythology throughout Egyptian history. You can see a carving of Isis nursing the child Horus on a wall of the Temple of Philae's birth house (*mammisi*), a chapel dedicated to the god's birth.

Myths of Isis and Horus

After murdering Osiris, Seth imprisoned Isis in the spinning house of Sais, condemning her to an eternity of weaving. But Isis escaped and fled to Khemnis, a marshland in Egypt's Delta. Shortly afterwards, as she slept one night, a flash of lightning awoke her. In that moment, Isis realized that she was pregnant with Osiris' child. She predicted that her son would defeat Seth and asked the gods to protect him in her womb. Re-Atum, the sun god in his most powerful and ancient forms combined, appeared and questioned Isis: 'How do you know that your child is a god?' he said. Isis, perhaps taken a little aback, emphasized that she was the most glorious (or powerful) of the gods – an attestation of her trustworthiness – and repeated her assertion: a god was within her body, the seed of Osiris. Re-Atum accepted that what she was saying was true.

The gods satisfied, Thoth, deity of wisdom, suggested that Isis continue to hide from Seth. It was a wise bit of advice, for at the moment of Horus' birth, ten months into Isis' pregnancy, Seth's bed began to shake and his heart trembled. He understood that a contender for his throne had arrived in the world – and he went on a rampage. He set the Delta marshes on fire. He destroyed papyrus plants. And because he (somehow) knew that Horus would be a falcon, he even went from nest to nest, scrutinizing chicks. Nothing would deter him from finding his foe. Yet, Isis and Horus managed to evade Seth by living always on the move in the Delta marshes.

One of the longer accounts of Horus' youth is found in a story called 'Isis and the Seven Scorpions'. It goes as follows: Isis and Horus were travelling by palanquin, accompanied by seven scorpions, their protectors. This isn't the best way to keep a low profile, admittedly, but Isis had at least instructed the scorpions not to speak to anyone until they reached their destination. She didn't want people spreading news of her movements to Seth. One day, as they passed through a village, Isis, Horus and the seven scorpions decided that they needed a place to rest for the night, so they stopped at the house of a wealthy woman. Isis asked the woman for help, but without a moment's hesitation, she slammed her door in the goddess's face. The scorpions fumed at this insult. They wanted revenge.

While Isis found lodging with a poor woman, the scorpions combined their venom on the stinger of Tefen, the most powerful among them. With Isis distracted, Tefen left the group. He snuck beneath the wealthy woman's front door. He scurried over to the woman's son. And in a moment of pure vengeance, he swung his tail at his target. Tefen's stinger pierced the boy's skin with ease. Pain erupted in the child's body. He felt on fire. His mother ran out into the street, begging for anyone to come to their aid. No one came. But Isis saw her and offered to help. She regarded the child as guiltless in the rich woman's selfish actions. Putting her arms around the boy, Isis commanded the poison to leave his body. She named aloud each scorpion's poison one by one, gaining power over them and compelling them to leave. The boy immediately felt better. When the emergency was over, Isis scolded her scorpions: 'You were meant to keep out of trouble!' she yelled. In thanks, the wealthy woman gave her possessions to Isis and filled the poor woman's house with wonderful things.

Isis' magic and the secret name of Re

As a goddess 'Great of Magic', Isis was often invoked in spells of healing, an aspect of her divinity that became more pronounced over the centuries. One papyrus describes her as practising the art of Re and as a physician of the god. Such spells often included an introduction citing a time when the goddess had used the spell effectively – a mythological precedent, 'proving' that it had worked in the past and would work for you in the present. One spell presents Horus and Seth fighting for the 'Unique Bush'. Horus develops a headache, so Isis gives him something to help. This introduces a magical cure for headaches, using buds from the plant called the 'Unique Bush'. In another spell, Horus eats a golden *abdu*-fish from the edge of the pure pool of Re. This leaves him with stomach pains, so he tells his mother, who provides a spell to cure him. In another, Horus runs across the desert, a place of flames, where he is confronted by a fire demon. He says that if his mother were there, she would help him. Isis then appears and threatens the demon, saying that its dwelling place is filled with water from her mouth. This spell was meant to cure a person of burns.

How did Isis become so powerful in magic? The myth of 'Isis and the Secret Name of Re', set during Re's reign on earth, provides an explanation. It was well known that Re could take many forms and had many names. But his true name, like that of all the gods, remained hidden in his belly. This ensured that sorcerers couldn't use its power against him, for if a person knew a deity's true name, it gave them access to their magic – and there was no god more powerful than Re. The goddess Isis, rebellious and smart, wanted to know the true name of the sun god. By this time, Re had become old and his mouth sagged. One day, as Isis watched unnoticed, a dribble of saliva trickled from Re's mouth to the floor. Knowing that all divine fluids are imbued with creative power, she kneaded the saliva with some earth to create a snake. It burst into life. She then placed the snake on a crossroads where Re walked each day, pondering the Two Lands (Upper and Lower Egypt). All she had to do was wait.

Later that day, as Re strolled with his entourage, the snake bit him. Re felt as if he were on fire. It was so hot that nearby pine trees burst into flames. Re called out to the other deities in his following. 'I've been stung,' he said. 'By something I didn't create! Yet I'm the ultimate creator! What's going on?' He began to suffer intense pain. His heart burned. His body shook. His lips trembled. Various gods, knowledgeable in magic, came to offer their help, but only Isis could truly cure the ailing sun god. She approached Re, and he explained his predicament and symptoms to her. He began to sweat. His vision was failing. 'What is your name?' Isis asked. 'I made the sky, the land and the water,' Re said, before listing further accomplishments as his names. But none of this relieved his suffering. The venom just burned more intensely. Once again, Isis asked Re for his name – his true name. With the pain worsening with every passing second, Re asked Isis to bring her ears close to him, so that his secret name could leave his belly and enter hers. She had to keep it secret, but could pass it to her son Horus, so long as he was bound with a divine oath. Once Isis learned Re's true name, she uttered a spell to cure the god, destroying the venom and saving his life.

Isis battles Seth

Although in Egyptian mythology it's normally Horus who battles Seth for the throne of Egypt, or Anubis who fights him to protect Osiris' corpse from mutilation, Isis fought Seth too. One such tale is recorded on the Papyrus Jumilhac. Seth had gathered his followers, so Isis decided to march against them. She hid on a mountain until the murderous god and his army neared, and when the right moment arrived, she transformed into the fearsome goddess Sekhmet (goddesses often took the form of Sekhmet when angry). Fire shot through the air. She burned nearly all of Seth's followers alive, but Seth escaped the flames and transformed into a bull, ready to fight. Two can play at that game, thought Isis, so she turned into a dog with a knife for a tail. Seth chased Isis, but she was faster than him. As Seth ran, he ejaculated onto the ground and his semen transformed into plants. Isis mocked him – being a divinity of pure testosterone and aggression could be embarrassing for Seth sometimes. Further north, and now in a safe location, Isis transformed into a snake. Again she waited. When Seth and his remaining followers arrived, she bit them all, killing them and spreading their blood across the mountain. In another version of this myth, Isis took the form of a rearing cobra and hid on a mountain waiting for Seth's followers. As they passed her, she bit them all and threw knives into their bodies, killing them.

Isis goes international

Isis was clearly an important goddess, central to Egyptian mythology, and worshipped in temples across the country, so why did the Temple of Isis at Philae specifically become so popular? And why did people from the world over visit it in such great numbers? For the answer, we need to look to the Hellenistic Age, the 300-year period from the death of Alexander the Great in 323 BC – when Greek culture spread across his fast-won empire – to the death of Cleopatra and Roman dominance. This represented a new phase in Eastern Mediterranean and Near Eastern history. Suddenly, the world became more interconnected than ever before. People moved great distances, far from their homes, in search of opportunities. Cultures mingled. At the same time, the loss of community fed a growing sense of anxiety. People felt alone. Extreme inequality and the rise of piracy only added to this fear. In response, people sought new ways to make connections – common social links that they could share no matter where in the world they found themselves.

Isis was a powerful goddess, of great antiquity and fame, magical, a mother and a healer, but more importantly, she had suffered. She had known fear and pain – the murder of her husband, her concern for her son's safety in the face of great dangers. She would heal and help you, because she understood your problems. In a turbulent time of high anxiety, she had the perfect qualifications to become a world goddess and saviour. Word of her powers spread, through traders and entrepreneurs, slaves and pirates, so that whether you moved to Athens or Alexandria, you'd be able to find people seeking comfort from Isis and performing rituals that they hoped would secure her favour. The mysteries of her religion, with its initiates and secret rites, created bonds between strangers in distant lands: a welcoming club within the cold reality of Hellenistic society.

As Isis' fame spread, her temples sprang up across Europe and the Levant, from Britain and Spain to Lebanon. There was a temple to Isis at Pompeii (which had a cistern allegedly filled with Nile water), visited by the city's estimated 2,000 Isis worshippers – though presumably not all at the same time, it being rather small. Another stood in Mainz, Germany, its remains now preserved for visitation beneath a shopping mall. A temple to Isis even existed at Piraeus in Greece before Alexander the Great's arrival in Egypt, reflecting the early spread of the goddess's popularity. Written works about Isis were popular among the Greeks and Romans. Plutarch's account of the myth of Isis and Osiris is an important source for our understanding of Egyptian mythology, and Isis' magic and cult plays a major role in the 2nd-century AD novel *The Golden Ass*, also known as *The Metamorphoses*, by the Roman writer Apuleius. The protagonist of this story, Lucius, uses magic to try to turn himself into a bird, but accidentally ends up as an ass. In the end, it's only through his initiation into the priesthood of Isis that Lucius is transformed back into his human form. He later travels to Rome to worship Isis and Osiris.

One of the Isis aretalogies – hymns that describe Isis' divine quali-ties – from Cyme in Turkey (modern Nemrut Limani), provides a neat insight into how believers saw the goddess at the end of the 1st century BC. It credits Isis with inventing laws and the hieroglyphic and demotic (a late cursive way of writing the Egyptian language) scripts, creating the cosmological order, and ending cannibalism (with Osiris). She invented marriage contracts, gave languages to the Greeks and barbar-ians, created punishments for injustice, was a queen of seafaring, war and thunderbolts, and was in the sun's rays. Similarly, a long and detailed 2nd-century AD papyrus from the Egyptian city of Oxyrhynchus describes Isis' many manifestations as various goddesses in locations across the known world, proving that all deities were effectively forms of her greater power. It goes on to describe her as ruler of the world, inventor of writing and calculation, discoverer of all things, who made the power of women equal to men, one with power over wind, snow, thunder and lightning. She made Osiris and Horus immortal, and appointed Horus as Osiris' successor.

This classical hyper-powered Isis is represented within Egypt's Ptolemaic- and Roman-Period temple inscriptions too. Various hymns inscribed on the north and south walls of Isis' sanctuary at Philae cover similar themes. Isis is praised as the mother of Horus and wife of Osiris, who protects her brother. She is the rain cloud that revitalizes the fields, who commands the Ennead (the nine major gods of Heliopolis) and causes the Nile to flood. She made the land, the sky and the afterlife realm of the Duat, creating them in her heart and forming them with her arms. She drives away darkness; kills the chaos snake Apophis; is the female Horus and destroys all enemies. By this time, then, thousands of years after her first appearance, Isis had taken on the role of sun god, while simultaneously acting as the sun god's protector and the female incarnation of kingship. It's no surprise that people travelled from across the ancients' known world to Philae to worship her.

Aswan in history and today

A small Predynastic village on Elephantine Island marks the earliest inhabited part of the Aswan region. After Egypt's unification *c.* 3100 BC, the Egyptians constructed a fortress on the island and built a protective wall around the settlement; this became the newly formed kingdom's southern boundary and capital of the first Upper Egyptian nome (a regional division, or district). This town, which continued to develop at Elephantine's southern tip over the course of the Old Kingdom, prospered because of its position as an important trading centre, dealing with goods travelling to and from Nubia. The governors of Aswan not only administered the region for the king, but also led military and trading expeditions into Nubia and defended the territory from raids. They were venerated by later inhabitants of the city: Hekaib, a governor of Aswan during the Old Kingdom, was deified and worshipped at Elephantine from the Middle Kingdom onwards. The Egyptians also exploited the Aswan region for its high-quality granite. Throughout the Pharaonic Period and into the Roman Era, this stone was quarried and carved into statues, obelisks, sarcophagi and chapels. During the Late Period, a Jewish population lived on Elephantine and built a temple to Yahweh. Aramaic papyri produced by this community have shed a great deal of light on Egypt during the Persian occupation (the 27th Dynasty).

With the construction of the Temple of Isis on Philae Island during the Ptolemaic Period, the Aswan region became an important centre of pilgrimage, a situation that continued even after the Roman Emperor Theodosius commanded the closure of all pagan temples in Egypt during the late 4th century AD. A peace treaty between the Eastern Roman Emperor Marcian and the Blemmyes – a Nubian group who frequently attacked Roman interests in the Aswan region – gave the Blemmyes the right to worship at the temple once a year, and to use the statue of Isis for oracles. Nonetheless, the temple officially closed its doors *c.* AD 537. By command of the Eastern Roman Emperor Justinian, its cult statues were sent to Constantinople and its priests arrested. It was the last of Egypt's pagan places of worship to abandon the old ways. Under Bishop Theodore, part of the Temple of Isis was converted into a church, dedicated to St Stephen – the faithful carved Christian crosses over the ancient depictions and hieroglyphs. Today, Aswan is a university town and governorate capital, famous for its souq, beautiful natural environment and ancient monuments that continue to draw tourists from around the world.

▲

Aswan's laid-back charm and beautiful surroundings urge you to relax and take your time exploring the area's many sites. On the east bank of the Nile, in the city of Aswan itself, the **Nubia Museum** presents monuments from the region in modern surroundings, while a little to the east, just after the Fatimid cemetery, the **Unfinished Obelisk** still rests on the spot where Egyptian workers abandoned it over 3,000 years ago. If it had been completed, it would have been the tallest obelisk known from ancient Egypt. Clustered at the southern end of **Elephantine Island**, ancient ruins are preserved from different phases of Egyptian history. Key sites include the remains of the **Temple of Khnum** (only its gateway is still standing); the various incarnations of the **Temple of Satet**; the **Temple of Hekaib** (more fully known as Pepinakht called Hekaib), a local governor of the Old Kingdom who was deified during the Middle Kingdom; and the **Nilometer**, a steep set of steps that enabled the Egyptians to record the height of the inundation. To learn more about the region's ancient history, there's also the **Aswan Museum**.

On the west bank of the Nile, you'll find the **Tombs of the Nobles** at Qubbet el-Hawa. These date to the Old and Middle Kingdoms, and are the final resting places of the governors of the Aswan region and other dignitaries. Among them is the **Tomb of Harkhuf**, whose

ASWAN

Key dates and remains

c. 3500 BC	Earliest settlement on Elephantine Island.
c. 3150 BC	Earliest sanctuary dedicated to the goddess Satet on Elephantine.
c. 2250 BC	The Satet temple now included a cult place dedicated to Khnum. First tombs built at Qubbet el-Hawa, on Aswan's West Bank.
c. 1500 BC	New temples to Khnum and Satet are built on Elephantine, replacing the earlier structures. The Unfinished Obelisk is cut at Aswan.
c. 1380 BC	The first mention of a settlement on the east bank: Aswan.
c. 664 BC	A Jewish settlement is established and a temple to Yahweh built on Elephantine.
c. 380 BC	The Khnum temple on Elephantine is rebuilt, obscuring much of the Jewish temple. A gateway and kiosk (a place of rest for a divine statue when on procession) is built on Philae Island.
c. 360 BC	A new temple to Khnum is under construction on Elephantine.
c. 240 BC	The Temple of Isis is completed on Philae.
c. 205 BC	The Famine Stele is carved on Sehel Island.
c. 180 BC	The Temple of Satet is rebuilt on Elephantine.
c. AD 394	The last recorded hieroglyphic inscription is carved on Philae.
c. 537	The Temple of Isis on Philae is closed.
1970s	The monuments of Philae, including the Temple of Isis, are moved to Agilkia Island.

autobiography, carved on the tomb's outer wall *c.* 2200 BC, records the young King Pepi II's excitement at the news that the governor was bringing a dancing pygmy back from Nubia. There is also the **Tomb of Hekaib.** His autobiographical text, again carved on the outer wall of the tomb, describes his mission to Sinai to retrieve the bodies of fellow Egyptians killed while building boats for a voyage to the land of Punt (perhaps located in eastern Ethiopia or Eritrea).

Philae Island is a short distance to the south of Aswan. The original island disappeared beneath the Nile reservoir that formed between the old **Aswan Dam** and the **Aswan High Dam,** completed in 1970. Luckily for us, between 1971 and 1979, a UNESCO-led project moved the entire temple complex and its associated buildings to nearby Agilkia Island, which was transformed to appear like Philae. There's no bridge connecting the island to the shore. The only way to reach the new Philae Island is the same one taken by every visitor for thousands of years before you: boat – motor these days, rather than sail. Various monuments are spread across Philae. There is the **Kiosk of King Nectanebo I** (r. *c.* 380–362 BC), a pharaoh of the 30th Dynasty; a small **Chapel of Imhotep,** the 3rd Dynasty architect and priest turned god; the ruins of a **Temple to Mandulis,** a solar god of Lower Nubia; a **Temple to Arensnuphis,** a Nubian god regarded as Isis' husband; the **Gateway of Hadrian,** from which the statue of Isis once departed on its frequent visits to the (originally facing) island of Biga; and the **Kiosk of Trajan** – once the island's formal entrance.

Philae's main attraction is the **Temple of Isis.** It is reached via a processional way, lined with colonnades. You enter the temple through a monumental pylon-gateway (two tall and wide towers, flanking a covered passageway that links them), leading to a courtyard with a colonnade and the *mammisi* (**birth house**), dedicated to the birth of Isis' child Harpokrates (Horus the Child). A second pylon gives access to a hypostyle hall – a room filled with columns – and from there, you progress towards the sanctuary, the most sacred part of the temple, where the priests kept the statue of Isis hidden in a shrine (naos). The **pedestal** that supported Isis' divine barque – her processional boat, carried by priests on festival days – is still present. Every wall of the temple is decorated and inscribed with sacred images, rituals and hymns celebrating Isis. In antiquity, it was all brightly painted, and embellished with gold leaf and precious stones. Among the many scenes, keep an eye out for Christian crosses carved into the walls – reminders that the temple was converted into a church.

Doorway to a chapel in the Temple of Horus at Edfu,
with winged sun disc on the lintel.

2

EDFU

^^^^^^^^^^^^^^^^^^^^

Revenge and Triumph at the Temple of Horus

𓃞

'Sail northward from the south and sail southward from the north to reach the quay of the Throne of Re [Edfu]. Go up to the temple of the divine winged disc to kiss the earth for the one with the dappled plumage [Horus].'

Inscription at the Temple of Horus at Edfu, c. 100 BC.

I am standing in the shadow of a giant stone gateway, referred to as a pylon by Egyptologists. Above me, carved into its yellow sandstone surface, loom massive twin images of King Ptolemy XII (r. *c.* 80–58 BC, 55–51 BC). He grasps his cowering enemies by the hair, ready to bring his mace crashing down into their skulls. The god of the temple watches on, impassive – or at least, as impassive as a hawk-headed man can appear. Niches built into the pylon once held flagpoles, kept steady by clamps that protruded from the windows in the pylon's facade. Close by, standing in front of the gateway like divine protectors, are two falcon statues, one wearing the Double Crown of Upper and Lower Egypt, a symbol of kingship. Images of the temple's god, they welcome visitors from across the world, but perhaps in secret feel a twang of disgust: in ancient times, only the purest of priests, shaven from head to toe and wearing the finest white linen, could enter the temple. Today it's all shorts and baseball caps. Such heresy.

It's a typically busy day at Edfu's temple. Tourists mill around, expensive SLR cameras slung around their necks or mobile phones in their hands. Pictures are taken by the thousands. The air smells and tastes of sand. All around, there is the gentle splish-splash of water in plastic bottles, either tipped into dry mouths or rocking to and fro in backpacks. On the path to the temple, people crane their heads to stare at the colossal images of the pharaoh and wonder what other marvels await within. Most of them have arrived by cruise ship, docked nearby on the west bank of the Nile. After disembarking, it's a short and speedy horse-drawn carriage ride through the town of Edfu to the temple. En route, the bustling streets, with their shops and restaurants, soon give way to the sight of the monumental pylon-gateway. Built during the Ptolemaic Period on the sacred location of earlier temples, this 'mansion of the god', as the Egyptians would have known it, is dedicated to one of the country's most significant deities, who in myth fought the god Seth for the throne and avenged the murder of his father Osiris: the falcon god Horus.

Horus who?

Before we delve into the myths and legends connected with Edfu, we should first learn a bit more about Horus, or should I say, Horuses. As we saw in Chapter 1, Horus is usually the son of Osiris and Isis, and the god who avenged his father's death to become king of Egypt. In life, every pharaoh was an incarnation of Horus, just as in death each one became Osiris (for the life and death of Osiris, see Chapter 6). Horus himself actually appears in a great many variations, some quite distinct from the famous Horus, son of Isis, though all are ultimately different manifestations of the same divine power. This can be rather confusing when reading the ancient myths. So, let's take a deep breath and dive in: it's time for a crash course in *some* of Egypt's different Horuses.

Horus ('The Distant One') is first found towards the end of the Predynastic Period, when, during their coronations, kings received Horus names in addition to their birth names, associating them with

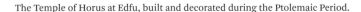

The Temple of Horus at Edfu, built and decorated during the Ptolemaic Period.

the god (there was Hor Aha, 'Horus: The Fighter', for example). Already, at this early time, the Egyptians visualized Horus as a falcon, usually perched atop the royal name, and his strong connection with kingship was well established. This early Horus appears to have been a god of Hierakonpolis, an important town in Upper Egypt. He was a sky god, whose left eye was the moon and right eye was the sun, and whose role expanded with the unification of Egypt under a single ruler.

But this was only the beginning. As time passed, the situation became more complex. By the end of the Old Kingdom, Horus had joined the Osiris myth as the son of Isis and Osiris. This is perhaps the most common form of Horus found in mythology. In addition to simply being referred to as Horus, he could be called Horus, Protector of His Father (Hor-nedj-itef in Egyptian, Harendotes in Greek), or often simply Harsiese (Horus Son of Isis) in Greek. Many stories describe Horus' upbringing by Isis in the Delta marshes following the murder of Osiris, his illnesses and troubles, and their attempts to evade Seth before the young god's ultimate triumph. This form of Horus is connected with images of Horus the Child (Hor-pa-khered in Egyptian, Harpokrates in Greek). He is normally shown sitting on the knee of Isis, but also featured on magical objects called *cippi*. These decorated stone slabs with a basin at the bottom were usually covered in magical healing spells, over which people poured water. By passing over the spells, the water was believed to become imbued with the words' power, which was taken into the body when drunk.

Confused yet? We haven't even got started. There was also Horus the Elder or Horus the Great, both translations of Hor-Wer (Haroeris in Greek). Depending on the myth, Horus the Elder became regarded as either Horus the child of Isis having grown up, ready to fight Seth for the crown of Egypt, or another Horus completely: the son of the deities Nut and Geb, and so a brother of Osiris, Seth, Isis and Nephthys. Sometimes, Horus the Elder is husband to Hathor, and according to the Book of the Dead, he fathered the Four Sons of Horus with Isis; these gods protected mummified internal organs. Horus the Elder was worshipped at Kom Ombo temple, which he shared with the crocodile god Sobek. Here, Horus was a healer, visited by people in the hope that he would cure their illnesses. Horus was also the rising and setting sun as Horakhty, meaning 'Horus of the Two Horizons'. This form of Horus later united with the sun god Re to create Re-Horakhty. And let's not get him mixed up with Horemakhet, 'Horus in the Horizon', another flavour of Horus as sun god, who in the New Kingdom came to be associated with the Great Sphinx at Giza.

Have you kept up? Well, here's one last Horus for you: Horus of Behdet was the god worshipped at the Temple of Edfu (despite the town of Behdet actually being in the Delta). He was an aspect of the sun god, usually shown as the sun disc, flanked by the wings of a hawk – an image often seen in Egyptian temples and at the top of stelae. He could also be shown as a hawk-headed man, wearing the Double Crown of Upper and Lower Egypt. As described in the myths of Edfu, this Horus helped Re to defeat his enemies, loved his weapons of war, and was an all-round tough guy. More about him later.

Horus fights for the throne of Egypt

To begin with, lets focus on Horus, son of Isis, and the mythology surrounding his attempt to avenge his father's murder and reclaim the throne of Egypt from his uncle Seth. This myth underlines the correct way for kingship to pass along a family line: from father to son, rather than brother to brother. Like much of Egyptian mythology, this story is reconstructed from mythological snippets spread across hymns and temple inscriptions, recorded over thousands of years of Egyptian history, from the Pyramid Texts of the 5th Dynasty through to the writings of classical authors. The walls of the Temple of Edfu, decorated during the Ptolemaic Period, include brief accounts too. One of these inscriptions has Isis and Nephthys telling Re, Thoth and Maat (goddess of balance and order) about the dispute between Horus and Seth over the throne. The gods pass judgment and Horus is awarded the kingship of Egypt.

One of the longest versions of the Horus myth was written down on a 20th Dynasty papyrus. It is today known as 'The Contendings of Horus and Seth'. The story goes as follows: Horus and Seth had been fighting for the throne for eighty years. Enough was enough, so the gods, weary from all the squabbling, decided to arrange a hearing, overseen by the Universal Lord – the combined manifestations of the sun god, including Re-Horakhty – to decide which of the two should be king of Egypt. Shu, one of the first generation of gods, opened proceedings by suggesting Horus as the best candidate. The wise god Thoth supported him – a sure sign of good thinking – as did Onuris, a hunter and warrior god. Isis, excited by the strong backing for her son, asked the north wind to head west – to the land of the dead – to take the good news to Osiris. But Isis' celebration was premature. The Universal Lord fumed – the gods weren't respecting his authority. He was the ultimate judge here, and he hadn't expressed his opinion yet. Seth, a being of pure aggression, also spoke up, challenging Horus to

fight him for the crown. Thoth intervened: why were they even consid-
ering giving the kingship to Seth when Horus, son of the previous king,
was still alive? The Universal Lord fumed some more.

Atum stepped in, proposing that the gods summon Banebdjedet
and Ptah-Tatenen to judge between Horus and Seth. Clearly with little
other business in their calendars, the two gods quickly arrived, but it
was a wasted journey. Neither wanted to make a decision (makes you
wonder why they bothered turning up). Their only input? Advising that
the gods write a letter to the goddess Neith to ask for her opinion. Neith
replied that the kingship should go to Horus, but in compensation,
Seth should receive the Universal Lord's daughters Anat and Astarte.
The Ennead – the nine major gods of Heliopolis – agreed with Neith's
decision. But the Universal Lord flew into another rage. 'You're weak
and have bad breath,' he spat at Horus. Chaos broke out at court.
Babi – an aggressive baboon god – told the Universal Lord that his
shrine was empty! (A particular insult to a god, implying that his divine
statue had gone missing.) Cursing to himself, the Universal Lord stormed
out and went to lie down. The gods yelled at Babi to leave, and grum-
bled off to their tents. To break the deadlock, Hathor, Lady of the
Southern Sycamore, visited the Universal Lord, and lifting her dress,
flashed her private parts at him. The Universal Lord laughed, and with
newfound cheer, returned to court.

Back to business. The Universal Lord asked Seth and Horus to
make declarations about their worthiness to rule. 'I'm strong,' said
Seth, his voice booming. 'And I defeat Re's enemies each day in his
barque – something only I can do.' Some of the gods agreed. Quiet
murmurings filled the room. But Thoth and Onuris remained unim-
pressed. They asked again why an uncle should be given the kingship
when the son still lived. Bah! The Universal Lord exclaimed something
so obscene that the scribe recording events refused to write it down.
Whatever the god had said, it shocked the Ennead. Horus and Isis complained, but were reassured that the kingship would be given to whoever
was righteous. Seth, not one for calm speech on the best of days, said
that he'd take his massive sceptre and kill one god each day until the
throne was given to him. On top of that, he refused to remain in court
as long as Isis was present. Her outbursts were getting on his nerves.
The gods relented. To escape Isis, they sailed over to the 'Island in the
Middle' and instructed the ferryman Nemty to refuse passage to any
woman that resembled Isis.

Now if there's one thing we've learned about Isis, it's that she's
powerful in magic. And a second: she doesn't give up easily. Unwilling

to accept her expulsion, Isis transformed into an old woman and approached Nemty. She pretended to be delivering flour to a hungry young man, who had been stuck on the Island in the Middle for five days caring for cattle. Nemty, playing the part of the gormless henchman to a tee, told her that although he wasn't *meant* to ferry any women across to the island, he'd be willing to ignore his orders if she'd hand over that lovely gold signet ring he'd spotted on her finger. Isis agreed, and Nemty ferried her across. Exploring the island, Isis spotted the Ennead in the distance. Seth was with them, and as soon as she caught his eye, she transformed into a beautiful woman. Seth being Seth, he desired her immediately and walked straight over. There's a reason why many of the myths about Seth focus on his testicles.

Seth sidled up to Isis and put on his best moves. Isis took the opportunity to tell him a story. 'My husband has died, and now a stranger is beating up my son and taking the cattle he inherited. Would you help me?' she asked. Seth was appalled: 'It isn't right that a stranger should own the cattle while the son still lives!' he exclaimed. Isis' trap had worked. Transforming into a kite, she flew up into a tree, keeping a safe distance from the aggressive Seth. 'Your own words have condemned you,' she said. Seth ran away, and complained to the Universal Lord about what had happened. The Universal Lord, at last admitting that Seth was to blame for his own actions, told him that he'd condemned himself. 'What do you want now?' he asked Seth. Revenge, obviously, was the reply. Seth wanted Nemty punished, so the gods cut off the front half of the unfortunate ferryman's feet. From that moment on, Nemty despised gold.

Their island hideaway rumbled, the gods moved again, this time settling on a mountain. The Universal Lord wrote to the Ennead saying that Horus should be crowned, otherwise Horus and Seth would spend their entire lives in court (and that's a waste of everyone's time). Seth, predictably, exploded. The gods were confused. 'What's your problem?' they said. 'The sun god has made his decision.' They crowned Horus, while Seth whinged and moaned. 'How come the son should be king when the crown should go to me, a brother?' Seth said. He made an oath, announcing that he'd remove the crown from Horus' head and throw him in the water. The Universal Lord gave in. The gods stripped Horus of his crown and the hearing began all over again. There was only one way to solve this problem: a series of outrageous challenges.

For their first challenge, Horus and Seth transformed into hippopotami and dove to the bottom of the sea: the one who failed to last three months underwater would lose. Time passed and the gods watched on – it can't have been the most exciting spectator sport. With the two gods out of sight beneath the waves, Isis worried that Seth might have killed Horus. She wept, but, being proactive, decided to take matters into her own hands. She fashioned a harpoon and threw it into the sea, but it hit Horus. He screamed. Isis panicked and commanded the harpoon to set Horus free. She then threw the harpoon back into the water. This time it hit Seth, who howled in pain. 'What have I ever done to you?' he yelled at Isis (seemingly without irony). In that moment, Isis felt great sorrow for Seth – her brother, let's not forget – and asked the harpoon to free him. Horus fumed. He waded out of the water and decapitated Isis. Then, leaving her body to transform into a flint statue, he stomped off up a mountain, her head in his hand. The Universal Lord missed all this drama; shortly afterwards, when wandering through the scene of the crime, he asked Thoth where this headless statue had come from. 'It's Isis,' Thoth told him. Astonished, the Universal Lord assembled the Ennead to scour the mountain for Horus, so that he could be punished. But Seth got to the young god first. He threw Horus to the floor, pulled out his eyes, and buried them in the ground, where they sprouted into lotuses. Seth left the beaten god on the mountainside, and when he bumped into the Universal Lord, pretended that he hadn't seen Horus.

Hathor, Lady of the Southern Sycamore, found Horus crying on the hills. Using milk from a gazelle, she poured it into his vacant sockets, reforming his lost eyes and restoring his sight. Then she rejoined the gods, and explained to the Universal Lord how Seth had attacked Horus. The gods summoned Horus and Seth and told them to dine together – they just wanted some peace for an evening, some time away from these two warring deities and their endless drama. Seth invited Horus over to his house, and that night, the two lay together in bed. Seth became aroused and slipped his phallus between Horus' thighs. When Seth ejaculated, Horus caught the semen in his hands. Horus then ran to Isis (whose revival isn't explained), telling her what had happened. When Isis saw Seth's semen on Horus' hands, she sliced them off and threw them into the water. Afterwards, she used her magic to create new hands for her son – it's useful having a magical mother. Isis suspected that Seth had other motives behind the sexual encounter, and decided to turn the tables on him. She made Horus ejaculate into a pot, then took the semen and dribbled it onto lettuce in Seth's garden. That night, Seth ate the lettuce and unknowingly fell pregnant.

The next day, Horus and Seth returned to court. Seth announced that he should be king of Egypt because he 'did a man's work' to Horus.

The Ennead yelled at Horus, but he laughed. He denied what Seth had said, and asked that they summon Seth's semen to see where it would emerge. Afterwards, they would be free to call for his own semen. Thoth used his magic, and Seth's semen rose up from the river rather than out of Horus' body. Then, he called for Horus' semen, and it erupted from Seth's head as a solar disc; it was clear to the gods who had 'done a man's work' to whom. Thoth took the solar disc and placed it on his own head.

Seth demanded another challenge. This time, he said, they should race stone boats. The winner would become king of Egypt. The two gods went to prepare for the race. The clever Horus carved his boat from wood, but plastered it to appear like stone. Seth, meanwhile, carved his ship from a mountain peak. When the race finally began, Seth's boat sank to the bottom of the Nile. In the water, Seth transformed into a hippo and fought with Horus. Horus fled north to the city of Sais and complained to the goddess Neith. In all the years of fighting, Horus said, he'd always been in the right. Something had to give. So, Thoth sent a letter to Osiris in the afterlife realm of the Duat, asking for his opinion on who should be king. Naturally, Osiris sided with Horus, and his influence was so strong that nobody could disagree with him. Soon after, Isis brought Seth to the gods in chains. Seth finally relented, saying that Horus should be crowned. Horus became king of Egypt, but Seth wasn't treated badly: he joined Re-Horakhty in the sky and his voice created thunder.

Episodes from this long tale can be found in other ancient sources. A fragmentary papyrus from Lahun, dated to the Middle Kingdom, presents Seth complimenting the beauty of Horus' buttocks, and Horus informing Isis that Seth wants to have sex with him. Isis' advice for Horus? Tell Seth it isn't possible, because Seth is too heavy for him. In a broken section, Isis advises Horus to place his fingers between his buttocks, perhaps another reference to the sexual episode in the Contendings of Horus and Seth. The episode of Isis cutting off Horus' hands is cited in the Book of the Dead and the Coffin Texts (see Chapter 9), and Horus decapitating Isis is found in various sources.

Further tales of Horus and Seth's dispute

Accounts of Horus and Seth's fight for the crown are spread across Egyptian history, and the details of the story vary widely in the telling. The Shabaka Stone inscription, carved in Memphis during the 25th Dynasty, presents the earth god Geb presiding over the hearing. Geb tried to make everyone happy by awarding Seth Upper Egypt and

Horus Lower Egypt. The two warring gods were thus separated, but Geb worried that he'd made a bad decision. Egypt was divided. It was wrong for Seth's territory to be the same size as Horus'. And because Horus was Osiris' first-born son, Geb decided that, actually, the entire country should really be given to him. He proclaimed his decision to the Ennead and Horus took his place on the throne.

In the Papyrus Jumilhac, it's Thoth who decides between the two warring gods. Isis and Horus complained to Re about all the evil deeds committed by Seth. So Re – perhaps too busy creating light and sailing along the sky to do the work himself – asked Thoth to decide which of the two gods had the most convincing claim to the throne. Thoth sat on his mat with his advisors. He summoned all of his wisdom, and after a deep think, decided that Horus was the best candidate. Re commanded that Seth be removed from the Nile Valley, exiling him to the desert. But Seth wouldn't give up without a fight. He gathered his followers, readied them for war, and in a petty act of revenge, stole Thoth's sacred writings and threw them into the Nile. When Thoth discovered what Seth had done, he remained calm. Wise as always, he replaced his writings and put everything back exactly as it had been before. Seth, meanwhile, transformed into a red dog and hid in a bush. The gods gave chase, and when they found him, thrust their lances into Seth's neck, killing him. Horus ascended the throne of Egypt and Thoth served him as vizier. Thoth removed all evidence of Seth: he killed Seth's followers, destroyed all cities and nomes allied with him, cut up his statues and even scratched away his name wherever it was found. He severed one of Seth's legs and threw it into the sky, where it became the constellation *meskhetiu* (the adze; today Ursa Major, the Great Bear). A hippopotamus goddess held the leg in place, so that Seth could no longer sail among the gods.

As one final example, we can look to the Greek writer Plutarch's account of Horus' triumph over Seth. After his death, Osiris returned from the next world to prepare Horus for his battle with Seth. (If it was a movie, this is where you'd insert the training montage.) Osiris asked Horus, what was the most noble thing to do. Horus replied that it was to avenge his father and mother because of the evil done to them. Osiris then asked which animal would be most helpful at war. To Osiris' surprise, Horus said the horse. 'Wouldn't you prefer a lion?' Osiris said. But Horus said no. The young god believed that a horse was better for cutting off an enemy, preventing them from running away. This would give him the chance to destroy them all. Osiris deemed his son ready for battle. After many days of combat against Seth, Horus prevailed, and Seth was dragged to Isis in chains, but she decided to set him free. Horus, in anger, took Isis' diadem from her head, so Thoth replaced it with a helmet. In the subsequent hearing, Seth argued that Horus was illegitimate, but Horus and Thoth spoke against him. In the end, the gods agreed that Horus was the legitimate heir to the throne. Two more wars followed, but Seth was defeated each time. Then, Osiris and Isis slept together and the child born from their union was Harpokrates – Horus the Child.

The Eye of Horus and Seth's testicles

The Eye of Horus, or the *wedjat* in Egyptian, symbolized the restoration of order after chaos. It was a popular symbol, often worn by Egyptians as a pendant. It also had a role in the afterlife, being placed over, or into, serious wounds on mummies, or over the spot where the embalmer had made an incision to remove the internal organs. Its importance is first mentioned in the Pyramid Texts, in which Seth takes the eye from Horus, damaging the god's face – an injury that could only be healed by a god spitting on it. Seth, meanwhile, lost his testicles, leaving him in great pain. Horus might have been responsible for this act of castration, but nowhere in the Pyramid Texts is it explicitly spelled out. When Thoth and various other gods visited Seth to ask for the eye back, they found that he'd stood on it and swallowed it. Seeing Thoth, the eye – now acting independently, and having somehow recovered from the whole trampling and swallowing incident – jumped to the other side of the Winding Waterway to escape Seth. It landed on Thoth's wing, where it found safety. There's little detail in the Pyramid Texts about the resolution of the dispute between Horus and Seth over the Eye of Horus, but there are hints that the gods held a tribunal, perhaps in the Official's Enclosure at Heliopolis (the sun temple's sanctuary). There's little resolution to the issue of Seth's testicles either, beyond that they must be returned to ease his pain. The Ebers Papyrus, however, mentions that Horus and Seth went to Heliopolis to discuss Seth's testicles.

According to the Book of the Dead, Seth injured Horus' face and Horus took Seth's testicles. It was then left to Thoth to restore the sacred eye. One spell tells us that Re gave the city of Pe to Horus as compensation for his injured eye. But when Re asked Horus to look at a black pig, Horus started screaming. 'The pain feels just like when Seth struck my eye!' he said, and fell unconscious. Re sent Horus to bed to rest. The gods wished that he would feel better. It turned out that the black pig was actually Seth, who had changed his shape and magically struck Horus' eye. Re announced that the pig was an abomination to Horus – if there were no pigs around, Horus might get better faster, the sun god reasoned. Because of these events, it became normal to hate pigs.

A myth recorded on the Papyrus Jumilhac also refers to the Eye of Horus. The enemies of the Eye of Horus stole Horus' two eyes and gave them to Seth, who hid them in boxes. To keep them safely in his possession, Seth placed these boxes on a mountain, and sat beside them in the form of a crocodile, watching, waiting. It fell to the jackal-headed god Anubis to retrieve Horus' lost eyes. He transformed into a winged serpent, with knives at the tips of his wings and extra knives in his hands. Six flaming serpents emerged from his body, three on each side. Despite his fearsome appearance, stealth was his first tactic. Anubis climbed the mountain at night, without Seth seeing, and found the boxes. He opened them and took the eyes, placing each in a new box of papyrus. Then, Anubis fled. After burying the boxes in a safe place, he returned to face Seth. Anubis' flaming serpents spat fire at the god, burning him. Later, Horus and Isis visited the spot where Anubis had hidden the eyes and found they'd grown into vines. To protect the eyes and keep them alive, Isis asked Horus to build a house nearby, a place for them to live while they tended to the emerging vineyard. One day, Isis stood on the roof of their home, and tilting her head to face the clear blue sky, asked Re to return the eyes to her son. Re, touched by her words, commanded Thoth to help them. The eyes were given back to Horus, but the vineyard magically continued to thrive. The wine it produced became known as the tears of Horus.

The scorpion wives of Horus

Although infrequently mentioned in Egyptian mythology, Horus had seven scorpion wives, each a manifestation of the scorpion goddess Serket: Sepertuenes, Ta-Bitjet, Ifdet, Wepetsepu, Sefedsepu, Metemet-neferetiyes and Betjeh. (These are a different group from the seven scorpions that assisted Isis during Horus' youth – see Chapter 1). In one myth, an unnamed scorpion wife and Horus are about to have sex, when she stings him, leaving him with a burning pain. The scorpion wife uses fluids to heal Horus, and shares with him names of power that enable him to work as a healer – 'Horus the Doctor'.

The creation myth of Edfu

To the priests of the Temple of Horus, Edfu marked the spot where creation began. They believed all creation to be a manifestation of Horus of Behdet – a form of Horus fused with Re, shown as a winged sun disc or winged scarab beetle. This Horus was husband to Hathor of Dendera, who together were the parents of Harsomtus (Hor-Sema-Tawy in Egyptian), who is usually shown wearing a tall feathered crown.

Horus of Behdet came into being on the 'first occasion' – at the beginning of time. Various waterways already existed in these early days, including the 'Water of Fighting' and the 'Water of Peace'. Unlike the unmoving, dark and inert waters of other Egyptian cosmogonies, the primeval state of the world at Edfu was a tumultuous and destructive flood. One day, a god, called He-who-is-on-the-water, saw a bunch of reeds floating along the water's surface. Hovering just above the torrent, a falcon called Heter-Her observed the reeds too. Then, the 'Beautiful-of-Harpoon' – a powerful weapon, brought by the flood – emerged from the water. As the hovering falcon watched, the harpoon collided with the floating mass of reeds, forcing a single reed to break away. The falcon circled the reed, and when it became stable in the water, perched on it. The Egyptian word *djeba*, meaning 'the reed float' or 'perch', was also the ancient name of Edfu. At the same time, the Egyptians called the floating reed, temple, town and nome of Edfu Wetjeset-Her, 'The Support of Horus' (also translated as 'Throne of Horus').

The Duat – the afterlife realm – now came into existence. Where there was once only eternal night and chaos, the falcon brought order by flapping his wings. He stretched the limits of the sky, and cried with joy when the constellation of the adze (*meskhetiu*) appeared among the stars above. There was now sky, Duat and water in creation, but no light or land. Horus flew into the dark sky and the 'Flying Disc' appeared – the first sunrise. This new light, sweeping away the darkness, revealed mounds of land, protruding from the floodwaters like small islands. To tame the dangerous floodwater and bring order to its chaotic flow, the gods cut canals. And as time passed, the floodwaters subsided, exposing more fertile earth for agriculture. Finally, deities, both major and minor, founded and built the Temple of Edfu – from Thoth, who planned the construction, to divine 'commanders' who personified the creative word (magical speech, believed to bring into being whatever was said). This temple would be the reed upon which the Horus falcon could rest, the culmination of creation. And as the world evolved all around, Thoth jotted down every development on a scroll, keeping a record for eternity.

The 'Legend of the Winged Sun Disc' (and its sequel) at Edfu

In addition to its cosmogony, the inscriptions at the Temple of Edfu record myths about Horus of Behdet. The 'Legend of the Winged Sun

Looking out over the peristyle courtyard of Horus' Temple at Edfu.
The winged sun disc, a symbol of Horus of Behdet, stretches across a lintel.

Disc' opens in year 363 of Re-Horakhty's reign over Egypt. Horus of
Behdet sensed something was wrong. He was sailing north with the
king and his army through Nubia to Egypt, and although he could see
no sign of trouble on the riverbanks, he felt someone was plotting rebellion. When they reached Edfu, he expressed his fears to Re-Horakhty,
who, trusting his advisor, sent him to investigate. Horus flew into the
sky as a great winged disc, and there, hovering in the air above, found
his enemies. A great sky battle raged. Horus inflicted blindness and
deafness on the rebels, and in the chaos and panic, each foe slew the
other and dropped from the sky. The battle won, Horus descended to
Re's boat in victory, and together they travelled to the spot where the
rebels had crashed into the ground. Smashed heads littered the surface.
Blood oozed from corpses. But not all of Re's enemies had died. Some
survivors had crawled away into the Nile, where they'd transformed
into crocodiles and hippopotami. Having regrouped, they were now
swimming towards the royal boat. Horus and his followers grabbed
their harpoons and hurled them at the creatures. Many enemies died
on the spot, their bodies carried away by the current. Horus took another
651 prisoner, only to execute them later. Again, some escaped, slipping
through Horus' feathery fingers.

The gods couldn't allow any of Re's enemies to get away, so Horus,
accompanied by the goddesses Wadjet and Nekhbet as uraei (rearing

cobras), gave chase, sailing northwards in the barque of Re. Near Thebes, Horus slaughtered another batch of Re's enemies, but still some escaped. This sequence of chase, slaughter and escape continued at cities across Egypt, from Dendera to the Faiyum Oasis, and all the way north to the Mediterranean Sea, where Horus offered the rebels' intestines to his followers and their flesh to the deities aboard Re's boat. With nowhere left to go, the chase turned south again. In one town, as the battle raged, Horus of Behdet captured followers of Seth among the enemies of Re. He gave them to Isis and Horus, son of Isis, to behead. Realizing his nemesis was part of the problem, Horus, son of Isis, decided to join the fight. Both he and Horus of Behdet were equal in appearance and power as they set off for war, but when they found Seth, there was no opportunity to use their skills; seeing the two Horuses, the trickster god transformed into a roaring snake and fled, slithering into the earth. Still, the war continued. On one occasion, Horus of Behdet transformed into a sphinx, and unleashing his claws, tore out his enemies' kidneys. Horus and his followers ate the rebels. Eventually, Horus of Behdet won the war, and as reward for defeating Egypt's enemies, Thoth installed the image of the winged sun disc across Egypt. That is why today it can be seen everywhere in the country's ancient temples and shrines. The winged scarab beetle, seen within divine shrines, was also Horus of Behdet, as were the morning and evening stars.

Another inscription at Edfu provides a short sequel to this myth. The enemies of Re had reappeared, in spite of Horus' long crusade, manifesting as Nubians, Libyans, Asiatics and Bedouin of the Eastern Desert. So, as before, Horus of Behdet chased them around Egypt, slaughtering them at different cities using his sacred lance. In the end, Isis asked Horus of Behdet for help: she needed him to defeat Seth to protect her son. They travelled together to Edfu, where Seth used his magic to create a storm against the gods, but he was defeated by Isis and killed by Horus of Behdet. This myth is tied with a ritual in which the performer, ideally the king, added grape juice, representing the blood of Horus' enemies, to water, just as during the mythological slaughter the rebels' blood dribbled into the Nile. The ritualist drank the mixture of grape juice and water, then ate a grape, symbolically destroying Egypt's enemies and taking in new strength.

One final short myth and the 'Edfu Drama'

Another short inscription in the Temple of Edfu tells how Horus of Behdet offered his assistance to the pregnant Isis and ultimately ensured Horus, son of Isis' place on the throne of Egypt. Fearing Seth,

Isis told Thoth that she was pregnant with Osiris' child. Thoth, ever willing to offer wise advice, suggested that she visit Edfu and request the aid of Horus of Behdet. Thoth would use his magic to protect Osiris (a little late, I'd say, given that he was already dead), and Horus of Behdet would protect the child once born. Isis gave birth, and years passed before Seth finally arrived with his followers to confront the gods. Seth accused Horus of not being Egyptian, but a foreigner, and transformed into a red hippopotamus, ready for battle. Isis and Horus fled north, leaving Horus of Behdet to face Seth. Standing on his boat, Horus of Behdet transformed into a young man and raised his harpoon, waiting for the right moment to hurl it at Seth in the water. When that moment came, he threw the harpoon with such force that it pierced deep into Seth's flesh. Seth, wounded, fled the scene, chased by Horus of Behdet. Meanwhile, Horus, son of Isis, was proclaimed King of Upper and Lower Egypt.

Also called the 'Triumph of Horus', the 'Edfu Drama' was a ritual play that celebrated Horus, son of Isis' defeat of the followers of Seth and his coronation as king of Egypt. It was performed at Edfu each

Carving from the Temple of Horus at Edfu. The pharaoh Ptolemy XII raises obelisks before the falcon-headed Horus, who wears the Double Crown of Upper and Lower Egypt.

year during the Festival of Victory. The play equates the king with Horus. Magically, its performance made the pharaoh victorious, just as Horus had been in the mythological past. The full 'script' of the play includes a prologue, three acts and an epilogue, complete with stage directions. There were various divine roles for members of the temple cult to play, a narrator, and probably even a chorus. The play's central event was the harpooning and killing of a hippopotamus, meant to represent the god Seth. This was attacked with ten harpoons, each plunged into a different part of the animal's body. Thankfully for Egypt's hippos, it's thought that the priests used a model animal during the ritual. Seth's body was then sliced into pieces, and eaten as 'hippo cake'.

The Coronation of the Sacred Falcon at Edfu

The ritual of the Coronation of the Sacred Falcon was an annual event at Edfu. The falcon (this time certainly a live animal, rather than a model) represented the reigning king and served as a vessel for the *ba*-spirit of Horus of Behdet – the *ba* being a force of movement and personality (see p. 72). The same rituals reconfirmed the falcon's selection and coronation each year until his death, when a new falcon was chosen by oracle. The falcon lived in the Temple of the Sacred Falcon in front of Edfu's pylon-gateway, though nothing remains of it today.

As the coronation ritual began, priests dressed as Egypt's ancestral kings silently carried the statue of Horus from his dark sanctuary at the rear of Edfu Temple to the Temple of the Sacred Falcon. Other priests brought falcons from a nearby breeding grove to meet them. The divine statue, resting in a small boat borne on the shoulders of the priests, slowly passed in front of each falcon, until finally, it tilted towards one, indicating which would become the new 'king'. The priests, the Horus statue and the selected falcon then returned to the main temple and proceeded up a narrow stairway to a window of appearance, known as the Balcony of the Falcon, at the centre of the pylon's roof. There, the priests installed the falcon on a special platform, so it could stare out at the world and be seen by the assembled crowd below.

Afterwards, the priests took the falcon downstairs for the coronation ceremony. They anointed the falcon, offered him bouquets and symbols of eternity, tied a piece of cloth around his head, and placed amulets on his body. Another piece of cloth, inscribed with magical protective symbols, was tied around his neck, along with more golden amulets. At the end of the ceremony, following further rituals of protection, the priests enjoyed a meal in the Temple of the Sacred Falcon. The falcon was offered the best meat (naturally). Finally, the priests returned the statue of Horus to his shrine, and the sacred falcon remained in the Temple of the Sacred Falcon, until next year.

The Festival of the Beautiful Meeting and the Festival of Behdet

During the Festival of the Beautiful Meeting (also sometimes translated as the Festival of the Joyous Union), Hathor of Dendera visited Edfu to meet her husband, Horus of Behdet. It took fourteen days for the divine statue of Hathor, sailing along the Nile accompanied by other sacred boats, to make the 180-kilometre (110-mile) journey south from Dendera to Edfu. Along the way, she visited the goddess Mut, wife of Amun-Re, at Thebes, and other sacred sites and deities. People watched the divine flotilla from the riverbanks, no doubt in awe of witnessing a deity floating by.

Horus of Behdet met Hathor at a quay near Edfu. From there, they travelled to a nearby temple, where priests performed sacred rituals, including an offering of *maat* (divine order) and the Opening of the Mouth ceremony – a ritual that enabled a statue to act as a vessel, whether for the manifestation of a deity or a spirit of the dead. Afterwards, the divine couple continued their journey to the Temple of Horus, sailing on a canal via a site sacred to the earth god Geb. Upon arrival, it was time for the Festival of the Beautiful Meeting's main event: Horus and Hathor's marriage ceremony, presided over by their priests. That night, the two divine statues rested together in the temple's sanctuary, marking the end of the celebration. For the next fourteen days, Horus and Hathor, their priests, and members of the local community visited the necropolis of Behdet for the Festival of Behdet, in which the two gods regenerated the nine divine souls, or ancestral gods, of Edfu. Once the rituals were complete, Hathor returned to Dendera.

Edfu in history and today

Today, Edfu's economy is based on tourism and agriculture. The town is particularly known for producing pottery and sugar cane, and for its famous, well-preserved Temple of Horus. This temple was built during the Ptolemaic Period, though as is often the case, it stands on the site of earlier temples dedicated to the same god. Construction began under King Ptolemy III (r. *c.* 246–222 BC) in 237 BC, but it wasn't completed until 57 BC, nearly two centuries later. We know a great deal about the temple's construction process because its decorators left inscriptions detailing its various sectors, how long they took to build, and under which king it happened. There's even a reference to a rebellion in Upper Egypt that halted work for years.

It's unclear when cult activity ended at the Temple of Horus, beyond that it must have occurred during Roman times, sometime after the introduction of Christianity. As the pagan ways faded, the nearby village expanded into the temple, transforming it into a place to live and work. Christians carved crosses and inscriptions on its walls, and after the Arab conquest, people built huts in the temple's courtyards and on the roof. Eventually, sand and the accumulated refuse of centuries filled the temple, hiding its carvings and leaving only the tips of its pylon and roof visible (where people continued to live). As the years passed, travellers mentioned the temple's existence in their accounts, but it wasn't fully revealed again until the 19th century, when French archaeologist and founder of the Egyptian Department of Antiquities Auguste Mariette removed the village from its roof and cleared the chambers.

The archaeological site is much more than just the temple. In ancient times, Edfu was the capital of Egypt's second Upper Egyptian nome. It has a necropolis that dates as far back as the Early Dynastic Period, and settlement remains from around 2400 BC. There's even a tiny step pyramid of 3rd or 4th Dynasty date. Such 'provincial pyramids' were not burials, but perhaps markers of royal authority in Egypt's districts. Recent excavations have unearthed two large official buildings from the late Old Kingdom. Quarrying expeditions into the Eastern Desert departed from Edfu – one of the reasons for its prosperity – and evidence for smelting has been found in its ancient town. Trade routes headed west from Edfu into the desert towards the Kharga Oasis and beyond. Archaeologists have excavated a probable governor's residence and administrative buildings of Middle Kingdom date, as well as silos from the Second Intermediate Period. New Kingdom and Late Period blocks have been spotted incorporated into a local monastery. Evidence for activity at Edfu continues all the way through to the Roman Period – the entire length of Pharaonic history – and beyond to the present day.

▲

Most visitors arrive at Edfu by cruise ship, then take a horse-drawn carriage to the **Temple of Horus**, which is surrounded by the town. Passing through the **pylon entrance**, you enter the temple's **peristyle courtyard**. Here, on the back of the pylon, you can see images of the Festival of the Beautiful Meeting, including carvings of Horus and Hathor's boats. From the peristyle court, you can access the **ambulatory** that passes around the main temple building. This is where many

EDFU

Key dates and remains

c. 3050 BC	Earliest cemetery at Edfu.
c. 2500 BC	Small step pyramid built, perhaps as a symbol of royal authority.
c. 2400 BC	Earliest urban remains at Edfu. Two large official buildings with workshops constructed.
c. 2000 BC	Governor's mansion constructed.
c. 1290 BC	Ramesside Era temple remains.
c. 360 BC	Shrine (naos) of Horus carved under King Nectanebo II.
237 BC	Construction on the current Temple of Horus begins.
57 BC	Completion of the current Temple of Horus

of the myths described in this chapter are carved. Within the **hypostyle hall**, there are scenes of the temple's foundation ceremony. Continuing along the central axis, you walk through the hall of offerings and vestibule into the temple's main **sanctuary**. A pedestal here once supported the barque of Horus. There's also the **granite naos,** or shrine, in which the statue of Horus – the vessel for the god – was kept. This was carved during the reign of King Nectanebo II (r. *c.* 360–342 BC). Various other chapels surround the main sanctuary. Outside the temple, you can visit Edfu's *mammisi* (**birth house**), where, among the scenes, you can see the child god Harsomtus suckled by goddesses.

The Hypostyle Hall in the Temple of Amun-Re at Karnak,
located on the east bank of the Nile at Thebes.

3

THEBES
EAST BANK

~~~~~~~~~~~~~~~~

Home of the Hidden God

'Thebes is the pattern for every city. Water and land were in it from creation. The sands came to mark out the fields, and its ground became the high ground, when the land came into being. People came into being on it, in order to establish every city in its true name. Their name is called "city" under the supervision of Thebes, the Eye of Re.'

Papyrus Leiden I 350, c. 1250 BC.

I'm enveloped by a forest of sandstone columns. They block the intense sunlight falling from above, splitting its rays and casting long shadows. Tiny brown sparrows dart between ledges and holes high in the ancient stones, tweeting to one another as they fly. Where the light strikes the columns, ancient carvings spring to life. Kings making offerings. Feathered plumes. Rearing snakes. Lapwing birds. Hieroglyphic symbols carved in honour of the god Amun-Re 3,000 years ago. Only the undersides of the architraves bear the remains of paint – yellows, greens, reds. It is a reminder of how garish this space once appeared. Such bright colours were necessary, for when the roof was still in place, this was a much darker place. The only light poured through small windows near the ceiling, or was cast by flames from torches, flickering in the dark. Despite the hall's size, it would have felt claustrophobic. Oppressive, even.

Tourists explore, circling columns in awe of the sheer spectacle, or perhaps just enjoying the ample shade. They admire the scale and ambition on show, perhaps a little overwhelmed. Egyptian guides speak of Ramesses the Great, of the passing of millennia. Their hyperbole is echoed by the stone. The excess and grandeur was designed to be brain-altering, you were meant to feel different; for this, the Great Hypostyle

Hall of the Temple of Amun-Re, was a place of transition, separating the temple's open courts, closer to the profane world, from the dark and mysterious divine sanctuary beyond – the beating, sacred heart of one of the world's largest religious complexes. This chamber represented the marshes of creation at the beginning of time. By walking through it, you left behind human concerns, and entered the world of gods.

Outside is the city of Luxor (Waset to the ancient Egyptians and Thebes to the Greeks), a tourist magnet built on the fame of its spectacular monuments. Whether you're staying in one of the East Bank's luxurious hotels or on one of the many cruise ships that line the riverfront, you don't have to venture far to meet someone trying to tempt you into their store to buy souvenirs, or offering you a horse-drawn carriage ride or sailboat on the Nile. There are shops and restaurants to suit all tastes – and wallets – as well as a fabulous museum, amazing temples and a hectic atmosphere that can prove energizing or overwhelming. (If the latter, you'll want to base yourself in the far more laid-back West Bank, for which see Chapter 4.) It's odd to think that none of this would exist today if not for Amun-Re, a creator of absolute importance in ancient times, but who no longer enjoys the same fame as gods like Osiris, Anubis or Isis. Being originally a god of darkness and hiddenness, a reclusive observer, perhaps he doesn't mind.

Amun-Re: King of the Gods

The Egyptians envisioned Amun – 'the Hidden One' – as a god in human form, sometimes with blue skin, wearing a crown of tall double plumes. He could also be shown as a ram or goose. Originally, Amun was one of the eight gods of pre-creation, known as the Ogdoad. But he didn't become especially prominent until the 11th Dynasty. This royal family line called Thebes home, and united Egypt under their rule after a period of political breakdown. Once in power, they raised Amun, their local god, to national significance. Within a short time, Amun became Amun-Re, the ultimate force of all hidden and visible power. Some 500 years later the 18th Dynasty kings, also from Thebes, raised Amun-Re's profile further. They made him the state god of Egypt. From this point on, Amun-Re was the pharaoh's divine father, and King of the Gods.

From c. 1200 BC, the Theban priests celebrated Amun-Re as the ultimate creator, the deity who existed beyond and behind the material universe. To them, Amun-Re was a god who made himself when nothing existed. And this wasn't your typical pre-creation nothingness – we're talking pre, pre-creation here, a time when there couldn't even be nothingness, because there was nowhere for nothingness to exist. There was a total absence of absence. An absolute lack of lack. (I'm sorry for giving you a headache. Let's move on.) In this unimaginable emptiness, Amun morphed into the eight deities of the Ogdoad. Each of these divinities embodied a concept or quality – such as infinity, or darkness – that when combined built something new in the emptiness: the pre-creation universe. There was now infinity. Great! But it was filled with a dull and dark expanse of motionless water, and not a lot else. Okay, thought Amun-Re, let's take this further. So, he manifested as the first mound of earth to rise from the waters. In turn, he became the sun, and then the gods of Heliopolis – the deities that together formed the physical world, our bubble of existence in the infinite waters (for more on this, see Chapter 11). We now had a place to live, and could spend eternity praising Amun-Re for it.

Amun-Re was thus responsible for both pre-creation and creation, and existed before either. He did an important job, but nothing else was known – or could be known – about him. No one knew his true appearance. He was hidden from the gods, more distant than the sky, and even further underground than the afterlife realm of the Duat. If you managed to comprehend Amun's secret identity, whether on purpose or not, you dropped down dead. This is perhaps why he plays almost no role in Egypt's myths and legends: he was beyond such things. Still, because of his cosmic importance, the Egyptians wrote many hymns for Amun or Amun-Re. One speaks of his self-creation. Amun (here identified with Re) is a creator, but was not himself created, the hymn says. He made everyone and caused them to live. He made the seasons and the months. He created heat and cold. And everyone sees the god when he sails across the sky. Another hymn says that Amun fashioned his body with his own arms. He is a god who made himself into millions, who is Atum, Khepri and Re – each traditionally manifestations of the sun god – Shu, Osiris and the moon. Amun had silver bones, gold skin, hair of lapis lazuli and teeth of turquoise.

Amun-Re's most important temple stood at Karnak, a short distance north of what is now central Luxor. The Egyptians believed this to be the spot where he created the first mound of earth at the beginning of time. This was a place of extreme wealth, where pharaoh after pharaoh donated treasures, chapels, statues and stelae in return and in thanks for Amun-Re's blessings. As a result, the temple complex expanded massively over the centuries. Within the main precinct stood the temples of Amun-Re and his son Khonsu, but there were separate precincts for the war god Montu (described in a hymn as eating raw flesh, drinking blood and burning with his eyes) and the goddess Mut,

The extensive ruins of the temple complex at Karnak. The temple was expanded over many centuries by kings wishing to praise Amun-Re.

wife of Amun. Together, the entire complex covered about 1 square kilometre (0.4 square miles).

The Karnak Temple complex was much more than just its buildings. Its priesthood owned fields, gardens, boats, building sites, livestock and even towns across Egyptian territory, which in the New Kingdom included Nubia and the Levant. They employed huge numbers of staff. By the time of King Ramesses III (r. *c.* 1185–1153 BC), 81,322 people worked for the Temple of Amun-Re – priests, administrators, hunters and boatmen among them. By comparison, in the same period, the Temple of Re-Atum at Heliopolis had 12,963 staff, and the Temple of Ptah at Memphis had 3,079. To please Amun and his divine family, the priests' daily offerings included 1,600 litres of grain, as well as fowl, wine, fruit, incense, honey, fat, flowers and vegetables. During the reign of King Amenhotep III (r. *c.* 1388–1348 BC), the Temple of Montu at Karnak alone received just under 2,300 kilograms of gold among the precious goods donated to the temple for its construction. (Just for comparison, at the time of writing, 2,300 kilograms of gold is worth £100 million, or $135 million.) Keeping the gods happy was an expensive, yet lucrative, business. Amun might be hidden, but he liked his bling.

Mut: Lady of Isheru
The goddess Mut represented the female side of kingship, and was wife to Amun-Re (though not his original wife – that was Amaunet, for whom see Chapter 8) and mother of his son, Khonsu. Mut was shown either in human form, as a lion-headed woman, or, in the later phases of Egyptian history, as a vulture. The vulture hieroglyph was also used to

write her name, which translates as 'mother'. In human form, Mut often wears a vulture-headdress or the Double Crown of Upper and Lower Egypt. She was closely connected with other lioness goddesses, such as Sekhmet and Tefnut, and like them she received many votive offerings of cat figurines.

Mut had her own temple precinct at Karnak, south of the Amun Temple. Dedicated to Mut, Lady of Isheru, this temple is notable because of its crescent-moon-shaped sacred lake, called Isheru, that curves around it. (Indeed, Isheru is the name of any sacred lake at which a feline deity was placated.) One of the temple's major features was its columned porch, used during the annual Festival of Drunkenness. To celebrate the appeasement of the country's dangerous lioness deities, celebrants drank to excess and fell asleep in the temple. When morning came, they sang, danced and had sex (presumably while suffering from a massive hangover).

On a less fun note, ceremonial executions may also have been held at the temple. At its back, archaeologists unearthed a male skeleton, his body arranged just like the bound captives shown in Egyptian art. This discovery isn't so surprising. Mut had long been associated with violent death: texts from different periods tell us that rebels were burned on the brazier of Mut, for example at Heliopolis. Mut, like other goddesses, could manifest as the fiery Eye of Re (see Chapter 5), and as the female side of kingship, she had a particular interest in punishing the king's enemies. Burning such rebels would destroy their bodies, barring them from an afterlife.

Despite this gruesome side to Mut's temple, most people who vied for the goddess's attention there were more concerned with avoiding death. When excavating the rubbish dumps in the temple's outer areas, archaeologists discovered broken nude female figurines, seemingly connected with healing. Sick people visited the precinct and purchased a figurine (probably manufactured on site), which absorbed the person's disease or illness thanks to the rituals and spells performed over it by the temple's priests. Once 'filled' with disease – an evil force – the priests broke the figurine to destroy or neutralize the threat captured in its fabric, and dumped it in the temple refuse.

Khonsu and his cosmogony

The god Khonsu ('The Traveller') was the son of Amun and Mut. He had his own temple at the south-west side of the Amun-Re precinct at Karnak. A moon god, Khonsu can be identified by the unified full and crescent moon resting on his head. He usually takes fully human form (though occasionally with a hawk's head), and sports a side-lock of youth – the hairstyle worn by children, reflecting his position in his triad. Despite his childlike appearance, Khonsu could be a pretty violent god, perhaps taking after his mother. In the Pyramid Texts, he strangles and eviscerates 'the lords' for the king, while the Coffin Texts describe him as eating hearts and heads. It is surprising, then, that later in Egyptian history, Khonsu and his temple became famous for healing, particularly in the Ptolemaic Period, when he is said to have healed King Ptolemy IV (rather than strangled, eviscerated or eaten him). The temple even issued 'oracular amuletic decrees' to protect people from illnesses.

Like many Egyptian gods, Khonsu had his own creation myth, known as the Khonsu Cosmogony, carved on the walls of his temple. It borrows from other cosmogonies at Heliopolis, Memphis and Hermopolis, and goes as follows: Amun-Re created all things as the

The divine triad of Karnak Temple: Amun-Re (left), Mut and Khonsu.

ram-headed Kematef snake, starting in Memphis. Having created the earth and the sky, the snake, who was simultaneously Amun and Ptah, spat out an egg. When it hatched, a second snake came into being. Amun/Ptah then fertilized another egg at Hermopolis, which created the Ogdoad. Next, Amun/Ptah transformed into Khonsu, and travelled to Thebes. Hathor now came into existence, and Khonsu – back in the form of Ptah – slept with her. Confusingly, their union led to the birth of the Ogdoad (again) – this was probably an attempt to explain why the Ogdoad were gods of both Hermopolis and Thebes.

'Khonsu the Exorcist'

Carved on a stele at the Temple of Khonsu at Karnak, this tale of possession is set during the reign of King Ramesses II (*c*. 1279–1212 BC). Ramesses was in the land of Naharin (roughly northern Syria and southeastern Turkey) to receive gifts from the princes of foreign lands. When the prince of Bakhtan approached him, he offered Ramesses not only his usual gifts, but something extra: the hand of his eldest daughter in marriage. Ramesses – who already had a large harem, and over 100 children – accepted the proposal. He gave his new bride the Egyptian name Neferure. Some time later, when Ramesses was making offerings at Luxor Temple, a messenger sent by the prince of Bakhtan arrived with gifts for Neferure and, more importantly, an appeal for help: 'Neferure's younger sister, the princess Bentresh, has fallen ill,' said the messenger. 'Please send a knowledgeable man from Egypt to help her.' Ramesses summoned his advisors. Could they suggest a suitable person to make the journey, he asked. They chose the royal scribe Thothemheb.

Thothemheb travelled from Egypt to Bakhtan, and upon arrival, visited the princess. His diagnosis? A ghost had possessed her. But don't worry, he said; he knew how to deal with this type of problem. He sent a messenger back to Egypt, requesting that the king despatch a god who could fight the ghost. By the time the messenger reached Egypt, it had been three years since the first news of the princess's sickness. Ramesses received the message in Thebes, which was lucky, because it meant that he could visit the god Khonsu-in-Thebes-Neferhotep. 'I'm here because of the prince of Bakhtan's daughter,' he said. The god listened to the king's story, and went to visit a friend, Khonsu-the-Authority, famous for exorcizing spirits. Ramesses followed. 'Can Khonsu-the-Authority visit Bakhtan to help the princess?' he asked. The god nodded.

Khonsu-the-Authority departed for Bakhtan with an escort. The journey lasted one year and five months. The god was honoured by the prince of Bakhtan and taken straight to Princess Bentresh upon arrival. Wasting no time, Khonsu used his magic to protect her. Within seconds, she became well again. The ghost emerged from her body and materialized before Khonsu. 'I am your servant,' the ghost said. 'I will happily return home, but first, will you and the prince of Bakhtan enjoy a meal with me?' Not one to pass up a celebration, the god agreed. Khonsu remained with the ghost while the prince and his soldiers, all rather terrified, made the party preparations. Both Khonsu and the ghost received their hosts' offerings, and the ghost departed happy. The prince and the people of Bakhtan cheered with happiness, relieved that their ordeal was over.

But that wasn't the end for Khonsu. Impressed by all that he'd witnessed, the prince proclaimed that the god must remain in Bakhtan. Three years and nine months later, the prince was sleeping in his palace, when in a dream, he watched Khonsu rise as a golden falcon from his shrine and fly to Egypt. It is a sign, the prince thought. The next morning, he allowed Khonsu-the-Authority to return to Egypt, sending him with gifts, horses and soldiers. And so, the god returned home to Thebes, arriving a whole ten years after the first messenger from Bakhtan had entered Egypt with news of Bentresh's illness.

Luxor Temple and the royal *ka*

Luxor Temple – the Southern Opet (Ipet Resyt) to the ancient Egyptians – is one of the most popular ancient sites visited by tourists in Egypt. It was dedicated to Amenemopet, 'Amun in Opet', a particular form of Amun specific to this temple, and the cult of the royal *ka*, the spirit of kingship that entered the king's body during his coronation. Each year, during the Opet Festival, the king visited Luxor Temple for a ritualized rebirth, in which the royal *ka* within him was reconfirmed and re-energized, proving his right to the kingship.

The festival began within Karnak Temple. After the king had made offerings to Amun-Re, Mut and Khonsu, priests placed the gods' statues on their processional barques, and took them by land or boat to Luxor Temple. The king and priests led the way. Soldiers marched. The people of Luxor watched and celebrated. Once at Luxor Temple, only those of sufficient ritual purity followed the king and the gods into the cult chambers. In the first chamber after the hypostyle hall – a place called the 'Chamber of the Divine King' (today the room with the Roman Period sanctuary) – the king knelt before Amun-Re, while priests purified him with water and re-enacted his coronation. Through these rituals, the royal *ka*-spirit passed from the god – the king's divine father – to the

The pylon entrance to the Temple of Luxor.

king, rejuvenating him. The king, gods and priests then proceeded into the barque sanctuary of Amun-Re, where the king viewed the god and made further offerings. To complete the rituals, the priests crowned the king a second time. The king and the gods now left Luxor Temple, re-emerging into public view to the sound of rejoicing on the streets of Luxor, to return to the Karnak temple precinct by land or river.

Amenemopet of Luxor Temple also played a key role in the Decade Festival, in which the god travelled across the Nile to the Temple of King Ramesses III at Medinet Habu. In mythology, this was the location where the Ogdoad of Hermopolis – the eight primordial creator gods – and a serpent form of Amun called Kematef were buried beneath a mound. Queen Hatshepsut (r. *c.* 1472–1457 BC) built a small temple on this spot, and later, Ramesses III constructed his mortuary temple there too. During the Decade Festival, Amenemopet visited the burial site (Hatshepsut's temple) to conduct a funeral for the Ogdoad. He merged with Amun-Kematef and joined the Ogdoad, re-energizing him and causing him to be reborn.

The 'Divine Birth' legend at Luxor Temple
Within Luxor Temple's 'birth room', close to the sanctuary, scenes and texts describe the divine birth of King Amenhotep III. The god Amun-Re took the form of the future king's father, Tuthmosis IV, and entered the queen's bed-chamber. His divine scent – a fragrance that smelled like the fine incense and myrrh from the land of Punt – awoke her. The

god became aroused, and the two slept together. It was from this union that Amenhotep III was born. The associated scene shows Amun-Re seated opposite the queen, offering an *ankh* – a symbol of life – to the queen's mouth, representing the conception of Amenhotep III.

An earlier version of the same legend decorates part of the mortuary temple of Queen Hatshepsut at Deir el-Bahri, on the west bank of Luxor (see Chapter 4). Other examples are also known, though they're not as complete, including one from the reign of King Ramesses II. Similar statements concerning the king's divine associations or selection from a young age can be found throughout Egyptian history. Texts make reference to a god choosing the king even before his birth, or to the king already ruling in the egg – an allusion to the birth of the falcon god Horus, whom every king embodied in life. King Horemheb (r. *c.* 1328–1298 BC), a military general who became pharaoh at the end of the 18th Dynasty, commissioned an inscription explaining that Horus of Hutnesu – the place where he grew up – chose him to be king.

'The Blinding of Truth by Falsehood'

The story today known as 'The Blinding of Truth by Falsehood' was written on a papyrus found in Thebes. After its lost beginning, in which it seems that Falsehood complained at court about Truth's failure to return his fabulous, massive knife, the story opens with a description of said knife. This knife was special. Its blade was like a mountain, its haft wood was from Coptos, and its scabbard was like a god's tomb. In the great hall of the gods, Falsehood stood before the divine Ennead to demand that Truth, his brother, be blinded. Without sight, Truth would serve as doorkeeper to his house. The gods agreed to his request. Truth was blinded and sent to work at Falsehood's house. But Falsehood could see that people still admired Truth; so he commanded his servants to abduct Truth and feed him to the lions and lionesses. They did as Falsehood asked, but took pity on Truth before the animals could tear him to shreds. 'Please feed a piece of bread to the lions instead,' Truth said to Falsehood's servants. This they did (no doubt to the lions' disappointment), and Truth escaped.

Later, while Truth lay beneath a thicket, a rich lady and her retinue passed by. The lady's servants saw Truth's handsomeness, and told their mistress about him. The lady asked that Truth be brought to her, and the moment her eyes fell on him, she agreed. She slept with Truth that night and fell pregnant. Nine months later, she gave birth to a boy. He was like a god: the best at writing in his school, and a master of the art of war. But the other students laughed at him, for he had no father.

One day, when the bullying became too much, the boy stormed home to confront his mother. 'Who is my father?' he demanded. His mother pointed to the blind doorkeeper. Furious at the treatment of his father, the boy took Truth aside, fed him, and gave him a chair and footstool. 'Who blinded you?' the boy said. 'I will take revenge.' Truth told the boy his story, explaining how his younger brother had blinded him. The boy listened, shaking his head in disbelief, and devised a plan to avenge his father.

The next day, the boy went to visit Falsehood's herdsman. He gave the herdsman ten loaves of bread, a staff, a waterskin, a sword and a pair of sandals. All he asked for in exchange was that the herdsman keep an eye on his ox until he returned. It seemed like a good deal, so the herdsman agreed. Months passed, until one day, Falsehood visited the herdsman to check on his oxen. Falsehood found the boy's ox extremely beautiful. 'Give me this one to eat,' he said to the herdsman. 'It's not mine to give away,' the herdsman replied. Falsehood didn't care: in his mind, all of these oxen belonged to him. Falsehood took the ox.

When the boy discovered that Falsehood had stolen his ox, he visited the herdsman. 'You can take any one of the remaining cattle in its place,' the herdsman said. The boy frowned. 'Are there any as large as the one that Falsehood took?' he asked. 'My ox was half the size of the Delta.' The herdsman scoffed: there couldn't possibly be an ox as large as the one that the boy was describing. The boy grabbed the herdsman, and took him to Falsehood. To solve the dispute, the three of them visited the tribunal of the Ennead together. The Ennead, too, were sceptical that the boy owned an ox as big as the one he described. 'Surely this could never have existed,' they said. The boy replied: 'Has there ever been a dagger as large as the one that Falsehood says he owned? I'm Truth's son, and I've come to avenge my father.' Falsehood made an oath: 'If Truth is alive,' he said, 'Let me be blinded in both eyes and made to serve as Truth's doorkeeper.' The boy led the Ennead to meet his father, proving that he still lived. An oath's an oath, so Falsehood was punished. He was beaten, given five open wounds, blinded, and made to serve as Truth's doorkeeper.

Thebes's East Bank in history and today

Ancient Thebes was a place worthy of hymns – a 'religious capital', designed so that divine processions could easily travel between its major temples. But beyond its temples and tombs, archaeologists know very little about its original appearance. The earliest evidence for construction at the Karnak temple precinct is a column erected by King Intef II (r. *c.* 2123–2074 BC) or King Intef III (r. *c.* 2074–2066 BC). Shortly afterwards, under the 12th Dynasty, a stone sanctuary was built there for Amun. It was during this phase – the Middle Kingdom – that Thebes grew into a large city, complete with royal palaces and houses laid out on a grid pattern.

In the New Kingdom, parts of Thebes were demolished to make way for the expanding temple precincts of Amun-Re and Mut, and for Luxor Temple to their south. Under the 18th Dynasty kings, builders extended the temple of Amun-Re along two different axes: one heading south towards Luxor Temple; the other westward, towards the bank of the Nile. Over time, reaching out from the divine hub of the New Kingdom sanctuary (just in front of what had been the Middle Kingdom sanctuary), successive kings built columned halls – including the Great Hypostyle Hall of the 19th Dynasty – open courts and pylon-gateways, as well as smaller temples, obelisks, statues, barque shrines, kiosks, chapels and a sacred lake. There was even a royal palace within the temple grounds. New housing sprung up around Thebes' temple complexes. If a painting from a now lost New Kingdom tomb is accurate, some of this housing was built in multistorey rows, reflecting a dense living environment. Meanwhile, excavations have revealed town houses of 18th and 19th Dynasty date that once stood on what is now the road to Luxor's airport.

After the apex of its wealth and influence in the New Kingdom, Thebes entered the Third Intermediate Period as an independent province, ruled directly by the oracle of Amun from the Karnak temple precinct. This phase didn't last long, however, and Egypt was again reunited under the Nubian 25th Dynasty. Soon after, in 663 BC, Thebes was sacked by the Assyrian army, who carried off many of the city's treasures to Nineveh. With Egypt's political focus now in the north, Thebes' importance began to wane. Nonetheless, after the Persian occupation of Egypt (the 27th Dynasty), successive kings returned to Karnak to leave their mark on the temple complex, a process that continued into the Ptolemaic Period and until the arrival of the Romans.

Due to intermittent rebellions against Roman rule in the Theban region, the Romans turned Luxor Temple into a military camp, and afterwards, left it to be engulfed by the surrounding town. The last hieroglyphic inscription at the Karnak temple precinct was carved under Emperor Domitian in the late 1st century AD. Just under three hundred years later, Emperor Constantius II sent one of the temple's obelisks to Rome (it is now known as the Lateran or Unique Obelisk).

Key dates and remains

c. 2120 BC	First evidence for construction at the Karnak temple precinct.
c. 1970 BC	The White Chapel of King Senwosret I is built at Karnak. A stone sanctuary is added to the Temple of Amun.
c. 1380 BC	Construction of the Precinct of Mut at Karnak begins. Construction also begins at Luxor Temple, replacing earlier buildings.
c. 1300 BC	Construction of the Great Hypostyle Hall in the Temple of Amun at Karnak begins.
c. 1185 BC	Construction of the Temple of Khonsu at Karnak begins.
663 BC	The Assyrian army sacks the Karnak temple precinct.
c. 332 BC	Barque shrine of Amun built under Alexander the Great at Luxor Temple.
c. 323 BC	Granite shrine of Amun-Re built under Philip Arrhidaeus at the Temple of Amun at Karnak.
c. AD 81	Last hieroglyphic inscription carved at the Karnak temple precinct.
c. 300	The Romans transform Luxor Temple into a military camp.
357	Emperor Constantius II sends an obelisk, originally from Karnak, to Rome.
c. 1200	Mosque of Abu'l Haggag built at Luxor Temple.
1903	The 'Karnak Cachette' – a huge collection of ancient statues and ritual objects – is discovered south of the Hypostyle Hall in the Temple of Amun at Karnak. The statues had been cleared from the temple and buried during the Ptolemaic Period.

Parts of the complex were later transformed into Christian places of worship. After Egypt's conversion to Islam, these monasteries closed, and Thebes' grand temples fell into ruin. Over the following centuries, travellers commented on the city's breathtaking wonders, but they weren't fully cleared and revealed again until the 19th and 20th centuries. Today, Luxor's economy is reliant on tourists, who come to see the ancient remains and to enjoy the beautiful surroundings.

▲

The East Bank's major attractions are the Karnak temple precinct, Luxor Temple and **Luxor Museum**, located between the two, which has an excellent collection of artefacts, including impressive statues. From the **Karnak temple precinct**'s main entrance and visitor centre, you pass along a row of **ram-headed sphinxes** through a pylon gateway into the first court of the Temple of Amun-Re. If you take a look at the back of this pylon, you'll find there's still a mud-brick ramp left from its construction. The temple's **first court** has **two 'way stations'**, places where the divine barques of Amun-Re, Mut and Khonsu rested and underwent rituals during their journeys in and out of the temple. The first, and simpler, one dates to the reign of King Seti II (*c.* 1201–1195 BC); the other – effectively a miniature temple – was built under King Ramesses III (r. *c.* 1185–1153 BC). Entered through the Second Pylon, one of the temple's highlights is its **Great Hypostyle Hall**. This was constructed at the start of the 19th Dynasty, particularly under King Seti I (r. *c.* 1296–1279 BC) and King Ramesses II (r. *c.* 1279–1212 BC). At the eastern half of the north wall, there's a nice image of Seti I in the sacred persea tree, while Thoth writes the king's name on its leaves. Scenes showing Seti and Ramesses in battle are carved on the exterior walls of the Great Hypostyle Hall.

Moving further into the temple, you pass **obelisks of Tuthmosis I and Hatshepsut** and into the holy of holies, with its **granite shrine of Amun-Re** erected under Philip Arrhidaeus (r. 323–317 BC), Alexander the Great's half-brother and immediate successor. Divided in two, the first part of the shrine was the sanctuary of Amun-Re proper, where his divine statue received offerings (note the offering scenes on the walls), while the second half was for the god's divine barque. On the walls of the passage that surrounds the shrine of Amun-Re you'll find the annals of the wars of King Tuthmosis III (r. *c.* 1479–1424 BC), detailing the booty that he brought back from the Levant for Amun-Re. Behind the shrine and its surrounding complex of chambers there's a ruined court, and beyond, a **memorial temple** from the reign of Tuthmosis III. Highlights here include a king list (in the 'Chamber of the Ancestors') and Tuthmosis' 'Botanical Garden' – depictions of flora and fauna from his campaigns in the Levant. In the temple precinct's **open-air museum,** you'll see the beautifully carved **White Chapel of King Senwosret I** (r. *c.* 1974–1929 BC), and images of Hatshepsut's coronation on the walls of her **Red Chapel,** originally erected in front of the sanctuary of Amun-Re. The **Temple of Khonsu** stands at the south-west corner of the Amun complex, while the **Temple of Mut** is in its own enclosure to the south.

A 3-kilometre (2-mile) long **avenue of sphinxes,** much of which has now been excavated, connects the Karnak Temple complex to **Luxor Temple's pylon-gateway** and the **first court** beyond, both built under King Ramesses II. The temple's **colonnade** comes next; it was started under King Amenhotep III (r. *c.* 1388–1348 BC) of the 18th Dynasty, but finished much later. This is succeeded by a **peristyle court** and a **hypostyle hall.** Behind the hall, you'll find the temple's main **cult chambers,** including the **'birth room'** where Amenhotep III's divine conception is described; a **barque shrine** constructed under Alexander the Great (r. *c.* 332–323 BC); and at the very rear, **the sanctuary of the god Amenemopet,** built under Amenhotep III. Among modern Egyptians, Luxor Temple is also famous as the setting for an annual festival connected with the **mosque of Abu'l Haggag,** which was built over part of the temple's first courtyard during the 13th century.

El-Qurn, the 'natural pyramid' that rises over the Valley of the Kings,
burial ground of the New Kingdom pharaohs.

4

THEBES
WEST BANK

~~~~~~~~~~~~~~~~~~

Celebrating with the Dead

'I oversaw the digging of his majesty's cliff-tomb,
alone, none seeing, none hearing.'

In his tomb, the courtier Ineni refers to his work in the Valley of the Kings, c.1465 BC

'See, I do not wish to leave Thebes. Take me away from what I hate.
Whenever I sail north, the city accompanies me. The Temple of Amun is
on my road.... Bring me to your city, Amun. I love it. I love your city, more than
food and more than beer, Amun. More than clothes, more than ointments.'

Written on a pot sherd (ostracon) found at Deir el-Medina, c.1200 BC

When you stand in a tomb, there's a sense of disconnection from the
world. Perhaps it's simply knowing where you are and where you'll one
day be, but something makes you feel like you're standing in a place
removed from reality. This is certainly the case in the Valley of the
Kings; and for me, particularly in the burial chamber of King Tuthmosis III
(r. *c.* 1479–1424 BC). Take a set of modern, metal steps through a rocky
crevice, then proceed down through ancient, carved corridors, and
you'll reach the king's final resting place. It isn't the most lavish or the
grandest tomb in the Valley, but it certainly feels the most adventur-
ous. At first glance, the burial chamber's moodily up-lit decoration
appears almost simplistic – inked hieroglyphs, stick figures, winged
snakes, boats and mysterious mounds, within borders of pink and
yellow, sit below a starry sky. But the paintings and writings that wrap
around the room like an unfurled papyrus scroll are anything but
simple. They are a complex guide to the king's afterlife in the netherworld realm of the Duat, including a detailed catalogue of gods and
demons and an explanation for the sun god's disappearance at night.

Most importantly, they represent the eternal struggle between order and chaos, in which the king, united in death with the sun god Re, fights to keep the cosmos active. The drama of these scenes is at odds with the quiet of the tomb. I hear the gentle hum of an air pump. The chatter of visitors, echoing from other corridors. The shuffle of the tomb guardian's sandals. For a moment, I am elsewhere.

This sense of quiet permeates Luxor's West Bank. It's a different world from the hectic East Bank. Where the East Bank is filled with hotels and restaurants, apartment blocks, souvenir shops, taxis, feluccas and horse-drawn carriages, the West Bank is a haven of small villages, swaying palm trees and dusty ancient monuments. From the moment your ferry or motorboat drops you at the docks, the distant fields and mountains beckon. Where the cultivation meets the desert, the mortuary temples of the New Kingdom pharaohs stand in various states of ruin. Beyond, the western horizon is dominated by el-Qurn, the pyramidal peak that rises above the tombs of ancient nobles cut into the hillside. And behind them, excavated into the wadis (dry riverbeds) of the desert, is the Valley of the Kings – once a place of untold riches, sealed away in dark chambers and corridors. Luxor's West Bank was a place of transition, of priests and funerals, where festivals celebrated the dearly departed and ghost stories cautioned the dangers of messing with supernatural forces.

The Valley of the Nobles: staying alive (in death)

Now that we've set the scene, it's time to get spooky. The Egyptians used Luxor's West Bank as a cemetery for thousands of years, starting perhaps as early as *c.* 2520 BC. The hills of the desert escarpment are dotted with rock-cut tombs – the burials of local families of importance: viziers, high priests, military men, scribes and everyone in between. But the Egyptians' relationship with the dead didn't end with the sealing of a coffin. A typical Egyptian tomb had two main sections: the burial itself, hidden from view underground, where the tomb owner's mummy, along with the mummies of his family, lay in their coffins, sealed away with their grave goods; and a public 'chapel' that any passer-by could enter. This was a space filled with painted scenes and inscriptions highlighting the deceased's good service for the king and gods.

What was the point of all this? The Egyptians believed that an individual was composed of various aspects that separated at the moment of death to explore their own destinies: there was the *ka*, a form of life-force or double that remained in the tomb; the *ba*, representing movement and personality, which entered the Duat but could return to the mummy at night to sleep and recharge; the shadow, which was a double of the person, present throughout life, but free in death (just like Dracula's shadow); the body, which needed to be preserved as a vessel for the *ba*; and the name, which identified the person. The loss of any one of these aspects caused the second (true) death: obliteration from existence. Destroy all copies of a person's name, and they vanished for ever. Burn the mummy and it was the same fate, unless that person had invested in ritually awakened statues, inscribed with their name. Sometimes, the Egyptians sealed these backup statues in special chambers within the tomb chapel to protect them from damage. Visitors could only see these statues through small holes or slits in the walls, installed so that the scent of burnt offerings or incense could waft in and be experienced by the spirit inhabiting the statue.

The *ka* and the *ba* required sustenance in the afterlife. The painted scenes and texts inscribed on the walls of the tomb chapel magically provided this sustenance, with the *ka* able to enter the scenes, like a form of ancient virtual reality. But the nourishment provided wasn't as potent as true, physical offerings made by a visitor. This is why the Egyptians dedicated so much space in the tomb chapel to advertising a person's worthiness: it was all an effort to tempt you to make offerings and say prayers to this obviously deserving individual. You were meant to be impressed. The inscriptions included plenty of copies of the deceased person's name, too, so that there were backups, just in case some nefarious visitor decided to scratch the name away. As you can see, the Egyptians developed many practical plans to ensure their afterlife existence. Every problem had a solution.

The Beautiful Festival of the Valley and ghost stories

Every year at Thebes, during the ninth month, the Egyptians celebrated a major two-day event called the Beautiful Festival of the Valley. The gods of the Karnak temple precinct – Amun, Mut and Khonsu – left their shrines and crossed the Nile to the West Bank, accompanied by the pharaoh. Together, they travelled to each of the royal mortuary temples, one by one, to visit the kings of the past, who in death had fused with local manifestations of Amun. Meanwhile, the people of Thebes celebrated in the necropolis, visiting their own lost loved ones and ancestors. At the tombs, families made burnt offerings for the dead, while the temples provided free food and alcohol for the celebration. Even the dead got drunk. This temple-sponsored intoxication wasn't just to ensure that a good time was had by all: the drunken haze was thought to blur the lines between the realms of the living and the dead, and to create a calm mood, just as alcohol had calmed the bloodthirsty Hathor-Sekhmet in myth (see Chapter 5). Inebriated families spent the night among the tombs, wearing flower garlands called *wah*-collars, which served as symbols of regeneration. They offered these garlands to the dead too.

Interactions with ghosts were not unusual in ancient Egypt. The dead played an important role in daily life. They were part of existence, just the same as anything else in the cosmos, from cats and priests to celestial cows. Unlike modern movies and literature, ancient Egyptian stories don't present encountering a ghost as a terrifying experience: most of the time, it's just like meeting an old friend. And the dead had access to the gods, so if you wanted a powerful divinity to improve your life, a conversation with a ghost who might be persuaded to pass on a message was a good starting point. At the same time, the dead had expectations of the living: they wanted a steady supply of offerings and a well-maintained tomb. And they could cause serious problems if their expectations weren't met – such as ruining your life. If you didn't know a friendly ghost, it was possible to summon one, as long as you knew the right spells. To summon a dead man (a zombie?), you placed the dung of an ass and an amulet of the goddess Nephthys on a brazier, forcing him to enter your chamber. To summon a spirit, you placed two specific types of stone (sadly difficult to identify) onto the brazier, and once the spirit had entered, it was a good idea to burn a hyena's or hare's heart on the brazier, too. Another type of stone, unidentified but said to be connected with the sea, summoned a drowned person.

Given that the Egyptians believed the person to scatter into various independent spiritual aspects at death, it's interesting that only the shadow, *ba* and *akh* – a status given to spirits who had passed Osiris' judgment – appear as ghosts in stories and spells, with the *akh* being the most commonly attested. There are no *ka*-ghosts or stumbling mummies. Artistic representations of spirits are rare. On a wall in the tomb of the workman Irinefer, at Deir el-Medina, the shadow is a standing man, thin and entirely black, as if in silhouette. Paintings of the dead as an *akh* are virtually non-existent, though texts describe them as manifesting in human form. Images of *ba*-spirits are more common, and usually show them as human-headed birds.

Various ghost stories have survived from ancient Egypt, though few are preserved well enough to reconstruct the story in full. One tale is today known as 'The Levitating Ghost'. Due to its fragmentary nature, we can only really say that its main characters were the king, his courtiers, a poor man and an *akh*-spirit, described as floating in the air. A few other ghost stories feature a son of King Ramesses II (r. *c.* 1279–1212 BC), Prince Khaemwaset, later popularly known as Setna-Khaemwaset. These are presented in Chapter 8. Two other stories, however, star priests of Amun-Re, so let's look at these here.

The tale of 'Khonsuemhab and the Ghost'

In the broken beginning of 'Khonsuemhab and the Ghost', the high priest of Amun-Re, Khonsuemhab, has travelled home after telling a ghost that he will provide him with offerings. From the roof of his house, Khonsuemhab called on the gods of the sky, land, necropolis and the four cardinal points to make the ghost appear before him. The ghost materialized, and Khonsuemhab asked him for his name and the names of his parents. He wanted to make offerings to them. 'My name is Nebusemekh,' the ghost said. 'My father is Ankhmen and my mother is Itemshaset.' Khonsuemhab offered to make a new tomb for Nebusemekh, complete with a wooden coffin, covered in gold. 'I am hungry and cold,' the ghost said. He had other problems too, but these are lost due to breaks in the text. Whatever they were, they were so intense that Khonsuemhab wept. 'In life, I served King Montuhotep II [founder of the Middle Kingdom, r. *c.* 2066–2014 BC] as overseer of the treasury and lieutenant-commander of the army,' Nebusemekh said. 'I died in the fourteenth year of his reign, and was buried in a tomb built for me by the king. It was provisioned with funerary goods. But now my tomb has fallen apart. The wind blows through it. Four times before, people have said that they'd rebuild my tomb. Nothing happened.' Khonsuemhab reassured Nebusemekh: the tomb would be rebuilt. After a break in the text, Khonsuemhab has sent his staff to Thebes' West Bank to search for the ghost's crumbling tomb. They discovered it close to Montuhotep II's mortuary temple at Deir el-Bahri, and returned to the Temple of Amun-Re at Karnak to report the good news to the high priest. The night was filled with celebration. The next day, the high priest summoned the deputy of the domain of Amun to assign him the work of rebuilding the tomb. Unfortunately, the story breaks off here. We'll have to assume it turned out alright for poor Nebusemekh.

'The Vengeful Ghost'

A priest of Amun-Re, his wife and their children had travelled to Thebes to attend a feast. While they were preparing themselves for the meal, a messenger arrived to speak with the priest: there were important matters to be discussed, matters that needed to be brought to the pharaoh's attention. Without delay, the priest left to deal with his business. The priest's wife decided to attend the meal without her husband, and sent the children ahead to arrive first. As soon as the children stepped through the doors of the banqueting hall, they were murdered. Soon after, the priest's wife arrived, only to face the same violent death. A slave witnessed the massacre and fled. He found the priest and explained all that he'd seen. The priest rushed to the hall, but he was no match for his assailants, who cut him down without mercy. The entire family was dead. The unidentified culprits roamed free.

Soon after, Prince Setna-Khaemwaset, son of King Ramesses II, was performing his royal duties, when a ghost appeared before him. The ghost was a priest of Sokar-Osiris, one of the sons of the murdered priest of Amun-Re. The ghost asked Setna to take revenge on the man who had killed his family. 'Meet me in Abydos,' the ghost said as he vanished, 'for this is where the murderer lives.' Setna visited his father, Ramesses, and explained all that he'd seen and been told. Ramesses was shocked to discover that the murderer hadn't been brought to justice. 'Go deal with this criminal!' the king said.

When Setna arrived in Abydos, the ghost appeared again. 'The murderer is a priest of Isis, called Petese,' he said. Together, they developed a plan. At the temple of Abydos, Setna asked the herald to summon Petese and his followers, enticing them to the temple with the promise of fabulous royal gifts. Setna made offerings to Isis and Osiris-Sokar (presumably to apologize for the blood about to be spilled in their earthly home), and waited. When Petese and his gang arrived, Setna shackled them and executed each conspirator with a spear. Wiping the fresh blood from his weapon, Setna asked the ghost if he needed anything else. 'Please bury my parents, for Petese stopped this from happening,' he said. 'And make my eldest son a priest of Osiris-Sokar, and my younger son a priest of Amun-Re.'

The Book of the Dead: a guide to the afterlife

During the New Kingdom, a deceased Egyptian nobleman wouldn't be caught dead in his tomb without a Book of the Dead. This composition, known as '(The Book of) Going Forth by Day' to the ancient Egyptians, provided the deceased with a guide to the otherworld realm of the Duat – the place through which the sun god travelled at night, and which in death spirits traversed to reach Osiris' judgment hall. The Book first makes its appearance shortly before the New Kingdom, and many of the spells can be traced back to the Coffin Texts of the Middle Kingdom, themselves developed from the Old Kingdom Pyramid

Texts. Spells from the Book of the Dead were written on papyrus, leather, linen, amulets, figurines and on the walls of tombs and coffins – items and locations that would be close to the deceased's mummy in the burial chamber. But there are indications that the Egyptians read the Book in life too, giving ample time for them to prepare themselves for the many oddities and trials that they would encounter in the Duat.

For the Duat was a terrifying place. It was filled with dangerous beings, whose sole purpose was to frustrate the deceased's progress, from men, gods and spirits of the dead to strange demons – creatures that walked upside down, drank blood and ate their own excrement and entrails. To make it through safely, the deceased had to call on the Book's magic – pronouncing its spells and performing rituals over specific objects – or rely on good old-fashioned weapons. But the afterlife wasn't all bad. In death, each person became an Osiris – they even used his name as a title – and so partook in the god's powers and regeneration. Some deities provided food and aid, while the deceased, through magic, could transform into certain gods – including Atum-Khepri, Shu and even Re – and use their powers and influence to aid their journey. The spirit could also change into various creatures: a crocodile, a snake, a falcon, a phoenix and a swallow among them. Because of the advantages such magic gave the dead, demons often tried to steal their magic and had to be repelled with spells.

The Book of the Dead provides details on specific otherworld destinations, including caverns, mounds, gateways, waterways, fields and mountains. The geographic links between these places aren't always clear – you can't use the Book of the Dead as a map of this mysterious world. Of the many locations described, the gateways were of particular importance, because the dead had to pass through them to reach the judgment hall of Osiris. Spell 144 says that there were seven gateways, each protected by a keeper, guard and announcer. The deceased had to announce the name of each demon in order to pass safely. Spell 146, however, says that there were twenty-one gateways, each with a guardian and doorkeeper. (Though these spells contradict each other, it was best to include both – one had to be correct!) Such demons might sound fearsome, but in the Duat, if a spirit pronounced a being's (or even a thing's) name correctly, it ceased to be dangerous, and became their supporter.

The deceased's goal was to pass Osiris' judgment (for more on this see Chapter 6), and so gain the rank of *akh*; this identified the person as a transfigured spirit in human form, an eternal being of

The Book of the Dead of a 19th Dynasty courtier named Ani, showing a number of the gateways through which the deceased must pass in the Duat to reach judgment.

light, with free movement within creation. In this form, many after-life destinations were available, depending on the spirit's mood. The dead could join Re on his solar boat and help him in his endless battle against chaos; take part in the tribunal judging between Horus and Seth; freely enter and leave the realm of the dead; transform into any shape; play the board game senet; and eat Osiris' food offerings. One afterlife destination prominently featured in the Book of the Dead's artwork, and sometimes on tomb walls, is the Field of Reeds. This was a heightened version of Egypt, literally – spirits were taller than in life, and the crops grew higher too. There, the dead ploughed their bountiful fields, sailed on their waterways, and worshipped their ancestors and gods, safe in the knowledge that the Field's walls of iron barred entry to any dangerous forces.

Deir el-Medina: contacting the ancestors and household deities

Deir el-Medina is the modern name for a small village known to the ancient Egyptians as Set Maat, 'The Place of Truth'. It is the well-preserved home of the artisans who dug and decorated the royal tombs in the Valley of the Kings, and a must for any visitor to Luxor's West Bank. Here, you can walk the village's ancient streets, explore the remains of its houses, and even visit the artisans' tombs, built overlooking their homes. Much is known about the Deir el-Medina villagers due to the excavation of their stone houses, but also because of the vast quantity of textual material found at the site. Being literate (unlike the vast majority of the ancient Egyptian population), these artisans jotted down their thoughts and letters on ostraca – broken pieces of pottery or chunks of stone – which were readily available, and cheaper than papyrus. The ostraca were dumped, once read, as garbage in an abandoned well (where archaeologists found them). Thanks to this unique (and accidental) archive, we know their work habits and families; who lived in which house at any given time; and which gods played a prominent role in their daily lives.

If you could travel back in time to Egypt's New Kingdom and visit the people of Deir el-Medina in their houses, you'd find that many families kept ancestor busts and stelae dedicated to 'Able Spirits of Re' (*Akh iker en Re* in Egyptian). Both were connected to the Egyptian belief in the *akh* – a title bestowed on anyone who had passed judgment by Osiris in the afterlife. The stelae usually show a seated male or female *akh* – a dead relative of the family – while the busts, which only display the upper torso and head of the deceased, seem to represent the totality of a person's ancestors. People placed offerings before both objects in the hope that the dead would provide help, perhaps by having a word with one of the more powerful gods on their behalf. Remember, though, this was a dangerous business: if you didn't make offerings to the satisfaction of the *akhu* (the plural form of *akh*), they could become angry and make life difficult for you, and perhaps even bring about your death. Luckily, insulted *akhu* could be warded off with magic, or with the help of friendly household gods.

As well as owning shrines to ancestors, ordinary Egyptians made offerings to deities that could influence their daily lives. The most famous Egyptian gods – ones like Amun, Ptah or Osiris – had big roles to play in the cosmos, but they weren't the obvious choices to appeal to when faced with more local or down-to-earth concerns, such as the harvest, health or starting a family. For such issues, people could approach an array of more relatable, household deities. For one, there was Bes, a bearded dwarf with a lion's mane and ears, who wore a plumed crown and held knives (or the less dangerous tambourine or harp). He was normally shown with his tongue sticking out, and protected mothers in childbirth and children. Unusually for Egyptian art, Bes is typically painted face on, looking straight at the viewer. His aggressive nature was thought to scare away dangerous beings. Archaeologists have found paintings of Bes on the walls of houses at Deir el-Medina, but also on head-rests – ancient pillows – where he would protect the sleeper from the evil forces that caused nightmares.

There was also Taweret, an upright-standing hippopotamus, invoked to help women through pregnancy and childbirth. Taweret often holds a symbol of protection, and has a pregnant belly and human breasts. Statuettes of Taweret could be kept by pregnant women, or dedicated to temples to ask for her assistance during birth. Amulets in the shape of Taweret were also popular. And Renenutet, a cobra deity, sometimes shown as a woman with a snake's head, was connected with royal protection since early Pharaonic times, but eventually became a goddess of the harvest – an important role that made her a popular figure of veneration among Egypt's predominantly agricultural population. Renenutet also had the power to set the limits of a person's lifetime, shaping their destiny.

Ordinary Egyptians, such as the people of Deir el-Medina, could access the gods through oracles too. On festival occasions, priests took a deity's statue from their shrine in the temple sanctuary and placed it aboard a small boat. This boat was flanked by two long horizontal poles that enabled the priests to carry it out of the temple in procession. As the priests marched, people approached the divine boat and asked the god questions. This could be done verbally, with the boat tipping backwards or forwards to give a 'no' or 'yes' answer. If the question was more complex, alternative responses, written on ostraca, would be placed on the floor. The god tipped towards the correct course of action to take. Scholars don't know how much the priests consciously manipulated the answers given, but Egyptian wisdom literature says that it was a great crime to fake an oracle. Perhaps it was like a Ouija board, with one priest's subtle movements influencing the others, leading all to move in the same direction. Or, more cynically, it's possible that the priests – particularly in smaller settlements – might have known the questions people were likely to ask, and coordinated beforehand over what answers to give.

Deir el-Medina's patron deity was the deified King Amenhotep I (r. c. 1524–1503 BC), who had a shrine just north of the village. The oracle of this divine king solved local disputes and crimes, and even appointed jobs. In the case of crimes, the accused had to admit their guilt; if the person refused, further oracles could be approached. There were also shrines near the village dedicated to various gods. One stood just west of Deir el-Medina, on the path from the village to the Valley of the Queens (situated in its own wadi, lower in the Theban hills than the Valley of the Kings). There, at 'the Beautiful Hillock', the villagers visited rock-cut stelae dedicated to the goddess Meretseger to petition for help. This goddess, whose name means the 'One Who Loves Silence', was usually shown as a snake and had the epithet Lady of the Western Mountain. Meretseger was associated with the peak over the Valley of the Kings (today called el-Qurn) and could be invoked for numerous reasons, including health issues (though this goddess could also cause health problems as a punishment). If Meretseger helped you, a way of showing your appreciation was to leave a small stele dedicated to her at the shrine.

The Valley of the Kings: the sun god's nocturnal journey

The Valley of the Kings served as the burial ground for the vast majority of the New Kingdom pharaohs, as well as some particularly favoured courtiers and even animals, who were perhaps royal pets. Rock-cut tombs had been a tradition at Thebes for centuries, and the choice to use such tombs for the New Kingdom rulers, rather than bury them beneath pyramids as in earlier times, may have been influenced by these local customs. The naturally pyramid-shaped hill of el-Qurn, looming over the Valley, might also have been a factor. It enabled each king to be buried beneath the same pyramidal peak, no extra construction necessary. Security was on the minds of these pharaohs, too. By the New Kingdom, the already ancient pyramids had been robbed, so a less conspicuous tomb would help to protect the king's mummy and burial goods. The royal mortuary temples that supported the king's afterlife needs, meanwhile, were built on the edge of the floodplain, below the hills, and so were visible to all. Early New Kingdom royal tombs are unmarked, lacking even a formal gateway. The courtier Ineni writes of constructing the tomb of King Tuthmosis I (r. *c.* 1503–1491 BC) with no one hearing or seeing. Kings being kings, over time, these hidden tombs began to be marked by increasingly elaborate carved gateways – they couldn't help themselves. Security now relied on the *medjay* – trained police who monitored movements in the Valley.

The entrance to a royal tomb in the Valley of the Kings.

Over the course of the New Kingdom, the royal tombs changed in size and complexity, and their decoration became more colourful and extensive. But the focus throughout remained on the king's association with the sun god, their unification in death, and their joint regeneration each night after merging with Osiris' divine force. The sun god's journey through the day and night skies was one of the most important aspects of Egyptian mythology. Re was locked in a never-ending battle with the chaos snake Apophis, who sought to overwhelm order with chaos. In death, each king joined the sun god in this struggle. The Egyptians explained this daily drama and its trials in various netherworld 'books', which they inscribed on the walls of the tombs in the Valley of the Kings to magically conjure eternal success – writing something down ensured it would happen. Each 'book' provided a different insight or a different focus on events. They include the Amduat (better known today as 'The Book of What is in the Underworld'), the Book of Caverns, the Book of the Earth, the Book of the Sky, and the Book of the Heavenly Cow. Here, though, I want to focus on the Book of Gates.

The first known complete version of the Book of Gates was inscribed on the sarcophagus of King Seti I (r. *c.* 1296–1279 BC), now in the Soane Museum, London. And indeed, though various tombs in the Valley of the Kings are inscribed with sections of this composition, only the joint tomb of Ramesses V and VI has a full edition. When visiting this tomb, you'll find the Book of Gates spread across its entire length. The Book is identifiable thanks to its division into three registers, with the sun god's boat always in the central section. On board the boat, the aged ram-headed sun god stands in a booth encircled by the protective *mehen*-snake. His booth is flanked by two human-headed gods, Hu and Sia, representing divine utterance and divine perception. Four figures usually stand in front of the sun boat, dragging it along through the Netherworld. The action takes place across the twelve hours of the night, with each hour divided by a gate, protected by a tall upright-standing snake, assisted by two further snakes.

At sunset, the sun god sailed on his boat below the horizon. Another day was over. The dark and mysterious Duat beckoned once again, just as it did every night. From dawn to dusk, the sun god had grown from an infant into an old man, sharing his light with the world. But now he was weary, in a state similar to death, and vulnerable. It was the first hour of the night when he entered the place of transition – not part of the living realm, not yet the Duat. The gods of the west – the dead – solemnly met him, standing in rows. Representing the changes he would experience on his way to rebirth at dawn, the sun god transformed into a scarab beetle – the hieroglyph read as 'becoming'. He sailed on, and as the hour reached its end, he approached the first of the Duat's gates; a portal protected by a monstrous snake, like each of the eleven that would follow. As the second hour ticked by, the sun god met the blessed dead. The terrain became difficult, so four men dragged the god's boat towards the 'gods of the entrance', past four weary beings, lying on their backs. Close by, the god Atum judged the bound damned. During the third hour, the god's boat, still dragged by men, passed a lake of fire, which burned the damned and fed the blessed. The sun's presence awakened mummies from their slumber – his radiance had not yet completely diminished. A more malevolent force awoke, too; the chaos snake Apophis slithered towards the sun's boat, intent on destroying the god and plunging the world into disorder. Atum, supported by two enneads of gods, attacked Apophis. Their protection enabled the god to continue his journey into the fourth hour of the night.

The sun god reached a row of slumbering mummies, waiting to be awakened by his light. Beyond them were two slopes, separated by a pit filled with snakes that symbolized the passage of time. Six goddesses stood on each slope, together representing the twelve hours of the night. Nearby were four more supernatural lakes; the first pair were lakes of fire, protected by jackal-headed gods, and the second lakes of uraei, protected by rearing cobras. Fiery pits, dug all around, burned the enemies of Osiris. The sun god sailed onwards. The fifth hour of the night arrived, and the gods gave fields to the dead, enabling them to grow their own food, while Horus and Sekhmet cared for the four peoples of the world: Egyptians, Asiatics, Nubians and Libyans. The gods realized that Apophis was about to launch another attack, so they captured him and put him in chains. Their arms turned invisible as they touched his skin. Before passing into the sixth hour of the night, the sun god observed the judgment hall of Osiris, where the king of the dead sat enthroned in front of an empty scale, attended by the blessed dead. He was waiting for the next soul to approach him, when the heart of the deceased would be weighed on the scale against the feather of *maat*. A pig – a symbol of disorder – broke into the hall, only to be chased away by two monkeys. Osiris didn't seem fazed.

As the sixth hour of the night unfolded, the gods held Apophis. Others kept guard, gripping their forked poles, just in case the snake made any sudden movements. Severed heads rippled across Apophis' body, occasionally bursting out into freedom; these unfortunate souls had been devoured by the snake. Now, thanks to the gods' help, they could escape his stomach. Men with invisible arms carried the sun god's equally invisible body in procession, while mummies lay on beds near a circular lake of fire. This was the most important hour of the night, when the sun god's *ba*-spirit reunited with his (invisible) body, re-energizing him for the journey to the dawn. The seventh hour arrived. The dead walked in procession, carrying sickles, baskets of grain and feathers of *maat*. Demons tied the enemies of the sun god to the 'stakes of Geb' and tormented them. The forces of order had succeeded for another night. The sun god, rejuvenated, had begun his journey to the dawn. In the eighth hour, people carried the rope of time, while the lords of the provision of the west gave food and drink to the blessed dead and punished the enemies of the sun god. Divine judges protected mummies.

In the ninth hour of the night, the *ba*-spirits of the dead raised their arms in adoration as the sun god sailed towards a large, rectangular pool filled with the waters of Nun – the infinite waters that surrounded creation. The drowned floated in the water, but what had once killed them now offered regeneration. Nearby, Horus stood before twelve bound enemies, condemned to be burned into non-existence because of their crimes against Osiris. A large snake called the Fiery One reared, ready to execute the sentence, the Four Sons of Horus standing in his coils. As the tenth hour unfolded, the sun god transformed into a griffin. Apophis, bound by a god called the Old One, was punished, a sentence that continued into the eleventh hour, when the gods tied the chaos snake and his followers with a rope, held by a giant fist emerging from the ground. Other gods held stars. The oarsmen of the god and the goddesses of the hours walked in procession.

The sun god reached the twelfth and final hour of the night. Gods carried sun discs and stars, and goddesses sat on snakes. Other deities, gripping knives and crooks, marched in front of the sun god's boat, Apophis tied before them. Behind Apophis, four baboons screamed for the new dawn. Nurses awaited the newborn sun god. The final gate opened. The god Nun emerged from the primeval waters, raising the solar boat upwards. Embraced by Isis and Nephthys, the sun god in beetle form rolled the sun disc towards Nut, goddess of the sky, who reached down towards him. Dawn had arrived. The sun god was reborn.

Thebes' West Bank in history and today
Relatively little is known about the early history of Thebes' West Bank. Settlements were established from the Predynastic Period, and tombs

A courtyard in the mortuary temple of King Ramesses III at Medinet Habu,
one of many royal mortuary temples that once stood on Thebes' West Bank.

of Old Kingdom date have been found in the el-Tarif and el-Khokha
areas. The mortuary temple of King Montuhotep II (r. *c.* 2066–2014 BC),
founder of the Middle Kingdom, at Deir el-Bahri – one of the major
monuments on the West Bank – was built under the 11th Dynasty, but
only a few tombs have been uncovered from the subsequent 12th Dynasty,
when royal attention returned to the north of the country. During the
New Kingdom, the West Bank saw the construction of the Valley of the
Kings, the royal mortuary temples and the many tombs of the nobles,
carved into the Theban hills.

Though the West Bank continued to be less developed than the
East, scattered villages existed around the monuments. The most famous
is Deir el-Medina, a state-sponsored settlement that housed the artisans
who cut and decorated the royal tombs in the Valley of the Kings and
their families. A papyrus from the time of King Ramesses XI (r. *c.* 1094–
1064 BC) describes further villages standing between the mortuary
temples of King Seti I at Qurna and King Ramesses III (r. *c.* 1185–1153 BC)
at Medinet Habu. The settlement around Medinet Habu was called
Maiunehes, where around 1,000 people – mainly administrators and

priests – lived in 155 houses. Other houses were spread between the temples, and tenant farmers lived along the cultivation.

Towards the end of the New Kingdom, royal power waned and Thebes fell victim to repeated attacks by Libyan groups. As the situation worsened, desperate – or opportunistic – people started plundering tombs and trading their treasures, leading to official investigations, trials and executions. General Piankh installed himself as high priest of Amun at Thebes and vizier, uniting military, bureaucratic and religious authority in himself. Faced only with a weak pharaoh in the north, he effectively separated the Theban region from the rest of the kingdom, creating an independent province. Tomb robbery, this time officially sanctioned, now began again in earnest. Priests reburied the New Kingdom royals in hidden caches, and 'recycled' the treasures they found, boosting the wealth of Thebes and funding Piankh's military campaigns.

The so-called 'Colossi of Memnon', a pair of statues that stood at the entrance to the mortuary temple of King Amenhotep III.

THEBES – WEST BANK

Key dates and remains

c. 3800 BC	Early settlements on Thebes' West Bank.
c. 2520 BC	Earliest tombs on Thebes' West Bank.
c. 2160 BC	Local rulers build rock-cut tombs in the el-Tarif area.
c. 2050 BC	Construction of King Montuhotep II's mortuary temple at Deir el-Bahri.
c. 1560 BC	Royal and private tombs established in the Dra Abu el-Naga area.
c. 1500 BC	Establishment of the Valley of the Kings and Deir el-Medina. Increasing numbers of private tombs built in the Theban hills, 'The Valley of the Nobles'.
c. 1340 BC	Palace complex built at Malkata under Amenhotep III.
c. 1300 BC	Queens and princes begin to be buried in the Valley of the Queens.
c. 1100 BC	The Deir el-Medina workmen move to the mortuary temple of Ramesses III at Medinet Habu to hide from Libyan raids.
c. 1050 BC	The Valley of the Kings abandoned. Royal mummies moved and reburied.
AD 130	Emperor Hadrian visits the Colossi of Memnon.

Over the following centuries, Thebes reunited with the rest of Egypt and tombs continued to be built on the West Bank. Under the Ptolemies and Romans, the area became a tourism hot spot, with visitors particularly enamoured by the Colossi of Memnon – two huge statues that stood in front of the mortuary temple of King Amenhotep III (r. *c.* 1388–1348 BC) – and the royal tombs in the Valley of the Kings. Many tourists left Greek and Latin graffiti on the monuments. The rise of Christianity led to the construction of monasteries, for example at Deir el-Bahri, though these closed after the arrival of Islam. Some early Christian communities lived in the ancient tombs. European investigations of the West Bank's ancient monuments began in the late 18th century, and magnified over subsequent decades as collectors and museums competed to make the most impressive discoveries for shipment back to their home countries. Today, the economy of Luxor's West Bank relies on tourism and agriculture.

▲

There's much to see on Luxor's West Bank, enough for an entire holiday on its own. One highlight is the **Valley of the Kings**, where you can get a feel for the artistic and architectural development of the New Kingdom royal tombs, built over the course of five centuries. One of the earliest is the 18th Dynasty **Tomb of King Tuthmosis III** (r. *c.* 1479–1424 BC). The decoration of his burial chamber imitates an unfurled papyrus roll, painted with simple stick figures. The king's quartzite sarcophagus is still present. The famous **Tomb of King Tutankhamun** (r. *c.* 1343–1333 BC), also 18th Dynasty, is surprisingly small, and contains paintings of the royal funeral; among the guests is the king's successor, Aye (r. *c.* 1333–1328 BC). He performs the Opening of the Mouth ceremony on the royal mummy – a ritual that enabled the dead king to see, speak and hear in the afterlife. The 19th Dynasty **Tomb of King Seti I** (r. *c.* 1296–1279 BC) is the longest in the Valley, and features beautiful raised-relief carvings and well-preserved painted scenes, the Book of Gates and the Amduat among them. Another of the Valley's highlights is the 20th Dynasty **Tomb of King Ramesses V** (r. *c.* 1146–1141 BC) **and King Ramesses VI** (r. *c.* 1141–1133 BC), with its detailed carved and painted decoration.

Where the cultivation meets the desert edge, you'll find the **mortuary temples of the New Kingdom pharaohs**, called 'Mansions of Millions of Years' by the Egyptians. These temples had a complex purpose. They weren't simply places where priests made offerings to the king's soul to keep him alive in the afterlife, but were dedicated to a form of the deceased pharaoh merged with Amun. Consequently, the temples were part of the wider processional journeys of Amun-Re, who travelled from the Karnak temple precinct across the Nile to visit them. The best-preserved mortuary temple is that of King Ramesses III (r. *c.* 1185–1153 BC) at **Medinet Habu**, which shouldn't be missed by any traveller to Egypt. Other well-preserved examples include the **Ramesseum** of King Ramesses II

(r. *c.* 1279–1212 BC) and the **Temple of Queen Hatshepsut** (r. *c.* 1472–1457 BC) at Deir el-Bahri. To the ancient Egyptians, Medinet Habu was known as 'United with Eternity in the Estate of Amun', and the god worshipped there was Amun of United with Eternity, a form of Amun merged with Ramesses III. In the temple's first court, a window of appearance connects with an adjoining **small palace**. The king ascended steps in this palace to appear at the window and bestow rewards and honours upon people assembled in the temple courtyard below.

Dotted throughout the hills of the desert escarpment are the **Tombs of the Nobles**. Many are open to visitors – too many to discuss here – but to provide a flavour of their appearance, one of the more interesting examples is the **Tomb of the Vizier Rekhmire** at Sheikh Abd el-Qurna. Rekhmire's tomb follows the typical layout for this period: an external courtyard, followed by a T-shaped rock-cut interior. A burial shaft, sunk into the courtyard, and six further ones within the tomb itself, perhaps served as the burial place of Rekhmire and his family. The entrance area bears prayers to gods such as Amun-Re, Osiris and Re-Horakhty, and in the entrance hall proper (the top of the 'T'-shape) there are scenes and inscriptions that explain Rekhmire's family background, including his autobiography and a text describing his appointment as vizier. There are scenes of Rekhmire receiving foreign tribute, as well as inspecting temple workshops – which produced weapons of war, items for royal burials and statues – and the fields of Amun. Along the tomb's passage (the lower part of the 'T'-shape), you'll find the craftsmen of the Temple of Amun, a grand feast, and a scene showing Rekhmire listening to the petitions of the people (which sounds nice enough, yet includes the poor being threatened by officials with sticks). At the end of the passage – below the niche, high in the wall, that once contained a seated statue of Rekhmire – there are ritual scenes, including funerary rites and spells to create food and incense for the dead.

The ancient village of **Deir el-Medina** stands at the bottom of a path that snaked its way up the Theban hills to the Valley of the Kings. Here you can explore the ruins of small houses, once occupied by the families of the men who cut and decorated the royal tombs in the Valley of the Kings. On the edge of the village is a Ptolemaic **Temple of Hathor**, and a **Temple to Amun** built under King Ramesses II. The villagers built their tombs on a hill overlooking the village. Of particular interest is the **Tomb of Sennedjem**, which contains extremely well-preserved paintings, including Sennedjem and his wife in the Field of Reeds. Next door, in the **Tomb of Inherkhau**, keep an eye out for a scene of a knife-wielding cat attacking a snake representing the chaos snake Apophis. Not too far from Deir el-Medina is the **Valley of the Queens,** where you can explore the beautifully painted **Tomb of Queen Nefertari,** and the **Tombs of Prince Amunherkhepeshef and Khaemwaset,** both sons of King Ramesses III.

The face of the goddess Hathor decorates columns in the
outer columned hall of the temple at Dendera.

5

DENDERA

~~~~~~~~~~~~~~~~~~~

Blood and Beer at the
Temple of Hathor

'O beautiful one, O radiant cow, O great one, O great of magic, O his glorious lady, O golden one of the gods.... See him (the king), Hathor, his lady, from the horizon.... See him, golden one of the gods, from the sky, from the land, from Asia, from Libya, from the western mountain, from the eastern mountain, from all lands, from all places on which your majesty shines.'

From the Temple of Hathor at Dendera, 1st century BC.

I look up in amazement. The temple's ceiling could have been painted yesterday – yet it is 2,000 years old. Bright tones of blue spring from its surface. Gods sail in boats among the stars, or stand in adoration of human-headed birds. A *wedjat*-eye, carved within a disc, symbolizes the moon and its phases. The sky goddess Nut, her body stretched across a full strip of ceiling, swallows the sun at dusk. She will give birth to him at dawn, just as she does every day. There are signs of the zodiac. Planets. Colourful hieroglyphs. Together, these diverse images represent a complex astronomical scene, a detailed compendium of the Egyptians' knowledge of the day and night sky. For centuries, these scenes had been obscured by a thick layer of soot and grime. Now, though, thanks to the meticulous work of conservators, they shine with new life. Cleaned, restored and revealed; it's as if the Temple of Hathor is reawakening from a long sleep.

All around, the mutilated face of Hathor glares out blankly from column capitals, her eyes, nose and mouth erased – the work of early Christians scraping away the pagan era. The goddess may have been silenced by chisel, but her distinctive heavy wig and cow ears remain. It's still obvious who owns the temple. Below, carved into the columns,

93

Looking into the outer columned hall of the Temple of Hathor at Dendera.
Construction of the temple began in the late Ptolemaic Period.

are repetitive images of the pharaoh before Hathor, her child Harsomtus,
Isis, Osiris and Horus – too many deities to remove, at least, not without
great effort. Elsewhere, Roman emperors in pharaonic garb offer an
obelisk to Hathor, a reminder of the temple's late construction. From
the ceiling to the base of the walls, the entire outer columned hall of
Hathor's temple at Dendera is a repository of ritual knowledge, carved
in the twilight of ancient Egypt, almost, it feels, as a last act of self-
preservation. And indeed, despite the best efforts of time, religious
vandalism and the accumulated dirt of centuries, nothing has succeeded in erasing Hathor from memory. As one of ancient Egypt's most
popular goddesses, and with Dendera as her most important cult centre,
she was far too prominent to simply fade away. So, rattle your sistrums.
Put on your finest. It's time to raise a glass to the original goddess of
the good times.

Hathor: Lady of Dendera (and of Drunkenness)

Hathor was Egypt's goddess of love, dancing, music, beauty, motherhood and drinking – indeed, one of her titles was Lady of Drunkenness.
She could be shown as a woman, normally wearing cow's horns on her
head, their shape curving around a sun disc; as an angry lioness; as a
cow, representing her nursing and caring side; and as the uraeus cobra
that protected the sun god Re. The barque shrine of Hathor's temple at
Dendera is decorated with images reflecting these roles. When a woman,
she is given mirrors and makeup; as a cow, she receives milk; and as
the angry lioness, she is offered musical instruments called sistrums
and a jar of wine to calm her. Hathor was also a tree goddess, providing
the king and the dead with food and drink, and was associated with

death as Lady of the West. But to most people in ancient Egypt, Hathor was a goddess devoted to fertility, children and healing. People left objects at small shrines to her across the country, in the hope of securing the goddess's favour. One stood near Deir el-Bahri on the Theban West Bank, where archaeologists uncovered figurines of women and children, phalluses and eyes, made from clay, wood or faience. These items represented appeals for fertility, a safe birth and health (the eyes, for example, were left by people who suffered from eye problems).

Hathor's name, Hut-her in ancient Egyptian, translates as the 'House of Horus', reflecting a close relationship between these two deities. It's possible that in early mythology, Hathor, rather than Isis, was Horus' mother, or that Hathor was associated with the sky (Horus being a sky god). At Dendera, Horus and Hathor were a divine couple, the parents of the god Harsomtus (Hor-Sema-Tawy). Every year, the Egyptians re-enacted and celebrated their marriage during a festival at Edfu (for which, see Chapter 2). Hathor was also mother to Ihy, a god of music. Hathor herself was a daughter of the sun god Re. Even so, at Dendera she is praised as the sun itself, and as mistress of all solar deities. She is the right eye of Re, shining light and bringing life, and also Re's weaker left eye, the moon. She is Rayt, daughter of Re, and Atenet, the female form of the sun disc. At the same time, she is a daughter of the god Nun – the primeval waters – and of Irta – a snake deity who helped to create the earth. Hathor, as one of the first-born divinities in this mythology, inherited these deities' creative powers, giving her the ability to make land and everything that grows on it. Through her regenerative milk, she influenced the annual flood and all that was nourished by it. Elsewhere, Hathor is said to have been born from the Eye of Re's tears, which fell to the ground and created her as 'Gold of the Gods'.

Until Isis replaced her (during the 1st millennium BC), Hathor was the best known of Egypt's goddesses beyond its borders. Hathor, Lady of Dendera, is mentioned on an offering plate of the 6th Dynasty King Pepi I (r. c. 2265–2219 BC), found at Byblos in Lebanon – the port from which the Egyptians imported high-quality cedar. A statuette from the same reign describes Hathor as living in Byblos. Later, she became known as Lady of Byblos, a role that she usurped from an earlier goddess. The Egyptians dedicated chapels and temples to Hathor on the fringes of Egypt, often in mining zones and quarries, such as at the Serabit el-Khadim turquoise mines in the Sinai, and the Timna copper mine in modern Israel. As a goddess of minerals, Hathor was variously Lady of Turquoise, Lady of Lapis Lazuli and Lady of the Malachite Country.

The king makes offerings to Hathor, Lady of Dendera.

She was also the Lady of Incense and the Lady of Punt, a land to the south of Egypt from which the Egyptians acquired high-quality incense and other luxury goods, such as ebony, ivory and animal skins.

The Book of the Heavenly Cow: sating Hathor's bloodlust

Hathor plays a prominent role in The Book of the Heavenly Cow, a myth set in a time when Re ruled as king on earth. Re had become old; his bones had turned to silver, his skin to gold and his hair to lapis lazuli. The people of earth tended to be suspicious of deities, and with the sun god advanced in age, they saw an opportunity to plot against his rule. But Re wasn't stupid. He knew that humankind were making plans against him, and called a meeting of the gods at his palace. He summoned his Eye, Shu, Tefnut, Geb and Nut, and the fathers and mothers who were with him in Nun (the waters of creation), as well as Nun himself. He ordered the gods to come in silence – he didn't want the people to suspect that he was onto them. With the gods assembled at court, Re asked for their advice. 'My instinct is to slay humankind,' he said. 'But I want to hear some opinions first.' Nun suggested that

Re send his Eye out against humankind (who by now had gone to hide in the desert – evidently the gods weren't that great at keeping secrets after all). The other gods agreed: 'Send the Eye in the form of the goddess Hathor,' they said.

Hathor transformed into the Eye of Re, and did as the gods asked. She flew to the desert and slew any people she found. But while Hathor was away, Re had a change of heart. Humankind aren't all that bad, he thought, and if they all die, who will I rule over as king? When Hathor arrived back at court to report on her mission, Re asked her to stop all the killing. By now, though, Hathor had developed a taste for blood. She transformed from the usually fun-loving Hathor into the dangerous goddess Sekhmet, and flew from the sun god's court to continue slaughtering humanity as the Eye of Re.

Re needed to act quickly if he wanted to save humankind. He ordered his servants to bring red ochre from Elephantine and told the High Priest of Re in Heliopolis to grind it up. Meanwhile, he tasked other servants with brewing vast quantities of beer. When all was prepared, Re mixed the red ochre with the beer, creating a concoction that appeared like blood – there was so much, it filled 7,000 jars. The gods knew that Hathor-Sekhmet was travelling south, and that she would continue her massacre the next morning; so that night, under cover of darkness, they filled the fields in which she slept with the red beer. When Hathor-Sekhmet awoke the next day, much to her delight, she found herself wading in fields of blood. Without hesitation, she slurped up the tasty surprise. Just as the gods had hoped, she quickly became drunk, and in her alcohol-induced haze lost all interest in exterminating humankind. In honour of the occasion (and perhaps slightly out of fear), Re decreed that from that moment on, beer would be produced for all of Hathor's festivals.

The stress of these events took a toll on Re. He didn't want to wipe out humanity, but given his weakened state, he feared that they would plan another uprising. The best thing for everyone, he decided, would be to leave the planet. Nun appointed Shu as Re's protector and asked Nut to transform into a cow to carry the sun god into the sky. But just before take-off, a delegation of humanity arrived, offering to fight against Re's enemies. The god, perhaps beginning to doubt his decision to leave, said nothing. He rode off to sleep in his palace, plunging the world into darkness. The next morning, Re awoke to find a crowd gathered outside the palace walls. People from all over Egypt had come to serve him, and in their zeal had invented weapons – bows and clubs. In that moment, murderousness came into existence. Appalled, Re decided that it was definitely time for him to get as far away from his creation as possible.

Nut carried Re high into the heavens, and there transformed into the day and night skies. Celestial locations burst into existence: the Milky Way, the Field of Offerings, the Field of Reeds, the planets and the stars, and, finally, the 'infinite ones', eight gods who helped to support Nut. Beneath Nut, Shu, as the atmosphere, watched over the infinite ones. Communicating from a distance through Thoth, Re told the earth god Geb to keep an eye on the world's snakes for him. These creatures had been afraid of Re when he ruled, but now that he'd departed, Geb and Nun were to watch them and stop them from doing harm. Keep an eye on sorcerers too, Re added, somewhat as an afterthought. Next, Re appointed Thoth as vizier, tasking the god with writing for him and calming the people. Various forms of Thoth now manifested: his ibis-form, the moon of Thoth and the baboon of Thoth. Finally, Re embraced Nun, and explained that all things in creation were a *ba* of the gods – a form of spirit manifestation. The wind was the *ba* of Shu, for example; crocodiles were the *bas* of Sobek. Re's rule on earth had come to an end. The cosmos had been reorganized. The sun god would shine in the sky during the day, and light the way through the Duat at night.

The 'Return of the Wandering Goddess'

Just to the north of Dendera's sacred lake, there once stood a small Ptolemaic barque chapel of which only the gateway and platform now remain. These monuments (just like many other parts of the main temple) are decorated with scenes and texts describing one of Dendera's major events: the Navigation Festival. The barque shrine was the focal point of this annual celebration, which honoured the return of Hathor as Eye of Re from Nubia. On this occasion, the divine statue of Hathor, carried in procession by priests, entered the barque chapel and was placed aboard her divine barque. She then sailed on the sacred lake, along with the barques of Horus, Re-Horakhty and Isis, and afterwards returned to her home within the main temple. Local people, free to attend the celebration, sang and danced with the priests.

A myth, often called the 'Return of the Wandering Goddess', explains the meaning of the Navigation Festival. It exists in numerous forms, often featuring other female deities in place of Hathor, including Tefnut, Mut and Sekhmet. The basic story revolves around a goddess in the form of the Eye of Re – the Eye is always a goddess, because the Egyptian word for eye, *iret*, is feminine – becoming angry and leaving for a distant location, sometimes in Libya or Nubia. In this aggressive state, she transforms into a lioness and causes trouble for the local people. The sun god, missing his protector, sends out a deity to bring her home. Just as the goddess featured in the tale changes depending on the telling, so does the god ordered to find her. In the earliest versions, the god Onuris (Anhur in Egyptian, his name meaning 'The One Who Brings Back the Distant One') searches for the goddess. In others, it is Shu, aided by Thoth, or Thoth alone. Whichever god tracks down the goddess, his first task is to calm her anger and persuade her to return to Egypt. When convinced, the goddess transforms from a lioness into a friendly cat, and then, once in Egypt, resumes the form of a woman, restoring order. Her return is met with celebration across the land, and Re decrees that a festival should be held, because her arrival ensures a good inundation. All the perfumes, food and drink that Egypt can provide are offered to the goddess, and she becomes the uraeus on Re's brow, protecting him from his enemies.

Scholars have attempted to explain the meaning of the Wandering Goddess myth, but have not yet reached a consensus. The Egyptologist C. J. Bleeker suggested that the story may have been inspired by a solar eclipse, a time when both the sun and moon became invisible, leading the Egyptians to believe that the moon had gone in search of the sun – the Eye of Re. The Egyptologist Joachim Quack, meanwhile, has argued that the myth describes the heliacal rising of Sirius, the star's appearance at dawn, just before the sun, after seventy days' absence from the night sky. This was a major event in the Egyptian calendar that heralded the coming inundation. On that day, the rising sun god was reunited with his missing daughter, represented by Sirius. At the conclusion of the Wandering Goddess myth, the goddess becomes the uraeus on the sun god's forehead, just as during its heliacal rising Sirius appears as if worn by the sun. Also, when Sirius rises, it first appears red, but slowly turns to its usual whitish-blue. As the Egyptians associated red with anger, and the colours green and blue with peace, this too connects the heliacal rising of Sirius with the goddess's anger and eventual calm.

Variations of the myth are found in the Coffin Texts, the Book of the Dead, and even much later in Greek, but the best-preserved version was written in demotic on a papyrus dated to the 2nd or 3rd centuries AD. After the tale's lost introduction, Thoth, travelling as a baboon, discovers Tefnut in the form of an angry Kushite cat in Nubia. The goddess's departure for this foreign land has brought cheer to the Kushites, but misery to the Egyptians. Thoth employs all his wisdom to try to convince the aggressive goddess to return to Egypt. He argues that every being, plant and stone is happiest on their home soil, in their place of birth – even northern gods get homesick in the south, he says. He proclaims the superiority of Egypt over all other lands. To help his case, and to impress the goddess with his eloquence, Thoth recites a series of animal fables (see below), and the two enjoy a meal together, which pacifies her.

Throughout the tale, Thoth is careful not to antagonize the goddess – he'd been lucky when they first met that she'd spared his life long enough to let him speak. At any moment, or with one wrong word, the angry cat could transform into a truly fearsome lioness (every cat owner knows this). When Tefnut does make this transformation – interrupting Thoth in the middle of one of his fables – her eyes blaze with a fire as powerful as the midday sun, her back turns as red as blood, smoke rises from her fur and her face becomes like the sun disc. Fearing for his life, Thoth calms her with a hymn of praise, and by telling her that one day he will help her in a time of need – a promise that he later keeps by saving the goddess from attack. The lioness then becomes a cat again. Ultimately, Tefnut agrees to return to Egypt, though along the way she tries to slow their progress. As they travel north, from city to city, the cat changes shape, first into a vulture, then a gazelle, and eventually, at Memphis, back into Tefnut as a woman. There, they are greeted by the sun god, and a great celebration is held.

One of Thoth's animal fables underlines his argument that the weak can help the strong (a claim initially dismissed by Tefnut, but later proven when Thoth saves her from attack). Whatever your strength, kindness is always a virtue. It goes as follows: one day, a lion was walking on a mountainside when he found a panther, barely alive, his fur flayed and his skin ripped. 'What happened to you?' the lion asked. 'Man did this to me,' the panther said. The lion was confused, he hadn't heard of 'Man', and asked the panther to explain. 'Nothing is as cunning as Man,' the panther said. 'You don't want to fall into Man's hands.' The lion – a great hunter – became angry, and ran off to find Man. Soon after, the lion met a horse and a donkey, each gripping a bit in their mouths. 'What happened to you?' the lion said. 'Man,' the animals replied. 'Is Man more powerful than you?' he asked; but they, like the panther, simply replied that nothing is as cunning as Man, and that they hoped that the lion would not fall into his hands.

The lion departed, and as he travelled met more animals. An ox and cow had their heads tied, their horns broken away, and their noses pierced. A bear had been tricked by a man to have his claws torn out and his teeth broken, convinced by the pretence that it would make it easier for him to pick up his food. Each time, the animals simply repeated that nothing was as cunning as Man. The lion then met another lion, his paw stuck in a tree trunk. A man had told the lion that he could create an amulet of eternal life for him, but only from the wood of a certain type of tree. After a brief search, the two had found this tree, and the man began sawing its wood. Pretending that he needed help, the man asked the lion to reach out his paw towards the split in the wood. But when the lion's paw was close enough, the man snapped the tree shut. The lion was stuck. The man threw sand in the lion's face and ran away. 'If I capture Man, I'll make him suffer, just like he made the animals of the mountain suffer,' the first lion said.

As he searched for Man, the lion encountered a mouse. He was about to squash him, when the mouse spoke. 'Let me live,' he said to the lion. 'And in return, I will one day return the favour.' The lion laughed. 'Who will ever attack me?' he said. Amused, he let the mouse go free, but the mouse insisted that he would help the lion in a time of bad luck. The lion continued his journey, but as he walked the ground fell away from beneath his feet. He tumbled into a deep pit, dug by a huntsman, who sprinted over to view his catch. The huntsman tied up the lion and left him in a net for the night. Darkness came, and the mouse visited the lion. 'I told you that I'd return to help in a time of bad luck,' the mouse said. He nibbled through the straps to release the lion. Once the lion was freed, the mouse climbed into his mane, and the two ascended the mountain together. The tale ends there, with the lion seemingly abandoning his quest for revenge. Thanks to the mouse, the lion had learned to put aside his arrogance. Perhaps one day Man would do the same.

The Navigation Festival wasn't the only major celebration in the Temple of Hathor's calendar. There was also the Festival of Re on New Year's Day, when priests carried Hathor's statue to the temple's roof at the eighth hour of the day. Rituals ensued, and when the sun's rays hit Hathor's statue, she was believed to join with her father Re and be rejuvenated. There was also the Festival of Drunkenness, when Ptah and Re-Horakhty ritually enthroned Hathor, observed by two forms of her son Ihy. As the rituals progressed, priests made offerings of alcohol, including beer and wine, to the goddess. She was then presented to the public, who were themselves rather tipsy by this point. Just as the goddess had become peaceful upon drinking beer in the Book of the Heavenly Cow, her followers calmed themselves through their own acts of drunkenness. The Festival of the Beautiful Meeting, when Hathor of Dendera visited Edfu to marry Horus of Behdet, was also a major annual event, and is described in Chapter 2.

The Dendera Zodiac

One of the Temple of Hathor's most famous monuments is the Dendera Zodiac. It was carved into two sandstone slabs that once formed part of the ceiling of a chamber on the temple's roof. Taken to Paris in 1822, and now displayed in the Louvre, it generated rather a lot of debate after its arrival in the city. Scientists caused particular controversy when they said it showed a time before the agreed date of biblical Creation; and oddly, it inspired a French play, *Le Zodiaque de Paris*, which opened at the Théâtre du Gymnase on 2 September 1822. The play's first moments boasted a choir of mummies, and Osiris was a main character. The Dendera Zodiac itself reflects a curious mix of traditional Egyptian, contemporary Mesopotamian–Greek and earlier, purely Mesopotamian constellations. Taken together, these form a view of the night sky as it appeared in 50 BC, early in the reign of Cleopatra VII (r. *c.* 51–30 BC). As a Mesopotamian invention, the zodiac isn't known in Egypt before the Ptolemaic Period, though it could have entered the country as early as the Persian Period (the 27th Dynasty, which lasted from *c.* 525 to 404 BC).

The Dendera Zodiac is a detailed artwork: four goddesses of the cardinal points hold up the night sky. Between them are pairs of hawk-headed gods. The sky is divided into thirty-six decans – each decan

The Dendera Zodiac.

being a ten-day-long subdivision of an astrological sign – represented by named figures. These form a ring around the constellations at the centre of the zodiac. Some constellations are purely Egyptian. The part of Ursa Major better known today as the Big Dipper or the Plough is a bull's foreleg, called *meskhetiu* by the Egyptians. Another traditional Egyptian constellation is the giant hippopotamus called Reret. Meanwhile, some foreign imagery has been Egyptianized: the twins of Gemini are Shu and Tefnut; and Aquarius is the god Hapy, pouring water from vases. Other constellations have kept their original foreign characteristics: Cancer remains a crab, Pisces is a fish, Aries is a ram, Taurus is a bull. Earlier Mesopotamian zodiacal constellations – first attested 1,000 years before the carvings at Dendera – can be seen alongside their contemporary equivalents. There are five planets – Mercury, Venus, Mars, Jupiter and Saturn – as well as eclipses. A *wedjat*-eye represents a lunar eclipse on 25 September 52 BC, while an image of Isis holding a baboon by the tail marks a solar eclipse on 7 March 51 BC.

The Seven Hathors: deities of fate and destiny

Though Hathor had no role in determining a person's destiny, the Egyptians believed that the Seven Hathors – children of Re – predicted the fate of newborn babies. These goddesses were normally shown in a similar way to Hathor, but wore red linen. In one of the southern crypts at Dendera (unfortunately not the one open to the public) they can be seen playing tambourines alongside a hymn to Hathor. In magical texts, the Seven Hathors protect the sick until they're cured. They also make seven knots from seven bands and hit scorpions that bite them. In the 'Tale of the Two Brothers', the god Khnum creates a wife for a man named Bata. The Seven Hathors then arrive to tell her that she will be killed by a knife. In the 'Tale of the Doomed Prince', when the king's son is born, the Hathors proclaim that the child will be killed by a crocodile, a snake or a dog.

The Seven Hathors were not the only deities connected with fate. Thoth was able to calculate the length of a person's life, while Meskhenet and Renenutet assigned a person's career at birth. Shay represented destiny. He could take the form of a human, a snake, or a human-headed birth brick – the bricks that women squatted on during childbirth. He fixed a person's lifespan, and is sometimes shown at the weighing of the heart in the Book of the Dead. One hymn says that Amun-Re could shorten or lengthen a lifespan, adding to what was fated, and could even save a person from their fate.

Dendera in history and today

A settlement existed at Dendera as early as 3500 BC. After the unification of Egypt, the area became capital of the sixth Upper Egyptian nome, and the town itself was called Iunet. Although the current Temple of Hathor dates to the time of the Ptolemies and the Romans, inscriptions and archaeological evidence reveal that a temple of some kind stood on the same spot from the early Old Kingdom. Reused blocks and inscriptions show that this complex was then renovated or rebuilt repeatedly from the late Old Kingdom through to the Late Period, though the appearance of these early temple phases is unknown. A wall in the small temple of Isis, and the birth house's sanctuary, each built under King Nectanebo I (r. c. 380–362 BC) of the 30th Dynasty, represent the only standing remains from the Late Period. A smaller temple of unknown purpose, but perhaps dedicated to Horus of Edfu and Harsomtus, stood to the east of the Hathor complex. Following the Roman empire's conversion to Christianity, a Coptic church was constructed beside the Hathor temple.

A large necropolis covers the terrain just south of the temple enclosure. The earliest cemetery dates to the Predynastic Period, with later burials and tombs from the Early Dynastic Period, Old Kingdom, First Intermediate Period, 17th Dynasty, the Late Period and the Greek and Roman Periods. The 11th Dynasty ruler Montuhotep II (r. c. 2066–2014 BC) built a royal *ka*-chapel beside the Hathor Temple, which provided nourishment for the king's soul, and gave him a lasting physical connection with the goddess and her cult. It now stands in the Egyptian Museum, Cairo. Today, the Temple of Hathor lies about 3 kilometres (2 miles) south-west of the town of Dendera, and about 5 kilometres (3 miles) west of the city of Qena, just across the Nile. Qena is a modern provincial capital, and a key transport hub between the Nile Valley and the Red Sea.

▲

The **Temple of Hathor**'s popularity has led to the construction of a **visitor's centre** and an **open-air museum**, where you can see sarcophagi and other carved pieces from the local area. Due to its excellent preservation, the temple remains atmospheric, with colourful decoration, dark corridors, rooftop chapels dedicated to Osiris and crypts for storing the temple's wealth. Because the temple lacks its entrance pylon, you enter directly through its **pronaos** (or outer columned hall), its ceiling decorated with astronomical scenes, including imagery of the goddess

DENDERA

Key dates and remains

c. 3500 BC	Early settlement and burials at Dendera.
c. 2500 BC	Probable founding of Hathor cult at Dendera. Tombs built at same time.
c. 2260 BC	Further development of town and temple.
c. 2050 BC	Royal *ka*-chapel built under King Montuhotep II.
c. 1450 BC	Renovation of the Temple of Hathor.
c. 380 BC	Birth house of King Nectanebo I under construction.
54 BC	Construction of the current Temple of Hathor begins.
50 BC	Dendera Zodiac designed.
29 BC	First religious rituals performed in the current Temple of Hathor.
c. AD 480	Coptic church built at Dendera.

Nut swallowing the sun disc at dusk. As you explore, notice the **columns** with their four-sided capitals; each side bears Hathor's mutilated face, with her distinctive cow ears, and a sistrum on her head. From there, you pass through a **small hypostyle hall** towards the **sanctuary**, where the statue of the goddess rested in her shrine.

The temple complex overall was once surrounded by a mud-brick enclosure wall, parts of which still remain. In this outer area, there is a huge **gateway**, originally part of the enclosure, built under the Roman emperors Domitian and Trajan; two **birth houses (*mammisi*)**, one built under the 30th Dynasty and the Ptolemies, the other under the Romans; a 5th-century AD **Coptic church** that separates the two *mammisi*; and a **sanatorium**, where sick pilgrims slept and waited for Hathor to pronounce a cure for their illnesses in their dreams. There's also a temple dedicated to Isis (the **Iseum**) at the back of the main temple.

A view of the banks of the Nile near Abydos. The ancient necropolis itself lies about 9 kilometres (5½ miles) further west, beginning at the edge of the cultivation and stretching off into the desert.

6

ABYDOS

^^^^^^^^^^^^^^^^^^^^^^

Necropolis of the Murdered God

ę

'Regarding this cenotaph, I made [it] in the desert of Abydos, this island that one draws near, walls begun by the Universal Lord, a glorious place since the time of Osiris, established by Horus for the forefathers, served by the stars in the sky, lady of mankind; the great ones of Djedu [Busiris] come to it, the counterpart of Heliopolis in glory, on which the Universal Lord rests.'

Intef, Son of Sent, c. 1950 BC.

I stare down into the Osireion at Abydos; a curious monument, it looks like a royal tomb in the Valley of the Kings with its ceiling removed. Below me, set in a deep pit, colossal grey stone slabs stand on a platform – an island – surrounded by a moat of green water. Some bear lintels, making it reminiscent of a rectangular Stonehenge. The overall scheme was meant to represent the eternal waters of Nun encircling the first mound of creation. At the centre of the platform are two niches sunk into the ground, as if still awaiting the delivery of a sarcophagus and a canopic chest, 3,000 years after its construction. (I think we can safely assume they aren't turning up.) No inscriptions or carvings are visible from this vantage point; but in the sections that remain underground, various chambers and the entrance corridor are decorated with texts and scenes from netherworld books, magically ensuring a safe journey for the deceased though the afterlife. And yet, no one is buried here. No one was ever buried here. With its compelling mixture of megalithic style and subterranean oddness, the Osireion is the type of monument that writers and visitors like to label an enigma. To unravel its mysteries, you have to take a wider look at Abydos, Egypt's city of the dead.

This was once a vast cemetery sacred to Osiris, Egypt's god of regeneration. The king of the blessed dead. And Abydos is as dead as dead

107

The second hypostyle hall in the Temple of Seti I, where
doorways lead into the temple's seven sanctuaries.

can get – Osiris hasn't used his regenerative powers around here recently.
Low beige hills cast long shadows, interrupting the empty plain as it
stretches towards the distant desert escarpment. The sand is dusted
with a layer of broken pottery, millions of sherds – the remains of celebrations and dedications past. You get the feeling that you've missed
the party by a few thousand years – probably because you have. Most
visitors today spend their time exploring the fabulously preserved
Temple of King Seti I (r. *c.* 1296–1279 BC), next door to the Osireion,
getting lost in its dark chambers and admiring its beautiful raised-
relief carvings. But in ancient times, people came from far and wide
to take part in the annual festival of Osiris. This was one of ancient
Egypt's most popular events: a celebration of the resurrection of the
god after his unjust death.

Many small monuments once dotted the landscape at Abydos,
erected by Egypt's elite as a means of eternally taking part in this festival. And Seti, too, wanted a monumental marker – a memorial
temple – to express his devotion. The enigmatic (there you go) Osireion
was all part of this grand scheme. It served as a fake tomb for Seti, who
would become 'an Osiris' in death, connected to his temple. The arrangement replicated the relationship between Osiris' nearby temple and
tomb, which both played a role in the Osiris festival. Originally intended

to be hidden by a ceiling and layers of earth, and accessible only by a tunnel, the exposed Osireion today welcomes a warm breeze. The rising water table regularly submerges its floor, like the annual flooding of the Nile, adding to its unusual appearance and atmosphere. Its bare blocks have been torn from the darkness. Like Osiris himself, the Osireion was dead and buried, but now enjoys a second life.

Osiris: Lord of Abydos

King of the blessed dead. Symbol of eternal life. Role model to pharaohs. Murdered by his own brother. Osiris is not lacking in significance or dramatic mythology. As one of Egypt's most important gods, his name and image are found on monuments spanning thousands of years. In art, whether standing or seated, Osiris is usually shown as a mummy, tightly wrapped up to his neck, with only his hands protruding to grip his crook and flail – symbols of kingship. Upon his green or black head – both colours symbolizing regeneration and fertility – he most often wears the *atef*-crown, distinct due to its feathers and bulbous shape, while around his neck he wears an elaborate collar of precious stones. Dressed in this recognizable form, Osiris oversaw your judgment in the afterlife, deciding whether you'd lived a worthy enough life to spend eternity among the blessed dead, and to call yourself 'an Osiris'.

Yet despite Osiris' prominence, the first indication of his existence dates to the 5th Dynasty – well after the appearance of other important gods, such as Seth and Hathor. Why Osiris suddenly rose from obscurity is unclear, but it's interesting to note that his elevation coincided with a point in the Old Kingdom when kings stopped building sun temples. This suggests a weakening of, or at least a step away from, the

Spell 125 of the Book of the Dead, painted on a wall in the lost tomb of Amenemib at Thebes: Horus brings Amenemib and his wife Irtyaat to be judged by Osiris.

importance of the sun cult. It's also interesting that Osiris was not the original major god of Abydos; that honour fell to Khentyimentu, 'Foremost of the Westerners', the 'Westerners' being the spirits of the dead – who had gone beyond the place where the sun sinks below the horizon in the west. By 2000 BC, Abydos' Khentyimentu temple had been rededicated to Osiris-Khentyimentu, representing a merging of these two gods' duties (no text explains how Khentyimentu felt about this). Osiris was also Lord of Busiris, a city in the Delta.

Collecting information from across Egyptian history, we can reconstruct a mythological biography of Osiris' reign on earth and family connections. One Roman Period papyrus even tells us his length at birth: 1 cubit (52.3 centimetres, or 20½ inches). A particularly detailed account of Osiris' life was inscribed on the walls of the Temple of Dendera during the Ptolemaic Period. Osiris was born in Thebes to Geb and Nut, and when grown stood 8 cubits, 6 palms, and 3 fingers tall (4.7 metres/15 feet and 5 inches). Crowned in Herakleopolis, he was assigned the fivefold titulary of an Egyptian king, and appointed Thoth as his vizier. Hu – divine utterance – served as his general in Upper Egypt, and Sia – divine perception – as his general in Lower Egypt. The sources also ascribe Osiris various children. Most famously, he fathered Horus the Child (see Chapter 2), who eventually succeeded him as king of Egypt, and represented all pharaohs in life. He was also father of the jackal-headed Anubis, the female Horus Horit, the violent baboon Babi, the jackal-headed god Wepwawet, and Sopdet, personification of Sirius, who could also be presented as Osiris' wife, Isis. One daughter of Osiris was said to mould mud bricks, and held the opinion that Osiris should eat poisonous herbs and honey, unpleasant to beings in the Duat. No reason for her vitriol is given – perhaps she just didn't like making mud bricks.

The life – and death – of Osiris
THE OSIRIS MYTH ACCORDING TO PLUTARCH
The most complete version of the myth of Osiris was recorded by the Greek writer Plutarch in the 2nd century AD, though an earlier account was given by Diodorus Siculus, also Greek, in the 1st century BC (see below). In Plutarch's version, as king, Osiris brought civilization to the Egyptians: he taught them laws and to honour the gods. Afterwards, he travelled the world, peacefully spreading his ideas through his charm, songs and music. In Osiris' absence, Isis ruled Egypt, but upon his return he faced opposition from his brother Seth, who had concocted a plan to steal the crown for himself, aided by an Ethiopian queen and

seventy-two co-conspirators. Seth secretly measured Osiris' body and made an ornate chest that fitted him exactly. He then threw a party, inviting many guests, including Osiris, and displayed the chest for all to see. Everybody admired its beauty. 'The person who fits in this chest perfectly can keep it,' Seth said. One by one, his guests lay down within the chest; but no one fitted exactly. Then came Osiris' turn. When he lay inside, Seth's conspirators ran forward, nailed the lid shut and poured molten lead over it. To finish the job, they threw the chest into the Nile.

When Isis learned of Osiris' miserable fate, she mourned. She wandered the country, lost in her grief, until one day she happened upon a group of children who had spotted the chest floating down the Nile. Hoping that Osiris might still be alive – or at least wanting to recover her husband's body – she decided to chart the chest's course. She found that it had floated off towards the Mediterranean Sea, and from there had made its way to Byblos in Lebanon, where it had washed up on the shore and a tree had enveloped it, hiding it from view within its trunk. Isis decided to travel to Byblos; if she could find the tree, she could recover her husband. What Isis didn't know was that the king of Byblos, out walking on the coast one day, had already discovered the tree. He'd so admired its beauty that he ordered it be cut down and sent to serve as a pillar in his palace. When Isis arrived in Byblos, all she found was a stump. She sat and wept, until maidservants of the Byblite queen came across her on the shore. Isis plaited their hair, and gave them a lovely fragrance, which so intrigued the queen that she invited Isis to the palace to nurse her baby.

Unexpectedly employed at the palace, Isis spent each night burning away the baby's mortality. She would then transform into a swallow and fly around the pillar that still bore the body of Osiris. This continued, until one day, the queen entered the chamber to find Isis burning the child. She screamed and Isis stopped the flames, preventing him from achieving immortality. 'I will take this pillar,' Isis told the queen (no doubt expecting that she was fired anyway). Pulling the pillar from the floor, she carried it outside and hacked away at the wood to reveal the chest within. She threw herself on it, and wailed so powerfully that the queen's youngest child died. Soon after, believing herself to be alone, Isis opened the chest. She wept at the sight of her dead husband, and touched his face. While she cried, another child of the queen of Byblos crept up behind her. Sensing his presence, Isis turned with such anger that he, too, died on the spot.

Isis took the chest – still containing Osiris' body – back to Egypt and gave it to her son, Horus, who was being raised in the city of Buto.

But Seth, out hunting one night by the light of the moon, discovered the chest, and tore Osiris' body into fourteen pieces. He sent each piece to a different location in Egypt, forcing Isis to go in search of the body parts. Over time, she discovered them all, except for Osiris' phallus, which had been eaten by Nile fish. Ever inventive, she moulded a replacement phallus, and fully reconstructed the body of her dead husband.

THE OSIRIS MYTH ACCORDING TO DIODORUS

In the account of the myth written by Diodorus, Osiris was born in a city called Nysa in southern Arabia, where he invented wine. Later, Isis discovered wheat and barley, and Osiris figured out how to cultivate it, and so he was able to convince the world to give up cannibalism. Now that people no longer needed to eat each other, Osiris founded Thebes in Egypt, established temples to the gods, and ensured that each deity had honours and priests. Isis and Osiris also patronized the arts, and created tools from copper, so that men and women could work the fields and kill wild animals.

With Egypt in order, Osiris assembled a large army and travelled the world, spreading the word of wine and agriculture. Isis remained behind to rule Egypt, aided by Thoth as her advisor and Herakles as Egypt's general. Anubis and Macedon, Osiris' two sons, accompanied him on his travels, along with musicians and experts in agriculture. He vowed to leave his hair uncut until he returned to Egypt. Osiris travelled through Ethiopia, Arabia, India, Asia and Europe, and wherever he went, he carved details of his activities on pillars and hunted elephants. In Ethiopia, Osiris taught agriculture and founded cities, leaving representatives behind to collect tribute and govern in his name; in Thrace, he killed a king named Lycurgus; and he left Macedon behind to rule Macedonia, a country named in his honour. When Osiris returned to Egypt, having become immortal and joined the gods, he arrived with souvenirs from across the world.

Despite Osiris' newfound immortality, Diodorus goes on to narrate an account of his murder. Seth, as usual desiring the throne for himself, killed Osiris and cut his body into twenty-six pieces (there's no chest-related trickery in this account). He gave a piece of the body to each of his co-conspirators, who then hid the relics across the country. Acting fast, Isis and Horus went to avenge Osiris. Isis killed Seth, became queen of Egypt, and then went in search of the pieces of her husband. She found them all, again except for the phallus, which had been thrown into the Nile. But instead of rebuilding Osiris, she took some spices and wax and created a fake corpse around each of the twenty-six body parts. Then, after summoning priests from temples across Egypt, she gave each group a fake body, telling them in secret that they had the true corpse of the murdered god to take back to their nomes. This is why many places across Egypt claim to be Osiris' true burial place.

Isis dedicated her life to ruling Egypt and to making discoveries that would help cure people of their illnesses. Among her discoveries was a drug that awarded immortality, which she gave to Horus after he drowned. In death, Isis, too, became immortal, and she continued to help the sick by appearing in their dreams, offering cures to heal them. Interestingly, a 2nd-century papyrus from Oxyrhynchus (see p. 29), bearing a long invocation to Isis, also describes Isis as making both Osiris and Horus immortal, and says that she appointed Horus as her successor.

THE OSIRIS MYTH IN ANCIENT EGYPTIAN SOURCES

Unlike the classical descriptions, ancient Egyptian accounts of the Osiris myth are quite fragmentary or abbreviated. This is because the Egyptians preferred to avoid mentioning dangerous topics in their religious writings, such as Osiris' murder by Seth, in case they were magically conjured into being; nonetheless, some texts do make allusions. The Hymn of Amenmose mentions Osiris' transition from ruler of the living to king of the dead, his mummification, and Isis becoming pregnant with Horus. Even more detailed is the 'Ritual for the End of Mummification Operations'. This relates that Osiris was in Tawer, 'The Great Land' (in Abydos), when Seth attacked him under an *aru*-tree and threw him into the water. The god Nun hid Osiris' body beneath the water and Re came to inspect what had happened. But it was too late; the world had already fallen into chaos. The earth tipped upside down, the sun was blocked from view, rivers couldn't be sailed upon. There was only night. The deities Shu and Tefnut screamed. The Shabaka Stone, meanwhile, says that when Osiris was drowning, Horus commanded Isis and Nephthys to grab him. They went to help, and managed to pull Osiris to the shore.

The Pyramid Texts also make allusions to the murder of Osiris. One section refers to Osiris being felled on his side by Seth, and to Geb searching the mountains and desert for his body, only to discover it in 'Gazelle Land'. In another spell, it is Horus who finds Osiris on his side in Gazelle Land. Osiris then fills himself with Horus' eye. Another section talks of Osiris being thrown into water, while yet another describes Seth kicking Osiris and throwing him to the ground. Isis and Nephthys, in the form of kites, search for the god's body. When they find him in a place called Nedit – thought to be near Abydos – they halt Osiris' decay, and use their magic to revive him. One spell describes Horus as gathering together Osiris' dismembered parts, just as Isis is said to have done in the classical accounts.

The trial of Seth for his assault on Osiris is also described in the Pyramid Texts. The land quaked and the sky shook, we are told. Thoth and Horus, in the presence of Geb, raised Osiris from his side, so that he stood upright among the Dual Ennead (comprising nine gods of Lower Egypt, usually those involved in the creation myth of Heliopolis, and nine gods from Upper Egypt). The gods cursed Seth for throwing Osiris to the ground, but Seth insisted on his innocence, proclaiming that Osiris had attacked and kicked him. The gods weren't convinced. Horus sentenced Seth to spend eternity carrying Osiris.

Osiris' body and relics

Even after being punished (and sometimes executed) for Osiris' murder, Seth continued to pose a threat to the god's body. On one occasion, Seth transformed into Anubis, who was protecting Osiris' body during its mummification in the embalming house, and stole the corpse. Horus and Anubis chased Seth, and Thoth used his magic to make the god fall to the ground. Anubis – no doubt insulted by Seth's impersonation of him – sentenced Seth to serve as a seat for Osiris, but the trickster god escaped, and fled to a desert wadi. Once again, the gods gave chase. Seth, ready for a fight, transformed into a panther, but Anubis seized him and Thoth (again) used his magic, this time to make Seth burst into flames, cooking him. Some distance away, Re and his followers smelled Seth's burning flesh, and found its odour pleasant. Now Anubis wanted revenge. He flayed Seth and wore his skin. In this fleshy disguise, he went to confront Seth's followers, who had amassed on a mountainside, searching for their leader. Anubis slaughtered and beheaded them all. Their blood flowed down the mountain. Another time, Seth attacked Osiris' corpse in the form of a panther, but was caught and branded; this explains how leopards got their spots.

A myth recorded in 'The Calendar of Lucky and Unlucky Days' presents Seth as wanting to cross the Nile so that he can steal the body of Osiris. The gods had told Nemty, the divine ferryman, that under no circumstances should he ferry worms, associated with Seth, across to Osiris' resting place – corpses and worms not being a good combination. Despite this, when Seth, assuming the guise of an old man and accompanied by an army of worms, approached Nemty, he was able to gain passage by offering a bribe of gold (Isis similarly changes her appearance and bribes Nemty in 'The Contendings of Horus and Seth', see Chapter 2). Upon reaching the other side of the river, he attacked the embalming place of Osiris. Luckily, the gods realized what was happening, and tried to stop the troublemaker. With everyone overwhelmed by worms, Seth managed to grab Osiris' relics. Seth had achieved his goal, but his victory was short-lived. When the gods had finally managed to squish the army of worms, they turned their attention to Seth, who lobbed Osiris' relics into the Nile, creating a nice diversion for his getaway. The gods flayed Nemty as punishment, presumably after fishing the pieces of Osiris out of the water.

According to a myth in the Tebtunis Mythological Manual, named for the Faiyum city in which various fragments of the text were found, Wepwawet, a jackal god whose name means the 'Opener of the Ways', lapped up the liquid putrefaction from the dismembered body parts of Osiris. Afterwards, he vomited onto the floor, then licked it up, then vomited onto the floor again, then licked it up again, and so on – a cycle reflecting the changing phases of the moon. Dangerous beings then arrived, forcing Wepwawet to gather Osiris' body parts in his mouth and run into a cave. Horus helped Wepwawet to find his way, and the jackal hid Osiris' dismembered corpse in a cavern, saving the god from destruction by his enemies. Wepwawet isn't the only god to chew on the body of Osiris; Thoth also had some nibbles. One night, the dead Osiris and Horus were floating along the Nile, when Thoth, in the form of an ibis, flew down to land on the elder god. Feeling peckish, he gorged on Osiris' relics until he had eaten too much. Although it isn't stated, Thoth was probably believed to throw up the pieces of Osiris – just like Wepwawet had done – on land, saving them (and so the god) from the river. Other myths refer to a crocodile who damaged Osiris' limbs by sitting on his relics, and to a pig called Matit who chased demons away from the relics.

Traditions vary as to where the pieces of Osiris ended up. The Egyptians regarded the Mansion of the Leg at the Temple of Edfu as the place where Osiris' – guess which piece! – leg was kept, while one of his fingers was in Asyut. His head is usually cited as placed in a reliquary at Abydos. One papyrus says that Osiris' buttocks, phallus and a leg were kept in a chest at Herakleopolis, while his arm, lips and hair were kept in a chest at Kheri-aha – probably what is now Old Cairo – and his heart, lung, spleen and breast were hidden at the necropolis of Athribis. Meanwhile, according to the Delta Mythological Manual – a papyrus without clear provenance, but perhaps from Heliopolis or

Elephantine – Osiris' shoulder blade ended up in Letopolis and lives there, without anyone hearing or seeing it. Such myths no doubt influenced Plutarch and Diodorus when they wrote that Seth tore Osiris' body into pieces, which Isis then had to find.

Adultery and sexual assault

Osiris is normally presented as a positive force in the cosmos – a god that helped humanity as the power of regeneration and judged the dead fairly as their king. Nonetheless, some myths do present him as a negative force. For one, Osiris committed adultery with Nephthys, wife of Seth. (Indeed, this could even be why Seth murdered him.) A 4th-century AD love spell presents Isis as crying while talking to Thoth. She has discovered a secret, she says: a female friend has betrayed her. Nephthys was sleeping with Osiris. So, together, Isis and Thoth created a spell, one involving Osiris' blood and an iron nail, to bring Osiris back to Isis. Plutarch mentions this affair, saying that Isis went in search of the child born of Osiris and Nephthys' adulterous union. She used dogs to track down the child, which Nephthys had left exposed, and afterwards brought him up as Anubis.

According to a myth recorded on the Delta Mythological Manual, Osiris raped his daughter Horit – the female Horus. She became pregnant from this assault and wept. She later aborted the child, who was given the name Hu-mehen. Osiris raped Horit on two further occasions, producing two further Horus gods. The child named Horus-Hekenu was taken by a lioness, torn to pieces and eaten shortly after his birth. Horit went looking for her lost child, and eventually found his body (or perhaps what remained of it) protected by a snake in Bubastis. Thoth and Nephthys killed the lioness, and after wrapping the child in the lioness' skin, placed him in a coffin. Seth also raped Horit, leading her to fall pregnant with 'Thoth who Comes from the Forehead', a child, born in water, that took the form of a malformed monkey. It is difficult to explain how such crimes by the gods, and Osiris in particular, became established in Egyptian mythology, and the reasons are still debated.

Osiris as god of the blessed dead and the judgment

Although magically resurrected after his murder, Osiris remained in the afterlife realm of the Duat as king of the blessed dead. In this role, he watched as each recently deceased person came before him in the hall of judgment, known to the ancient Egyptians as the Hall of Two Truths. Depictions and descriptions of this location and event are found in the Book of the Dead, specifically spells 30B and 125. The vignette that often accompanies Spell 125 shows the central event of the after-life journey: the moment when the deceased's heart was weighed against the feather of *maat*. Typically in such scenes the enthroned Osiris over-sees proceedings within the hall. Isis and Nephthys stand behind him, while Thoth waits to jot down the results of the weighing on his papyrus scroll. Anubis or Horus (sometimes both) tend to the scales. The deceased is sometimes escorted into the chamber by Anubis. If judged worthy, the person was taken by Horus to Osiris, and became an *akh*-spirit, a being of light with free movement in creation. If, however, a person had led an unworthy life, they were eaten by a composite creature called Ammit – part crocodile, part hippo, part lion or panther.

Despite its famous vignette, the text of Spell 125 doesn't actually describe the weighing of the heart, but rather the 'negative confession', when the deceased came before forty-two assessor gods and proclaimed sins that they had not committed in life. Spell 30B, however, does mention the weighing, and is often carved on the underside of the deceased's heart scarab – a stone amulet, shaped like a scarab beetle, suspended from a chain worn around the mummy's neck. It magically ensured that the heart didn't testify against the deceased during the divine tribunal. (That's a nice way of saying that it helped people to cheat their way to eternal life.)

The tomb and Temple of Osiris

One of the major attractions for anyone visiting Abydos in ancient times was the tomb of Osiris (though around sixteen other places in Egypt claimed to be the location of Osiris' tomb, too). As of writing, this area of the site – today called Umm el-Qaab, and Poker in ancient times – isn't open to tourists, so modern pilgrims will be disappointed. But don't worry, it's not *really* the tomb of Osiris. It actually belonged to King Djer (r. *c.* 3000 BC) of the 1st Dynasty, and stands among the burials of Egypt's earliest kings. It isn't clear when or why the Egyptians started to regard Djer's tomb as the tomb of Osiris, but it may have been as early as the 11th Dynasty. To make Djer's tomb fit for a god, the Egyptians made certain alterations, including the addition of a stairway and a new roof. During the 13th Dynasty, King Khendjer (r. *c.* 1700 BC) installed a statue of Osiris within the tomb, showing the god lying on a lion bed, impregnating Isis, who has taken the form of a kite.

Abydos' temple to Osiris, built in an area called Kom es-Sultan, was originally dedicated to Khentyimentu, the necropolis's first god. It was rededicated to Osiris-Khentyimentu under the 12th Dynasty, and continued in use into the Roman Period, occasionally being rebuilt over the years. It is badly preserved today, mainly because, unlike other Egyptian temples that were built from stone, Osiris' temple was made from mud brick. A sacred way connected the Temple of Osiris to the tomb of Osiris, and according to a 13th Dynasty stele, only priests were allowed to walk on it; anyone else received the definitely-not-over-the-top punishment of being burned to death.

The Festival of Osiris

During the Middle Kingdom, Abydos became a major centre of pilgrimage, particularly during the annual Festival of Osiris. This was such an important event that if you couldn't make it there in life, you made sure you could in the afterlife – all you needed was a model boat, placed in your tomb, to magically transport you to the necropolis in death. Those that did manage to make the pilgrimage often left behind a symbol of their visit to this sacred place, ideally one that enabled the donor to eternally participate in the celebration of Osiris and be forever connected with all the gods of Abydos. Wealthy people left stelae, some within cenotaphs, constructed near the Temple of Osiris in an area called the 'Terrace of the Great God'. Those less well-off bought ready-made stelae and had their names carved into blank spaces left in the inscriptions.

Thanks to the Stele of Ikhernofret, a Middle Kingdom official who served King Senwosret III (r. c. 1881–1840 BC), we can reconstruct the major events of the annual Festival of Osiris. It began with the procession of the god Wepwawet, during which enemies tried to attack Osiris and had to be fought and killed (though being a ritual performance, no one would actually have been harmed). This was followed by the 'great procession', when Osiris' cult statue, resting aboard a divine boat carried by priests, travelled to the tomb of Osiris. Given the statue's destination, it's probable that Osiris' death was re-enacted during the festival's first part, but Ikhernofret wouldn't have wanted to mention this event on his stele for fear of causing magical harm. Along the way from temple to tomb, the procession passed through the 'Terrace of the Great God' and down into the 'sacred land', a dry river bed. Then, safely within his tomb, Osiris regenerated himself overnight, and his enemies were defeated at the place of his murder. The next day, Osiris made his way back to his temple, met by much rejoicing.

Abydos in history and today

For thousands of years, Abydos – Abdju to the ancient Egyptians – remained one of Egypt's most sacred locations, primarily due to its association with the god Osiris. The earliest hieroglyphs currently known were

The ruins of the (today restored) second portico of the Temple of Seti I at Abydos.

found on labels in Tomb U-j, dated to *c.* 3200 BC. This large burial probably belonged to a powerful ruler named Scorpion, though the extent of his territorial control is unknown. Egypt's first kings were buried at Abydos *c.* 3150 BC – a line designated 'Dynasty o' by scholars, because they ruled before the traditional dynasties of Egypt – followed by the kings of the 1st Dynasty. In addition to their tombs, these kings built huge mud-brick enclosures, seemingly as venues for funerary ceremonies, and buried boats for use in the afterlife. It was at this time that Abydos became a popular place of burial for Egypt's nobility.

Old Kingdom rulers built *ka*-chapels at Abydos, while from the Middle Kingdom onwards the necropolis attracted pilgrims, who wished to take part in the grand celebrations connected with the temple and tomb of Osiris. The monuments they left behind to commemorate their presence came to dominate the landscape. At some point in the Second Intermediate Period, a line of local rulers declared themselves kings at Abydos, but very little is currently known about them. Scholars refer to these rulers as the 'Abydos Dynasty'. During the New Kingdom, King Ahmose I (r. *c.* 1549–1524 BC) built a pyramid complex at Abydos, and Kings Tuthmosis III (r. *c.* 1479–1424 BC), Seti I (r. *c.* 1296–1279 BC), and Ramesses II (r. *c.* 1279–1212 BC) all constructed temples. The Temple of Seti I in particular was unusual due to its L-shape, seven sanctuaries (including one dedicated to the deified Seti himself in death), and the cenotaph tomb known as the Osireion beside it.

Throughout Abydos' existence, settlements sprung up at different times and locations: one town was founded during the Early Dynastic

ABYDOS

Key dates and remains

c. 4000 BC	Earliest burials at Abydos in the Umm el-Qaab area.
c. 3200 BC	Earliest hieroglyphs found on labels in Tomb U-j, perhaps the burial of a ruler named Scorpion.
c. 3150 BC	First kings of Egypt buried at Abydos. Early town built, probably along with the earliest version of the Temple of Khentyimentu.
c. 2300 BC	Temple of Khentyimentu probably demolished and rebuilt.
c. 2150 BC	Probable date of transformation of tomb of King Djer into the tomb of Osiris.
c. 1970 BC	Temple of Osiris-Khentyimentu demolished and rebuilt. The Festival of Osiris starts to become particularly popular.
c. 1880 BC	King Senwosret III builds a cenotaph complex with associated temple town.
c. 1540 BC	Pyramid of King Ahmose I built at Abydos. Temple of Osiris-Khentyimentu probably demolished and rebuilt.
c. 1290 BC	King Seti I builds his cenotaph temple and the Osireion.
c. 1279 BC	King Ramesses II builds his cenotaph temple.
c. 250 BC	Serapis worshipped within Temple of Seti I.
c. AD 150	Last evidence for belief in Osiris at Abydos.
c. 359	Oracle of Bes, operating within the Temple of Seti I, shut down by order of Emperor Constantius II.

Period, close to the spot where the Osiris-Khentyimentu temple would be built. It continued in use throughout Abydos' history. Other short-lived towns developed around particular monuments, such as the Temple of King Senwosret III, where excavations have revealed housing for the local mayor and elite. Abydos, then, shouldn't be viewed purely as a 'city of the dead', but as a vibrant place where transient visitors enjoyed festivals of national significance and locals made their livings among the tombs of the area's more permanent residents.

After its heyday in the Pharaonic era, Abydos retained some of its importance. Under the Ptolemies and Romans the Festival of Osiris stopped taking its traditional route, and instead was perhaps centred on the Temple of Osiris and the Osireion. The Temple of Seti I was rededicated to the god Serapis, and later, a Roman cemetery was established along the processional way to Umm el-Qaab. The oracle of Bes, operating within the Temple of Seti I, was shut down in AD 359 under the Roman Emperor Constantius II. After the arrival of Christianity, part of the Temple of Seti I was transformed into a church and a Coptic monk named Moses founded a monastery nearby; and in medieval times, anchorite cells were cut into the Shunet el-Zebib, a great mud-brick enclosure built at the end of the 2nd Dynasty. Today, beyond the desert edge, villages, mosques and fields occupy the cultivable land.

▲

Most of Abydos' archaeological site is protected, off limits to tourists, but the monuments that remain accessible are stunning. The site's main draw is the **Temple of Seti I**, built during the 19th Dynasty. Unusual due to its L-shape, it's one of the best-preserved New Kingdom temples in Egypt, and includes an impressive king list, carved into its walls. This records the names of many of Egypt's rulers, from Seti I himself, right back to the first kings of the Early Dynastic Period. It was probably a way for Seti to legitimize his family's right to the throne; after all, they had only recently risen from commoners to pharaohs. **The Osireion**, to the side of the Seti temple, is closed to visitors, but you can stand above it and look down. It served as a cenotaph for Seti, and resembles a royal tomb in the Valley of the Kings. Seti's Osireion and temple perhaps imitate the relationship between Osiris' temple and tomb nearby. The final monument usually visited by tourists at Abydos is the **Temple of Ramesses II**. It's not as well-preserved as the neighbouring temple of his father, Seti I, but vibrant painted scenes survive in places. This temple had a king list too, which can now be seen in the British Museum.

Akhenaten and Nefertiti, along with three of their daughters,
bask in the rays of the Aten.

7

TELL EL-AMARNA

〰〰〰〰〰〰〰

Doomed City of the Sun Disc

'Making a presentation of many offerings: bread and beer, long-horned cattle,
short-horned cattle, birds, wine, fruit, incense and all good vegetables on the
day of founding Akhetaten for the living Aten, who receives praise and love on
behalf of the life, stability and health of the King of Upper and Lower Egypt....
From the eastern mountain to the western mountain is Akhetaten itself.
It belongs to my father [the Aten], given life forever, with mountains,
desert necropolises, fields, new lands, arable lands, fresh lands, pastures,
waters, towns, riverbanks, people, cattle, copses and all things
that the Aten, my father, has caused to come into being forever.'

The Later Boundary Stele of Akhenaten, c. 1354 BC.

I walk along a rough path at Tell el-Amarna, following the edge of a
cliff face to the tomb of a priest named Panehesy. To my right, a steep,
rocky slope descends to the huge beige expanse of the desert plain,
around 80 metres (260 feet) below. The sun beats down on this flat, dry
moonscape. It is a place of emptiness, the sand criss-crossed by the
tyre tracks of vehicles long since departed, and the vein-like imprints
of water channels carved by the occasional winter rain. The odd hut
interrupts the void. Other shapes in the sand may be nothing more
than tricks of the imagination. The only green I can see is in the far
distance, tracking the course of the Nile, its blue shape lost in the haze.
You'd be forgiven for thinking that nothing had ever existed in this
barren place, but Panehesy's tomb, and other similar rock-cut burials
nearby, suggest otherwise. For although it appears lifeless today, a few
thousand years ago, Tell el-Amarna was Egypt's latest up-and-coming
royal city: Akhetaten, 'Horizon-of-the-Sun-Disc'.

Beneath the moonscape lies one of the world's greatest archaeological sites: the remains of a city of 20,000 people, thrown up in haste

on the whim of King Akhenaten (r. *c.* 1360–1343 BC), who ruled during the 18th Dynasty. The construction of a new royal city usually marked a fresh start, and Amarna was no different. Akhenaten had revolutionary ideas about how the Egyptians should interact with their gods. Well, gods at first. Over time he whittled them down to one: the Aten. Scholars still argue over whether this was a true monotheism or some other form of 'theism', but what is clear is that Akhenaten felt that Egypt's other gods were irrelevant. On a state level, everything became streamlined: officially, the only god to worship was the Aten, the visible sun disc in the sky, and you reached the Aten through the king. But after only twenty years, Akhenaten's religious experiment failed, and the Egyptians tore down Amarna just as hastily as they had erected it. The city's stonework was recycled, transported elsewhere – many blocks ended up in nearby Hermopolis – leaving its foundations and mud bricks to be eroded by time and covered with sand.

From my vantage point on the side of the cliff face, in the late morning haze, I can barely make out any sign of ancient Akhetaten, though its central quarter once stood only 3 kilometres (2 miles) away. It is hard to imagine that Panehesy, the priest buried in the tomb behind me, lived in this desolate place, worshipping a newly elevated god under the pharaoh's radical regime. It's even harder to imagine a bustling city. But excavations over the past century have revealed the ghosts of Amarna's grand temples, palaces and houses, providing a rare snapshot of a single, dramatic period in Egyptian history. This was a place where kings, courtiers and foreign delegations mingled in sumptuous palaces and enjoyed great festivals. It was also a place of extreme poverty, where malnourished skeletons reveal lives spent in backbreaking labour. From this work, we also gain an insight into Akhenaten's teachings – religious thoughts that upturned tradition, and so infuriated later generations that they would refer to him only as 'that enemy of Akhetaten'.

Akhenaten's religious revolution

The new state god of Akhenaten's religious reforms is referred to as the Aten, the physical sun disc that we see crossing the sky. But it's a bit more complicated than this. The god's name changed over the course of Akhenaten's reign. At the beginning, he was called 'The Living One, Re Horus of the Two Horizons, who Rejoices in the Horizon, in his Name of Shu who is the Aten'. By the end of his reign, the god was 'The Living One, Re, Ruler of the Two Horizons, who Rejoices in the Horizon, in his Name of Re, the Father who has Come as the Aten'. Clearly, as time passed, Akhenaten had wanted to remove the deities Shu and Horus

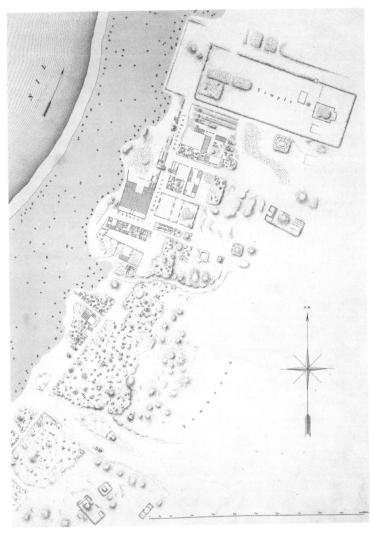

Plan of the city of Amarna, built by Akhenaten and abandoned
at the end of his reign. The long, rectangular enclosure wall of the
Great Temple to the Aten is at the top.

from his god's name; but what's more important is that Akhenaten's
god, throughout this period, is still called Re, with the Aten being the
sun god's physical form. As we will see again and again while exploring
Akhenaten's revolution, innovation mixed with tradition.

This god of Amarna was one of light, depicted as a disc from which
rays emanated, each terminating in small hands, sometimes offering

life in the form of the *ankh* symbol. In this way, the Aten was distant, yet present. Except at the start of Akhenaten's reign, when the Aten was represented as a hawk-headed man, this image was the only way in which the god could be shown in art. There's no indication that the Aten travelled across the sky in a boat, as Re was traditionally thought to do, and no suggestion that he fought enemies along the way as part of a daily struggle for *maat*. The Aten had no wife or child, and never speaks in texts. He was a god alone. The traditional myths took a back seat in favour of Akhenaten's teachings – he was the sole source for people to understand the Aten. If you had a question about life, the universe and everything, you had to visit the king. But he didn't offer many clear answers. Akhenaten's answer to 'where does the sun go at night?' was that it remained in his heart. His new religion focused on what could be seen, on a daily basis, in the world around you.

Even creation – normally described in mythic terms as taking place in the distant past – was an act of the Aten alone, re-performed every morning when the first light shone again on the land. Because of Akhenaten's focus on the present, we receive no insight into how the Aten itself was created – it seems simply to have made itself. We are told that the Aten is the source of everything in creation, the mother and father to all. Nonetheless, there is a single reference in the tomb of a nobleman named Ahmose at Amarna to creation coming from the Aten's mouth (despite the Aten not having a mouth), implying the creative power of speaking. Akhenaten, meanwhile, is sometimes said to have come from the Aten's rays or its body. The Aten was his father, and he was loved by the god.

What happened to Egypt's traditional pantheon? Were they banned, their temples closed, their assets redirected? Had they retired? Never existed? Did Egypt's priests end up unemployed, or find a sudden love for the Aten? Certainly the names of Amun and his wife Mut were attacked wherever Akhenaten's followers found them, hacked out of temple inscriptions and stripped from statues, most notably at his grand temple in Karnak (described in Chapter 3). These attacks later expanded to include the names of other deities too, and the word 'gods' was often amended to make it singular. Temples to the Aten were built around Egypt and Nubia, spreading the cult, including in front of the Temple of Amun-Re at Karnak. Perhaps, purged of the names of Amun and Mut, the Karnak temple precinct continued in use under 'new management'.

Nonetheless, many of Egypt's gods remained unaffected, their names left untouched. Even a prominent god like Thoth, whose main

Standing beneath the Aten's rays, Akhenaten, Nefertiti, and three of their
daughters throw gifts to courtiers from their window of appearance.
From the tomb of Aye at Amarna.

cult centre was next door to Amarna at Hermopolis – so an easy target
for any attacks – survived unscathed. At Amarna itself, people were free
to continue wearing amulets of traditional gods, and the sacred Mnevis
bull – an incarnation of the sun god – was buried at Amarna rather
than Heliopolis, highlighting Akhenaten's manipulation of tradition
rather than its wholesale dismissal.

Hymns to the Aten

If the evidence is to be believed, Akhenaten personally composed hymns
to the Aten, or at least, produced a base of writings from which his
scribes or priests could extract shorter hymns and prayers (something

assumed given the similarity between them). The most famous are the Great Hymn to the Aten, found on the walls of the tomb of Aye at Amarna, and the Short Hymn to the Aten, known (with variations) from the tombs of five Amarna courtiers. Shorter hymns were inscribed on the walls of other Amarna tombs as well. These hymns, overall, emphasize that the Aten – its power and its strength – is in Akhenaten's heart and that no one knows the god but him. The Aten taught Akhenaten his ways, and in turn, Akhenaten taught them to his courtiers. The courtier Aye, in his tomb at Amarna, says that the king put *maat* inside him, taught him, and now he does the king's teachings. It appears that Akhenaten was preaching, something unusual in ancient Egypt. Egyptian kings and priests didn't normally travel around spreading the word of their favourite deities; there was no need, they weren't seeking converts.

These hymns describe the cosmos as envisioned by Akhenaten (via the Aten, of course). The Aten somehow created himself and is mother and father to all his creation. Everyone and everything lives because the Aten gives them the breath of life. In particular, the Aten created Akhenaten; he is a child of the Aten's rays. The god listens to the king's wishes and the king offers *maat* to the Aten's face. The Aten is distant, yet present; or, as the Great Hymn puts it: 'You are far, but your rays are on the land.' The Aten made all things, from cities, towns and fields to the course of the River Nile. When the sun rises, everyone celebrates. People are able to work again. Trees and herbs grow, birds fly, and fish swim. Life returns.

In the Great Hymn, the Aten is the beginning of life that fills every land with its beauty in the morning. That the Aten touched every land is emphasized; the Aten was not just the god of Egypt, but the god of all people: 'You create the land according to your heart, alone, all people, large cattle, and small cattle; all those on land that move on legs, and those who are raised up, flying with their wings; the foreign lands of Khor (Syria) and Kush, and the land of Egypt. You put every man in his place, and you make their requirements. Everyone possesses his food, and his lifetime is counted. Tongues are distinguished in speech, and their characters likewise. Their skins are made distinct, and you distinguish foreign lands.' The Aten was an international god for an international age. This theme is highlighted again, later in the Great Hymn, when it refers to the god Hapy, bringer of the annual inundation. The Aten created Hapy as the inundation that comes from the Duat – the Egyptian underworld or netherworld. But foreign people have a Hapy, or inundation, from the sky: rain.

The Great Hymn compares the rising and setting of the sun to life and death: 'When you have risen, they live. When you set, they die.' Indeed, darkness is generally thought to be like death. The night was a time of danger, when a person could be robbed, when lions emerged from their dens, and when you could be bitten by a snake, says the Great Hymn. The absence of the Aten was the absence of safety. We will return to Akhenaten's approach to death.

The temples of Amarna

Akhenaten didn't just modify Egypt's religion, he adapted the layout of the country's temples too. During the New Kingdom, the Egyptians had developed a standard temple plan. Moving from front to rear, you first passed through a pylon-gateway, then a peristyle courtyard and a hypo-style hall, before finally reaching the sanctuary at the back of the building. As you progressed through the temple, the floor level rose and the ceiling lowered. The space became darker and more confined. At Amarna, this was quite different, though familiar elements from earlier tradition remained. During ceremonies and rituals, offerings were made to the Aten. Unlike in traditional temples, where priests brought food to the god's statue three times per day in his dark sanctuary, at Amarna, the king wanted the Aten to be dazzled by an abundance of offerings, visible on the ground below as he crossed the sky. So, he commanded that Amarna's temples be fitted with a huge number of open-air offering tables, places where the Aten's rays could directly touch his vast donations of food, drink, flowers and incense. To Akhenaten, a gloomy, confined sanctuary was no place to worship a sun god.

Taking the Great Temple to the Aten (known in ancient Egyptian as 'The House of the Aten in Akhetaten') as an example: within this vast, 750 × 270 metre (2,460 × 885 foot) enclosure, there were a number of discrete structures, each separated by a lot of open space. First, directly in front of the enclosure's entrance, was a small stone palace, and a series of mud-brick pedestals set within troughs, almost all divided into basins that probably contained water. Offering tables stood in this area, with around 920 more to the south. The site's excavators propose that these offering tables may have been maintained by the people of Amarna. Egyptians may even have placed corpses on some of these tables as part of the funerary proceedings, enabling the bodies to receive purification from the Aten.

Immediately after this area came the 'Long Temple'. Here, the visitor first entered a columned hall, known as the 'House of Rejoicing'. This had sixteen colossal columns, eight on each side of a central path, which probably featured a staircase leading to a raised platform where Akhenaten stood and looked out eastward towards the rising sun at dawn (visible between each of the subsequent pylons). After the columned hall came six open courts, each separated by its own pylon entrance (unlike traditional pylons, these were not joined at the top), where around 750 stone offering tables stood; this area was called 'The Aten is Found'. Unlike traditional Egyptian temples, none of these structures had roofs, enabling Akhenaten's priests to perform their rituals and worship in the sunlight – it must have been sweaty work. To the east of the Long Temple, but still within the overall enclosure, there was a pedestal, upon which rested a *benben*-stone, a symbol of the first mound of creation in traditional religion, and so another holdover from the past (see Chapter 11). A slaughterhouse stood beside it. Nearby, there was the temple sanctuary – a walled courtyard with around 150 offering tables.

Amarna's smaller Aten temple was called 'The Mansion of the Aten'. It stood to the south of the Great Temple to the Aten, beside the palace known as the 'King's House', and copied the larger temple in its overall layout, just on a smaller scale. Its first courtyard contained a structure called a 'Sunshade', where Akhenaten could worship the Aten, while a building in the second court may have been a royal robing room. Akhenaten perhaps used this temple for private worship; otherwise, it may have served as his mortuary temple.

Queen Nefertiti: her temples and role as priestess

The bust of Queen Nefertiti, discovered in a sculptor's workshop at Amarna and now in Berlin, is one of the most iconic symbols of Egypt. Its fame has made Nefertiti, the Great Royal Wife of Akhenaten, one of the ancient world's best-known names, up there with Tutankhamun, Ramesses and Cleopatra. She had particular prominence in Akhenaten's new religious movement. For one, unlike other queens, Nefertiti displayed her name in a royal cartouche – an honour normally reserved for kings – often preceded by the epithet Neferneferuaten, 'Beautiful is the Perfection of the Aten'. On the walls of the Aten temples that stood at Karnak, she was shown making offerings to the Aten with her daughters, a ritual role that was typically the preserve of kings. Indeed, one of these structures, the Mansion of the Benben, lacked any image of Akhenaten or any male figures. One temple block discovered at Hermopolis even shows Nefertiti smiting a female enemy – a carving unique in all Egyptian history. And at the corners of Akhenaten's sarcophagus, where images of protective goddesses were traditionally carved, we find Nefertiti. Unlike in the Valley of the Kings, where tombs were usually designed for an individual king, at Amarna, Akhenaten's royal tomb was to be a family crypt.

At Amarna, royal women, and in particular the Great Royal Wife, represented divine fertility and regeneration. Consequently, each high-level female member of the royal family – Nefertiti, Kiya (another wife of Akhenaten) and the princesses – had their own 'Sunshade of Re', temples that drew on the power of fecundity embodied in the Amarna royal women to ensure the rebirth of the Aten each day. Sunshades of Re were not an Amarna innovation; the first one was built as part of the mortuary temple of Hatshepsut at Deir el-Bahri, earlier in the 18th Dynasty. These structures were traditionally a form of Re chapel, dedicated to the re-energization of the sun god during the night and his rebirth at dawn. They were built within royal mortuary temples to connect the rebirth of the king with the rebirth of Re. Only two of the Amarna sunshades have so far been excavated, one owned by Princess Meritaten (but originally for Queen Kiya), called the Maru-Aten, and one for Queen Nefertiti, built in an area of Amarna called Kom el-Nana. Nefertiti's sunshade was designed as a huge enclosure divided into two sections. In the north section, archaeologists found the remains of a probable well, a brewery and a bakery, as well as the foundation of a building called the North Shrine. In the southern section was the South Pavilion, which had stepped entrances and sunken gardens. There was also the Central Platform, which may have featured multiple windows of appearance – places where the queen could appear to amassed crowds below.

An Amarna trinity?

Some scholars have argued that the Amarna belief system recognized a trinity, formed of the Aten, Akhenaten and Nefertiti. This would reflect the traditional first gods of Heliopolitan creation, with the Aten in place of Re-Atum, Akhenaten equated with Shu and Nefertiti as Tefnut. This association can be seen in Amarna art, in which early statuary showed Akhenaten wearing the feathered plumes of Shu. The Aten may even have been connected with Akhenaten's father, King Amenhotep III (r. *c.* 1388–1348 BC). After thirty years as king, Amenhotep celebrated his *sed*-festival, a grand ceremony that proved his continuing fitness to rule. He then held this same festival every three years until his death. When Akhenaten came to power, he continued to celebrate *sed*-festivals every three years in honour of the Aten and himself, following the pattern from his father's reign. Does this mean that Akhenaten believed

Amenhotep III had merged with the Aten in death? The god's name was carved within a royal cartouche – an honour traditionally reserved for pharaohs – and Akhenaten did refer to the Aten as his father, so it's possible, but cannot be proven at this time.

Household religion at Amarna

To what extent did Akhenaten impose his beliefs on ordinary people? In the northern part of Amarna, in a sector of residential housing, one shrine contained a stele dedicated to the major gods of Elephantine: Khnum, Satet and Anuket (see Chapter 1). This wasn't hidden away, kept secret from the new believers; it stood within sight of the villa of one of Amarna's key military officials – hardly someone who would allow the old religious ways to continue if they'd been forbidden by the king. Similarly, at the Workmen's Village – one of two workers' settlements at the eastern side of Amarna, thought to have been home to the families of the men who cut and decorated the tombs – there were twenty-four shrines dedicated to ancestors and deities. The gods worshipped there included the Aten, of course, but also Isis, Shed, Hathor, Renenutet and even that most hated of gods, Amun, all probably painted by the artisans housed in the village. Cult statues of Hathor may have stood in the workmen's shrines too.

Finds excavated from the houses of both the rich and poor at Amarna also attest to the continuation of tradition. Symbols such as the *wedjat*-eye adorned rings. Stelae, jewelry and figurines associated with Isis, Sekhmet, Ptah, Mut and Thoth have been found. Amun-Re's name appears on scarabs. People continued to wear pendants in the shape of the protector god Bes, who could also be seen on headrests, vessels, statuettes and even on objects buried with the Amarna royals. Archaeologists have discovered images of the goddess Taweret, female figurines connected with fertility, and a bronze stamp and figurines of Sobek. So, although the Amarna elite erected shrines dedicated to the royal family and the Aten in the grounds of their elaborate villas (you've got to keep in with the king, after all), for most people traditional religious life continued as normal. Too much evidence for this continuity has been uncovered for it to have been a hidden practice.

The Amarna tombs and cemeteries: afterlife beliefs under Akhenaten

Despite the various changes in life under Akhenaten, the dead still had to be buried somewhere. Akhenaten couldn't reform death itself, but he could reform how people dealt with it. Many of the elite members of Akhenaten's entourage had rock-cut tombs carved and decorated for themselves in Amarna's eastern hills, the direction of sunrise – as opposed to the traditional west, direction of sunset and symbolic of death. The decorative scheme of these burials is quite different from those of the earlier New Kingdom tombs at Saqqara or Thebes. For one, their main focus is on Akhenaten, the royal family and the Aten, rather than the tomb owner, his achievements in life and the gods. You wanted that fabulous painting of Osiris in your tomb chapel? Tough luck. You're getting Akhenaten on a chariot. You don't like that? What about Akhenaten and his family worshipping the Aten, or eating together? No? Well, it's not like you can use the wall space to show yourself, not unless you're commemorating a time when Akhenaten gave you rewards. Your death isn't about you.

The afterlife beliefs prevalent at Amarna are hard to reconstruct, being so short-lived. It seems, at the very least, that the dead were believed to awake at sunrise and wander from their tombs in the form of *ba*-spirits to the Great Temple of the Aten, where they consumed offerings left by the living. This new system is neatly summed up by the courtier Tutu in his tomb inscriptions at Amarna: 'You stand up at dawn in your place of eternity (tomb) to see the Aten when he rises. You purify yourself and receive clothes, as was your custom when you were on the land.'

Though this indicates an afterlife existence quite different from traditional belief, there remained continuity with the past. The dead still asked the living for provisions. Religious inscriptions mention *ba*- and *ka*-spirits, and embalmers continued to mummify bodies. Officiants performed the Opening of the Mouth ritual, which 're-activated' the corpse and enabled images to be used as a vessel for the spirit, and scribes copied out spells from the Book of the Dead. Artisans produced shabtis – statuettes of magical workers who performed tasks for the deceased in the afterlife – including for Akhenaten, who had over 200, and made other traditional items of burial equipment, such as canopic jars to contain the internal organs after mummification. Osiris, too, survived relatively unscathed. Akhenaten's followers didn't consistently attack his name and images. In fact, an offering table from the Workmen's Village at Amarna bears a prayer to Osiris. There are also references to the afterlife realm of the Duat during Akhenaten's reign. It is mentioned in the tomb of the standard-bearer of Akhenaten Suti at Amarna, while the high priest of the Aten Meryre I, in his Amarna tomb inscriptions, says he wants to be an *akh*-spirit in the Duat. All of this suggests that Akhenaten's reforms weren't perhaps as radical as sometimes thought.

The lack of eclipses in Egyptian texts

Given the importance of the sun god in both traditional Egyptian religion and Amarna religion, it's unfortunate that very little about the Egyptians' thoughts on eclipses is preserved. We know that they referred to solar eclipses as the sun growing dark, while a lunar eclipse was the sky swallowing the moon or the moon growing dark, but references to specific events are rare. Scholars usually state that the earliest solar eclipse mentioned in the Egyptian evidence dates to 30 September 610 BC, shortly after the death of King Psamtik I (r. *c.* 664–610 BC) of the 26th Dynasty. This event is recorded on a papyrus from the 1st century BC, which bears a fictitious tale about a priest set in the 26th Dynasty, so it may be unreliable in its details. Furthermore, the Egyptologist Mark Smith has argued that the text actually refers to a lunar eclipse that happened on 22 March 610 BC, not a solar eclipse. The 22nd Dynasty Chronicle of Prince Osorkon also refers to an eclipse, saying that although a bad omen such as a lunar eclipse didn't happen, civil war broke out anyway. Because the Egyptians didn't like to mention dangerous or 'un-*maaty*' events in religious contexts – the source of much of our evidence – and because eclipses were bad omens, it's unsurprising that we don't have further specific references to them; however, there's no reason why such events weren't recorded in archives, among non-religious writings.

Tell el-Amarna in history and today

Akhenaten started building his new royal city in the fifth year of his reign. It was arranged along the 'Royal Road', which acted as a sort of backbone, running roughly north to south along the east side of the Nile. At its north end, Akhenaten and his family probably resided in the fortress-like North Riverside Palace, within a sector called the North City. Nobles, courtiers and officials lived in large villas nearby. Further south along the Royal Road, the North Palace was probably originally home to Queen Nefertiti or Queen Kiya, but was later used by Princess Meritaten. Continuing south, after the North Suburb, you reached the Central City. Here stood Akhenaten's Great Palace – a large construction, with state apartments, a harem, magazines, servants' quarters and a coronation hall. It was perhaps where royal audiences and ceremonies were conducted. The Great Palace was linked by a bridge over the Royal Road to the King's House, perhaps a smaller, more private residence for the king. This had a window of appearance, where the king and his family stood to bestow honours and promotions upon loyal supporters. In the Central City, there was also the Small Temple

TELL EL-AMARNA

Key dates and remains

c. 2500 BC	Small settlement at Amarna (indicated by pottery).
c. 1360 BC	Akhenaten becomes king of Egypt.
c. 1355 BC	Akhenaten founds Akhetaten (Tell el-Amarna). Construction begins.
c. 1343 BC	The death of Akhenaten.
c. 1339 BC	Amarna abandoned. Tutankhamun erects his Restoration Stele at Thebes.
c. AD 500	Cemetery and constructions at Amarna. The tomb of Panehesy becomes a Coptic church. Monastery established at Kom el-Nana.

to the Aten and the Great Temple to the Aten, a records office, military posts, and bakeries. Then, in the South Suburb, there was another sector of housing. Two workers' settlements existed on the eastern edge of Amarna, one known as the Workmen's Village and the other as the Stone Village. Both seem to have housed artisans who cut and decorated the tombs of the elite and royal family. Why two settlements were needed remains a mystery, though it is possible that the artisans from Deir el-Medina in Thebes (see Chapter 4) moved together as a community to the Workmen's Village.

Excavations in Amarna's various non-elite cemeteries – where thousands of ordinary Egyptians were buried – have recently shed light on the city's population and their daily struggles. The North Tombs Cemetery, for example, contains many burials of young people (at least, younger than twenty-five years old). They were buried quite simply, often wrapped in a mat, with few or no burial goods. Sometimes, multiple bodies were placed in a single grave. Bodies here displayed spinal fractures, trauma to the arms and malnutrition. The site's excavators suggest that these were conscripts, working in such harsh conditions that it ultimately led to their deaths at a young age. If multiple people died on the same day, they seem to have been dumped in the same grave. It is perhaps no coincidence that Amarna's main limestone quarries were just north of this cemetery. Amarna's fast growth, and apparent opulence, was built on the backs of its suffering, poorest inhabitants.

With the death of Akhenaten after seventeen years as king, there was a brief period of two ephemeral rulers before his (probable) son, Tutankhamun (r. *c.* 1343–1333 BC) – originally named Tutankhaten – came to power, and re-established Egypt's traditional religion. On his Restoration Stele, erected at the Karnak temple precinct, but now in the Egyptian Museum, Cairo, Tutankhamun describes the challenges he faced: Egypt's sacred places had disintegrated into rubble and become overgrown; the gods had turned their backs on Egypt; the land was ill; deities didn't respond when people appealed to them; and soldiers sent to Syria failed in their missions to expand Egypt's borders. It was a dire situation, and Tutankhamun's early death meant that he never completed his restoration efforts, leaving this work to fall to his successors. To make matters worse, Hittite sources suggest that a plague spread through the Near East and Anatolia during the Amarna phase, lasting for about twenty years. Though we cannot say for certain, Egypt too may have been affected. If so, perhaps the Egyptians saw this as divine punishment for Akhenaten's religious experiment.

Akhetaten was dismantled during the early 19th Dynasty, and its stonework was reused in other constructions. The names of the traditional gods were reinscribed on temples across the country, and their statues were re-carved or repaired. The Amarna kings were purged from history. King lists jumped from King Amenhotep III to Horemheb (which seems a bit unfair on Tutankhamun and his successor Aye). After its abandonment, Tell el-Amarna was rarely occupied. A temple seems to have continued to operate, at least until the reign of King Seti I (r. *c.* 1296–1279 BC); a few people were buried there during the Third Intermediate Period; and *c.* AD 500, Christians converted the tomb of Panehesy, among the North Tombs, into a church and established a monastery at Kom el-Nana. They also built housing and cemeteries. Today, the archaeological site exists primarily as a place of study and tourism.

▲

If you're visiting Tell el-Amarna, remember that the city's sites are quite spread out, so it's a good idea to arrive with a taxi. The first stop on any visitor itinerary is normally the **North Tombs**, made for Amarna's highest officials, and reached via modern steps up the cliff face. Among them is the well-preserved **Tomb of Huya** – who served as a steward to Queen Tiye, mother of Akhenaten – which includes carvings of the royal family, and of Huya receiving rewards from Akhenaten at the palace's window of appearance. The king and queen are also present in the **Tomb of Meryre II**, overseer of the royal harem of Nefertiti. One scene shows the royal couple at the window of appearance, while another depicts Nefertiti pouring a drink through a strainer for Akhenaten. The outer hall of the **Tomb of Panehesy**, chief servitor of the Aten, is also of interest, because it was transformed into a Coptic church.

After visiting the North Tombs, you can briefly stop at the **North Palace**, and peer over its mud-brick outer wall to see the remains of chambers and courts. Originally, the palace was filled with colourful paintings, and at its centre, there was a relaxing pool. A short drive south of the North Tombs, following the cliffs, is the **Tomb of Akhenaten**. Little remains of the tomb's original decoration – the attacks on Akhenaten's names and images were quite thorough. Two suites of chambers break off from the tomb's main axis. The one closest to the tomb's entrance is thought to have been cut for Queen Nefertiti, but no decoration remains. The suite further along was made for Princess Meketaten. Preserved scenes show the royal couple mourning the princess, and there is an image of a dead child, perhaps indicating that Meketaten died during childbirth.

Afterwards, you can visit the **Central City**, much of which remains covered by sand. Here, the **Small Temple to the Aten** gives a sense of the shape and scale of Akhenaten's religious architecture, with its three huge courts and a restored column standing in its sanctuary. Nearby, you can ascend a modern set of steps and peer down into the well-preserved remains of an **Amarna villa**, once owned by an elite family. Then, if there's still time, end your day by visiting the **South Tombs**, where highlights include the **Tomb of Aye**, a courtier who became pharaoh after Tutankhamun, and the **Tomb of Mahu**, who served as Amarna's police chief.

Colossal statue of Thoth in baboon form at Hermopolis.

HERMOPOLIS AND TUNA EL-GEBEL

~~~~~~~~~~~~~~~~~~~~

The Wisdom and Magic of Thoth

◎

'Thoth, put me in Hermopolis, your town that is pleasant to live in.'
Papyrus Sallier I.8, c. 1100 BC.

'Hail to you, moon, Thoth, Bull in Hermopolis...who judges every person...who
knows what a person says and causes [their] acts to accuse the one that did it.
The one who causes Re to be content and forwards [matters] to the Sole Lord.
You cause him to know all that happens. When the land becomes bright, he
makes summons in the sky and he is not forgetful about yesterday's reports.'
From a statue of General (later King) Horemheb, c. 1340 BC.

The baboon mummy stares back at me through the glass, his rock-
cut niche illuminated by a bright bulb above. His skeletal brow appears
almost quizzical. I think he wants to ask a question – probably something like: 'How do I get out of here?' Reached by a small set of steps,
and wrapped in a yellowing linen shawl, this baboon has observed
every visitor to Tuna el-Gebel for Thoth knows how long. He's not so
much a mummy these days as a skeleton, and he's many years past
retirement. Above him, rearing cobras are carved as a defence against
dangerous forces. Below, there's an empty offering-slab and a pair of
stone columns, the cult setting for gifts of drink and burnt offerings
to this divine animal. On the other side of the room, beyond a broken
wall of blocks, a perfectly intact baboon statue squats in another
niche, out of reach. He rests on his hind-legs, hands gently placed
against his knees, sun disc on his head. There's no decay here – he
knows he's a highlight of the tour. It's almost insulting to the poor
dead baboon.

This is a baboon chamber within the catacombs of Tuna el-Gebel, a place where animals sacred to the god Thoth – Egypt's god of wisdom, divine scribe and vizier to the sun god – were once interred in great numbers. It is one of many cultic areas dedicated to the sacred baboons buried in the catacombs, which sprawl over two subterranean levels. And baboon mummies weren't the only creature feature locked in Thoth's dark basement. Along the sand-strewn, rock-cut corridors that connect the chambers, row upon row of small niches have been carved into the walls, giving the impression that you're walking through a dusty honeycomb. Many of these niches contain ibises, their mummified bodies placed in wooden coffins or tiny stone sarcophagi. More of these birds were laid to rest in pottery jars piled up in side chambers, where their souls chirped away eternity, safely blanketed in darkness. I again feel sorry for the poor dead baboon. He, too, was once privately sealed away, hidden from view in a coffin behind a limestone slab.

Above me, at surface level, is a desert necropolis. Among the ever-shifting dunes, tombs built like small temples stand on streets of the dead, the art within mixing Greek and Egyptian influences. There's a Roman-era waterworks that once supplied a nearby town, and not too far away, a boundary stele from the reign of King Akhenaten (r. *c.* 1360–1343 BC), marking one limit of his doomed ancient city (for which see Chapter 7). About 7 kilometres (4 miles) further north-east is Hermopolis, where you can see the sad remains of the once grand Temple of Thoth, the god's main cult centre. Though often overlooked by visitors to Egypt today, both locations – Hermopolis and Tuna el-Gebel – were once prominent places of worship in ancient Egypt, and their shared deity Thoth featured in many of the country's key myths.

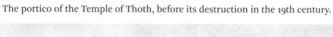

The portico of the Temple of Thoth, before its destruction in the 19th century.

Thoth: wise scribe of the gods

Known to the ancient Egyptians as Djehuty, Thoth was famous in Egypt for his wisdom. He loved *maat* – truth, balance and justice – and even taught *maat* to other divinities. But this doesn't mean that he was a peaceful character. Thoth was moved to anger whenever anyone broke *maat*, and he punished those who tried to frustrate it. Thoth created all languages – not solely ancient Egyptian – and invented hieroglyphs; this made him well qualified to serve as scribe for the gods. His wisdom meant that he was powerful in magic and healing, and could be called on by the sick for cures. The gods also benefited from his medical knowledge – he cures Horus' damaged eye in various myths, either by returning it to Horus, spitting on it, or 'filling' it, just as the moon, a manifestation of Thoth, fills and 'heals' when waxing.

In art, Thoth usually takes the form of an ibis-headed man, a full ibis or a baboon. As a moon god, his association with the ibis is probably due to its curved beak, reminiscent of the crescent moon. As for why Thoth takes a baboon form, one text rather unsatisfactorily explains that Re sent Thoth around the Greek islands, and as a result the baboon came into existence (more detail would have been helpful here). Thoth is sometimes referred to as a son of Re. At Esna Temple, dedicated to Khnum, one myth describes how Re was bitter because of a rebellion against him, and in that moment Thoth exited his heart, ready to face the god's enemies and restore order. In other myths, he emerges from the skull of Seth, or is born from an egg. He's said to have no mother, and his wives differ depending on the myth, sometimes being Maat, sometimes Nehemtawy.

Thoth served as deputy to Re, just as the moon was believed to be a weaker form of – and thus assistant to – the sun. But Thoth's association with the sun god's movements wasn't restricted to the night hours; he ensured the course of the sun god's boat in the day sky too, and helped to ward off any dangers it might face. Thoth's lunar connection is mentioned by the Greek writer Plutarch. When the sun learned that Rhea (Nut) and Cronus (Geb) were sleeping together, he cursed the goddess, stopping her from giving birth during any month or year. Hermes (Thoth) decided to help Rhea. He played draughts with the moon, and each time he won, he received one seventieth of her phases of illumination. From this, he created five new days of the year – an addition to the 360 that already existed. During these five days, Rhea gave birth to her children: Osiris, Arueris (Apollo/Horus the Elder), Typhon (Seth), Isis and Nephthys.

Thoth as an ibis-headed man (right) pours symbols of life and dominion over the king, aided by Horus (left).

Thoth often appears in mythology as a mediator. In the dispute between Horus and Seth for the throne of Egypt, Thoth tried to keep things civil between the two gods, and in one account acted as judge over proceedings. In the Pyramid Texts, Thoth sentences Seth to carry Osiris on his back as punishment for his crimes against the god. In some myths, the diplomatic Thoth is sent to calm the 'Wandering Goddess' and convince her to return to Egypt (see Chapter 5). Thoth was also present after a person's death. He stood watching, papyrus roll and pen in hand, when the deceased's heart was weighed against the feather of *maat*, ready to record the result of the judgment. He ensured that the deceased was refreshed by the cool north wind during the journey through the Duat, and sometimes performed the Opening of the Mouth ritual, which enabled the dead to regain their faculties in the afterlife.

Magic in Egyptian society and stories

As well as his association with scribes and healing, knowledge and wisdom, Thoth was highly regarded for his magic. To the ancient Egyptians, magic, or *heka* as they called it, was a gift from the gods, a weapon to help face the trials and tribulations of daily life. Even the gods themselves were susceptible to its effects. To prove their efficacy, many spells begin with a mythological introduction – a form of guarantee, because if the spell had worked for a god in the distant past, it would work again today. For instance, spells composed to cure sick children of their illnesses or to heal them from the effects of stings and bites often begin with an account of the infant Horus falling ill and Isis using her magic to cure him. Some spells in the Book of the Dead are described as having been found beneath a statue of a god at Hermopolis – presumably Thoth – written in the god's own handwriting, again as reassurance of mythological antiquity and thus quality. (And as Thoth was believed to have invented writing, we can assume that his handwriting was impeccable.)

The use of magic was widespread among Egypt's population. Most people probably knew simple invocations or rituals, but for more complex spells and specialized learning, they called on local wise women or men, and if need be, lector priests – men versed in sacred writings, who knew temple spells and rituals. The Egyptians used magic for a variety of reasons, from causing people to fall in love to summoning gods and demons. To cast a spell, you often first had to create a figurine or draw an image of a person, animal or god. If the figurine was meant to represent a specific individual, it was useful to add something associated with that person's body, such as their spit, hair or clothing. Rituals then magically made the figurine 'live', standing in for the intended subject of the spell's effects. When casting the spell, it was important to recite the correct words, sometimes at a specific time, day, or phase of the moon, and to be ritually pure.

Many Egyptian stories feature characters who were powerful in magic – and particularly lector priests. One tale revolves around a man who was sleeping with a chief lector priest's wife. Upon learning of the affair, the lector priest moulded a wax crocodile, only seven fingers (13 centimetres or 5 inches) long, and recited a spell over it. When the adulterous man went to wash himself in a nearby lake, just as he did each day after sleeping with the priest's wife, a servant threw the wax crocodile into the water. It immediately grew to 7 cubits long – over 3.5 metres (11½ feet). It lunged at the man, grabbing him in its mouth, and plunged into the dark depths of the lake. The two vanished. Seven days later, the lector priest and the king were walking along the lake shore. Wanting to show off his powers, the priest summoned the crocodile. It plodded onto the shore, and spat out the man. He was still alive. The priest shrunk the crocodile back to its original tiny size, and showed the king that it was formed of wax. 'Who is this man?' the king said. 'He was having an affair with my wife,' the priest replied. 'Oh! I see...' The king told the crocodile to return to the bottom of the lake, the man clamped in its mouth. Neither was seen again. As for the lector priest's wife, the king had her burned and her remains thrown into the Nile.

In another tale, following his chief lector priest's advice, King Sneferu (r. c. 2520–2470 BC) went sailing with twenty palace women, each chosen for their beauty. They rowed the boat for him, wearing nothing but nets. As one of the women rowed, her oar collided with her braided hair, causing a fish-shaped pendant to fall into the lake.

Plop! She stopped rowing, and refused to start again. 'What's going on?' Sneferu said. 'Your pendant fell? I can replace it! Keep rowing!' The woman refused. She didn't want a replacement, she wanted the one that she'd lost. So the king summoned his chief lector priest. Using his magic, the priest raised one half of the lake into the air and pushed it on top of the other half. Then, looking down at the empty lake bed, he spotted the pendant resting on a pot sherd (probably among some confused flapping fish). He retrieved it for the woman, and put the water back in its place.

To give a final example, one day, King Khufu (r. *c.* 2470–2447 BC) learned that there was a man in Egypt powerful enough to re-attach a man's severed head to his body, and thus bring him back to life. This magician's name was Djedi. 'I've got to see this,' Khufu said; so he summoned Djedi to his court. 'Bring a prisoner, and lop off his head,' the king commanded. But Djedi protested, saying that it shouldn't be done to a person. The king relented. 'Fine. Have a goose brought instead then,' he said. A courtier cut the goose's head off. He placed its body on one side of the hall, and its head on the other. Djedi recited his words of power. The goose's body raised itself up on its feet, and began to walk. The head began to wobble, and rolled itself towards its body. When the two goose-parts met, they recombined, as if nothing had ever happened. The goose cackled. Khufu was impressed. He sent for a larger goose, and witnessed the same miracle. Then an ox was brought, and the same happened again. Djedi definitely deserved his reputation.

The moon and moon gods

The Egyptians linked various gods with the moon. Because the moon was the sun god's deputy, Thoth, as divine vizier, was the most prominent of these, though there were also Khnum, Min, Osiris, Duau, Shu, Iah (whose name translates as 'moon') and Khonsu, who was regarded as moonlight, and simultaneously wore a crescent moon and full moon on his head. The moon also had various designations, such as 'the old man who becomes a child,' 'the one that repeats its form', and as one who repeated its births. Like other heavenly bodies, the moon was also thought to be a god sailing across the sky in a boat.

The moon's phases provided the Egyptians with a way to measure the passage of time. They developed a lunar calendar, with the first day of each lunar month marked by the new moon, when it vanished from the sky. Certain rituals and festivals were held at specific phases of the moon, giving this calendar an important religious function. The day of the full moon was called the 'union of the two bulls', when the light of the moon and sun merged together. Whenever a god entered a celestial body – whether the moon or another – its light became enhanced. Various deities performed this function within the moon, including Osiris, Hathor, Sekhmet and the sun god. The Egyptians also believed that the Nile inundation rose during a full moon.

Various myths explained the moon's weakness compared to the sun, and its changing shape. Observing its phases, the Egyptians saw a process of damage and healing, a cycle of disorder and order, following the familiar Egyptian theme of *maat* – the struggle for balance and order in the cosmos. The moon was a visible symbol of regeneration. They equated the moon with the left eye of Horus, torn from its socket by Seth and healed by Thoth (or another god), sometimes through spitting on it – spit being a key ingredient in Egyptian magic. The *wedjat*-symbol, often worn as an amulet, represented the Eye of Horus' return to order after this period of chaos.

The restoration of Osiris' dismembered body parts (see Chapter 6) was also part of lunar mythology. Seth ripped Osiris' body into pieces, represented by the waning moon, but Isis restored him, represented by the waxing moon. This final act of restoration was sometimes depicted as Anubis mummifying the lunar disc. In a similar myth, on each of the fourteen days of its waxing phase, a different god was believed to enter the moon and heal it. Each of these gods was created by Isis. The process of waxing could also be referred to as 'filling' the 'sound eye'. On the fifteenth day of the month, when the moon was full, Thoth completed its healing and Osiris entered the sound eye. At this moment, animals were at their most fertile – texts refer to bulls ejaculating and cows conceiving.

Thoth and Babi

Although Thoth usually had a good relationship with his fellow gods, one myth presents a confrontation between Thoth and the violent baboon-shaped deity Babi. Babi accused Thoth of stealing the food of Re – rather un-Thoth-like behaviour – and ran off to tell the Two Enneads. But the Enneads refused to believe Babi, because no one had seen it happen. 'Babi is wrong, and Thoth is right,' Re declared. Like a movie, the scene then abruptly cuts to Babi having sex with an unnamed woman. Thoth, angered by Babi's accusation, interrupted and used his magic to ensure that Babi couldn't retract his phallus. Then, to embarrass Babi further, Thoth summoned the Two Enneads to witness what was happening. 'We can see your testicles,' Thoth said to Babi, adding insult to injury. Babi – now able to retract his phallus, we must assume, and more than a little angry – grabbed his weapons and attacked Thoth. But Thoth was unaffected. He uttered another spell, compelling Babi to bash his weapons over his own head. The gods laughed. From that day forward, Babi became known as an enemy, perhaps a comical reference to the hieroglyph for 'enemy', which depicts a figure holding a staff up to his head, almost as if he's bashing himself. Re then gave Thoth permission to execute Babi on a slaughter block.

The god Babi, also known as Baba, is found early in Egyptian history, when he appears in the Pyramid Texts as a baboon. Here, he is described as red-eared and with a purple behind. Later depictions show him with a human body and a dog's face, carrying huge knives. His fearsomeness is emphasized in the Book of the Dead, where he's said to live on entrails. Less scarily, he is also the first son of Osiris (don't tell Horus), and his phallus served as the bolt of the doors of the sky. Babi's phallus turns up again as the mast of the Duat's ferryboat, a symbol of fertility. Given Babi's twin violent and sexual characteristics, the Egyptians often linked him with Seth. This is perhaps why Babi served on the sun god's boat – it is a protective role normally played by Seth.

Setna's search for the scroll of Thoth

Because of Thoth's magic and secret knowledge, objects and texts associated with him made good plot devices for stories. In the Westcar Papyrus, written in the Middle Kingdom but set in the Old Kingdom, King Khufu seeks to copy the secret chambers of the sanctuary of Thoth when making his own temple. The only problem? He has no idea how many secret chambers there are or where to find them. Luckily, the magician Djedi, who as we have already seen impressed the pharaoh with his powers of resurrection, does know where the king can discover the number of Thoth's secret chambers – a knowledge that highlights his own magical power. The book or scroll of Thoth is another popular plot device, featured in a tale written down during the Ptolemaic Period and starring the fourth son of the New Kingdom pharaoh Ramesses II (r. c. 1279–1212 BC), Khaemwaset, better known to the late Egyptians as Setna-Khaemwaset, hero of various epic stories (see also Chapters 4 and 10). In the lost opening to this tale, Setna and his foster brother Inaros are searching for the lost scroll in the Memphite necropolis, and have tracked it to the tomb of Prince Naneferkaptah...

Setna and Inaros entered the tomb, and after descending into its burial chamber discovered the mummy of Prince Naneferkaptah. This wasn't unexpected; it was his tomb, after all. What they didn't expect to find were the ghosts of Ihweret, wife and sister of Naneferkaptah, and Merib, his son, standing waiting for them. Ihweret wanted to tell them a story. 'During my life, I sent a steward to ask permission from my father to marry my brother,' Ihweret said. 'He wouldn't allow it. He wanted us to marry others. But he soon had a change of heart.' After the couple had married, they slept together. Ihweret became pregnant, and later gave birth to Merib. Naneferkaptah spent his days walking around the necropolis of Memphis, reading the ancient tomb inscriptions, until one day, during the Festival of Ptah, a priest laughed at him. 'Why are you reading inscriptions of such little importance during the procession,' he said. The priest invited Naneferkaptah to go with him to see something more worthy of his attention: the scroll of Thoth, a powerful magical document, written by the god himself. To entice Naneferkaptah, the priest told him about its incredible powers. The scroll bore two spells, he said. The first, when read, enchanted the sky, the land, the Duat, the mountains and the seas. It gave the reader the ability to hear the words of birds and reptiles, and to see fish 21 cubits (11 metres or 36 feet) beneath the water's surface. The second spell, whether you were on earth or in the Duat, enabled you to see Re and his Ennead appearing in the sky, and the moon too.

Naneferkaptah was hooked. He wanted to know where the spell was hidden. The priest would only tell him in exchange for 100 *deben* of silver towards his burial costs, and if he made his two brothers priests (and exempted them from paying tax). Naneferkaptah did all that was asked. 'It is under the waters of Coptos,' the priest told the prince. 'Inside a chest of iron, inside a chest of copper, inside a chest of wood, inside a chest of ivory and ebony, inside a chest of silver, inside a chest of gold.' And it's surrounded by 10.5 kilometres (6½ miles) of snakes, scorpions, and other assorted reptiles, he added. Oh, and one more thing: there's an enormous, eternal snake protecting it, too. Naneferkaptah wasn't fazed. He decided to make the journey to Coptos, no matter the risks involved, and convinced his father, the pharaoh, to foot the bill. Ihweret was upset that the priest had suggested such a dangerous mission to her husband and tried to dissuade him from going. But Naneferkaptah didn't listen, so she decided to join him on the expedition, and brought Merib along too.

Once in Coptos, Naneferkaptah celebrated with the priests and prepared for his mission to the waters of Coptos. He created a boat and rowers from a block of wax, spoke words of magic to vivify (and presumably enlarge) them, and filled the boat on which he had arrived with sand. Tying the two boats together, he then set off, leaving Ihweret and Merib behind. He soon found the spot beneath the waves where the scroll was hidden. Naneferkaptah threw the sand overboard to create a dry space in the river, and with the water drained, he could see the snakes, scorpions and reptiles, the eternal snake, and – most importantly – the chest below. Using his magic, he quickly neutralized the snakes, scorpions and reptiles, but the eternal snake was a more formidable foe. Each time Naneferkaptah fought and killed the snake, it returned to life, unharmed. After some time, Naneferkaptah had a clever thought: he sliced the snake in two, and before it could reform, piled sand between its two halves. Unable to join its head to its tail, the snake remained dead. Success.

Naneferkaptah opened the chests, one by one, and took the scroll from within. He read its magical words and received its powers. Suddenly, he could understand the words of birds, fish and animals, and could see Re in the sky with his Ennead. He returned to his boat and, being environmentally conscious, used his magic to restore the lake to its normal form. Then, he commanded his wax rowers to set sail for Coptos. Upon reaching Coptos, Naneferkaptah gave the scroll to Ihweret to read, and she too gained its magical powers. He copied the magic words onto a new papyrus, which he then burned, dissolving the ashes in water. He drank the mixture, taking the magical utterances into his body. The victorious couple celebrated.

When Thoth discovered what Naneferkaptah had done, he flew into a rage. Furious at the death of his guardian and the plundering of his treasures, he asked Re to judge Naneferkaptah. Re decided that Naneferkaptah should be punished by Thoth, along with everyone belonging to him. So the gods sent a powerful demon to earth, commanded to prevent Naneferkaptah and anyone associated with him from ever reaching Memphis. The demon acted swiftly. When Merib left the shade on the royal boat to stand on the deck in the sunlight, he immediately fell into the river and drowned. Naneferkaptah rushed to help his son, but it was too late. Using his magic, he raised Merib from the water, placed him on the deck, and used another spell to make him speak. Through the water-soaked words of his dead son, Naneferkaptah learnt of the curse placed on his family by Thoth and Re. Naneferkaptah and Ihweret turned the boat around and returned to Coptos, where they embalmed and buried Merib. Afterwards, the couple decided to sail north once more, to tell their father all that had happened. But disaster struck again. Upon reaching the spot where Merib had died, Ihweret stepped into the sunlight. When the sun's rays touched her, she too fell from the boat and drowned. Just as he'd done with Merib, Naneferkaptah magically lifted his wife from the water, and revived her just long enough to hear her speak of the anger of Thoth and Re. Defeated and wracked with grief, Naneferkaptah returned to Coptos, where he embalmed and buried his wife alongside Merib.

Despite all that had happened, Naneferkaptah once again attempted to sail north to the royal court. Reaching the spot where his wife and child had drowned, sitting safely in the shade, he pondered his own fate. He wondered what he would say to his father if he made it to court alive. How could he explain that pharaoh's daughter and grandson had died, yet he lived? He took a sheet of linen and tied the magical scroll of Thoth to his body. Then, stepping out from the shade into the sunlight, he fell from the boat and drowned. The crew, unable to find Naneferkaptah's body in the water, sailed onwards to Memphis, where they told the king all that had happened. The king and the people of Memphis mourned. But there was one last surprise. One day, at the docks, there was a great commotion, when Naneferkaptah's body was spotted still holding onto the royal boat's rudder. The scroll remained attached to his corpse, so the king had it removed and sent the prince's body for a proper burial.

Ihweret finished her story. She warned Setna that evil things had happened to them because of the scroll – the same scroll that Setna now desired for himself. But Setna still wanted it. 'I'll take the scroll by force if I have to,' he said. Naneferkaptah, shocked that Setna had completely ignored Ihweret's caution, now raised himself from his burial to confront the prince himself. 'Let's play a game,' Naneferkaptah said. 'If you win, you can take the scroll.' Setna agreed, and they sat down to a game of senet. Naneferkaptah won the first round, uttered some words of magic, and bashed Setna on the head with the board, knocking him into the ground up to his ankles. After winning the second game, he bashed Setna a second time, knocking him into the ground as far as his penis. The third time that Naneferkaptah won, he knocked Setna into the ground as far as his ears. The prince needed help, so (perhaps spluttering dirt), he sent Inaros to pharaoh to collect amulets of Ptah and magical scrolls. Inaros returned to the tomb with everything requested. He placed the amulets on the prince's body, magically launching him back to ground level. As Setna flew upwards, he grabbed the scroll of Thoth. The two men fled into the daylight. Ihweret wept. 'Don't worry,' Naneferkaptah said. 'I'll make Setna return the scroll.'

Setna sealed the tomb behind him, and went to visit his father, the pharaoh. He told him everything that had happened. 'You should return the scroll to Naneferkaptah,' the king said. 'If you don't, he will force you to bring it back to him.' Setna didn't listen. He wanted to read the scroll aloud so that everyone could witness his success. Soon after, Setna was walking along the forecourt of the Temple of Ptah when he saw a beautiful woman with her servants. He sent one of his own servants to find out her name. 'She is Tabubu,' the servant told Setna, 'daughter of the priest of Bastet, Lady of Ankhtawy. She is in Memphis to worship Ptah.' Setna sent the servant back to Tabubu with a message: if she slept with him, he'd give her ten *deben* of gold. Tabubu raised her hand, interrupting the servant before he could finish his message. 'If Setna wants me,' she said, 'he should come to my house himself in Bubastis.'

Setna travelled to Bubastis to meet Tabubu. After greeting one another in the garden, they entered her house. Servants brought food and wine. As bluntly as before, Setna asked Tabubu to sleep with him. 'Not until I have legal documents showing that your property will be given to me,' she said. Setna agreed. He summoned a scribe to make the deal. Setna's children arrived at the house too, so Tabubu demanded that the documents block them from any access to the property. She didn't want them arguing with her own children about the inheritance. Setna again agreed, and had his children agree to the deal. Perhaps now Tabubu would sleep with him? 'No,' was her reply. She had one final request. 'If you want to sleep with me,' she said, 'you must kill your children.' This would ensure, in a rather definite way, that they couldn't ever argue with her about the property. Setna agreed, so Tabubu had the children thrown from the window. The dogs and cats below devoured them, chewing on their flesh. Setna listened to their screams, sipping wine with Tabubu.

Setna asked again that Tabubu sleep with him, so the couple sailed to the treasury and lay beside one another on a bed of ebony and ivory. But as Setna reached out his hands to touch Tabubu, she opened her mouth and let out a great scream. Suddenly, Setna was awake. Naked. His penis inserted into a jar. The pharaoh, wandering by, asked his son what had happened. 'Naneferkaptah did this to me,' Setna said. 'You must go to Memphis,' the king replied. 'Your children are looking for you.' Pharaoh brought Setna a new set of clothes, and the two departed for the royal court. When Setna found his children alive, he hugged them. 'Were you drunk?' Pharaoh asked, perhaps doubting Setna's story. Setna told him the full tale of Tabubu and Naneferkaptah. Pharaoh listened carefully, and after pointing out 'I told you so,' suggested (again) that Setna return the scroll to Naneferkaptah.

When Setna arrived at the tomb, he was met by Ihweret and Naneferkaptah. Sunlight filled the room as he lifted the scroll and handed it to the ghosts. 'Is there anything I can do for your family?' Setna asked. 'The ghosts of Ihweret and Merib are only here in my tomb because of a scribe's magic,' said Naneferkaptah. 'Please bring their bodies from Coptos, and bury them here with me.' Once Pharaoh had approved the expedition, Setna travelled to Coptos. He spent three days and three nights searching the necropolis for the tomb of Ihweret and Merib, but had no luck. So Naneferkaptah, following invisible in spectral form, decided to help the prince by transforming into an elderly priest. When Setna saw the priest, he asked if he knew anything about the tomb. 'Generations of my grandfathers have said that this burial lies beneath the south corner of the chief of police's house,' he said. Setna was sceptical: 'Maybe you hate the chief of police, and just want me to demolish his house.' The elderly priest was taken aback. He would allow Setna's men to watch him, he said, and if a tomb wasn't found, he'd be willingly punished. Setna ordered the house demolished, and discovered the tomb beneath. He took the mummies of Ihweret and Merib from within, and transported them to his royal boat. Then, having ordered that the chief of police's house be rebuilt, he returned north to Memphis. Along the way, Naneferkaptah appeared to Setna, explaining that he had been the elderly priest. Upon his arrival at Memphis, Setna told the pharaoh all that had happened. Ihweret and Merib's bodies were interred in the tomb of Naneferkaptah, and all were sealed within, together at last for eternity.

The Hermetica and the Book of Thoth

Hermes Trismegistus ('Thrice-Great Hermes'), the founder of Hermeticism, is a Roman Period fusion of the Egyptian god Thoth and the Greek god Hermes, messenger of the gods and wearer of a fancy winged hat. The Egyptians called Thoth 'twice great' from around 580 BC, but he only received the title of 'thrice great' hundreds of years later, in the 2nd century BC. And though Thoth never wore a fancy hat, he did have some similarities to Hermes, such as escorting the dead in the underworld and serving as messenger of the gods. This is perhaps why the Greeks identified Hermes with Thoth from as early as the 5th century BC.

Hermes Trismegistus was believed to be the author of a collection of wisdom texts, derived from ancient Egyptian learning, that became the foundations of Hermeticism. These were compiled in various works that have survived through the centuries, including the eighteen

Wrapped ibis mummies. Ibis mummies were offered to Thoth at various locations across Egypt, but particularly at Tuna el-Gebel and Saqqara.

tractates of the *Corpus Hermeticum*, which date from the 1st to the 4th centuries AD, and *The Asclepius*, which dates to the 2nd or 3rd century AD. Other Hermetic writings have also been discovered, particularly among the Nag Hammadi texts.

Who created these hermetic texts? Scholars argue that members of a lodge in Alexandria produced them – a secret society accepting people of all origins, whether they be Egyptian, Greek or Jewish, as long as they were men. The 'cult leader' was the god Hermes Trismegistus, and there were various levels through which initiates could progress in the cult. There was even a form of baptism and prayers spoken together. Traditions vary on the number of hermetic books produced, but we know that they covered alchemy, spirituality and astrology, among other topics. According to Clement of Alexandria, a 2nd-century AD Christian theologian, there were forty-two books (thirty-six for Egyptian philosophy and six on medical issues).

One of these compositions was the Book of Thoth, a modern title given to a text presenting a discussion between Thoth (here 'Thrice-Great', i.e. Trismegistus) and a 'lover of knowledge' – his student. This work is known from various papyrus fragments found across Egypt, produced from the 1st century BC to the 2nd century AD, that reflect both Egyptian and Greek influence. Written in demotic, though hieratic (cursive hieroglyphic) versions also existed, the text was perhaps an attempt to preserve the sacred knowledge of traditional Egyptian religion, similar to the way that temple walls were used in the Ptolemaic Period. Egyptian scribes may have read it, and it might have served as a form of initiation for those entering into its world of sacred knowledge. The Book of Thoth's subjects are wide-ranging, from temple ritual to descriptions of the Duat and works of ancient wisdom literature. There's also a great deal of detail on sacred geography, both in Egypt itself and in the afterlife realm.

The Asclepius was translated from Greek into Latin, and it is the Latin version, in fragments, that survives today. Its ancient title was *Teleios Logos*, 'The Complete Revelation', and it was probably written in Alexandria. It is a discourse providing the information required by an initiate to make progress towards revelation. Reading the works of Hermes Trismegistus – these secret teachings – the initiate learned the true nature of the universe, god and humanity: that each are interconnected.

Ibises and baboons of Thoth

Though the African sacred ibis is not found in Egypt today, and hasn't been for about 150 years, its association with Thoth means that you can still see it in art and statuary from across ancient Egyptian history. Classical writers were also struck by these sacred birds, despite their sometimes not-so-sacred behaviour: Strabo, for example, talks of tame ibises standing on every one of Alexandria's crossroads, eating the garbage from bakeries and meat-shops. As with other sacred animals, killed and dedicated as votive offerings to the gods, ibises were bred at temples. Hermopolis was no different, with around a dozen breeding areas so far identified. During the Ptolemaic Period, each of these was independent of the others, and had its own fields that grew cereals to feed the ibises, maintained by local villagers. Thoth's baboon form, meanwhile, was typically the hamadryas baboon, probably already extinct in Egypt by 3000 BC, but present in other parts of north-east Africa to the present day.

The Ogdoad: the eight gods of pre-creation

In addition to honouring Thoth, Hermopolis was associated with the worship of the Ogdoad – eight gods who personified the pre-creation universe, presented as four frog-headed male gods paired with their female counterparts, four snake-headed goddesses. These were Nun and Naunet, the infinite and inert waters; Amun and Amaunet, hiddenness; Huh and Hauhet, infinity; and Kuk and Kauket, darkness. These divinities are described in Ptolemaic sources as the oldest of the gods and as the parents of the sun disc. They came to rest on the first mound of creation, we are told. A lotus grew on this mound (itself worshipped as Nefertum) and the sun emerged from it. In a late version of this myth, the four male gods united to become Amun as a black bull, while the goddesses became Amaunet as a black cow. But unable to copulate with Amaunet, Amun ejaculated into the water, creating a lotus flower. Another version, recorded in the Tebtunis Mythological Manual, presents the Ogdoad as creating a scarab that became a lotus and opened to reveal the newborn sun god inside. The god then rested between the horns of the sky cow and created sunlight, dispelling the darkness.

Hermopolis in history and today

Hermopolis, today known as el-Ashmunein, lies about 7 kilometres (4¼ miles) west of the Nile. The ancient Egyptians knew this city as Khemenu, meaning 'eight', a reference to the Ogdoad. Though covering a large area (the archaeological site is almost as big as the modern village), little remains of the ancient city today. Excavations have revealed a Middle Kingdom gateway, burials from around 2070 BC, and ruined monuments from the reign of King Ramesses II (r. c. 1279–1212 BC). Like other temples in Egypt, the city's Temple of Thoth was expanded and adapted under various rulers over the centuries, right through to the end of the Pharaonic era. A smaller temple dedicated to Amun and Thoth, and another to Ramesses II, were built during the New Kingdom. The city's importance continued under the Greeks and Romans, and into the Christian era, when the Great Basilica Church was erected. Today, el-Ashmunein is a large village surrounded by agricultural land.

Though there is some evidence for earlier use of the site, the necropolis at Tuna el-Gebel – still standing in the desert, just beyond the cultivable land – was firmly established during the New Kingdom, when officials of the 18th and 19th Dynasties built their tombs there, and the animal cult and catacombs were established. It continued in use into the Late Period. Under the Ptolemies and Romans, local nobles erected their tombs near the 26th Dynasty animal catacombs. The Egyptians built various impressive tombs in this southern part of the site, particularly that of Petosiris, a high priest of Thoth, which resembles a Ptolemaic temple and bears Greek-inspired carved scenes. A settlement with a church existed in the northern part of Tuna el-Gebel from the 2nd to the 7th centuries AD.

▲

To fully see all the sights connected with Thoth, you'll have to split your time between Hermopolis and Tuna el-Gebel. At Hermopolis (near el-Ashmunein), major sights include the **colossal statues of Thoth as a baboon**; the **pylon** and **hypostyle hall** of a Temple of Amun, built in the 19th Dynasty; and a Middle Kingdom **gateway**. Unfortunately, little survives of the **Temple of Thoth**, much of which dates to the reign of Nectanebo I (r. c. 380–362 BC) of the 30th Dynasty. The most impressive

Key dates and remains

c. 2070 BC	Tombs built at Hermopolis.
c. 1930 BC	Temple gateway of King Amenemhat II erected at Hermopolis.
c. 1500 BC	Tuna el-Gebel becomes the necropolis of Hermopolis.
c. 1380 BC	Colossal statues of Thoth as baboon carved.
c. 1270 BC	Ibises and baboons begin to be buried at Tuna el-Gebel.
c. 1210 BC	Small temple of Amun built at Hermopolis.
c. 650 BC	Expansion of animal catacombs at Tuna el-Gebel.
c. 380 BC	Much of Temple of Thoth at Hermopolis rebuilt under King Nectanebo I.
c. 300 BC	Large 'temple-tombs' built at Tuna el-Gebel for the high priests of Thoth.
c. 30 BC	Roman town established in northern Tuna el-Gebel.
c. AD 200	Church built at Tuna el-Gebel.
c. 450	Great Basilica Church built at Hermopolis.

remains at Hermopolis are those of the Coptic **Great Basilica Church**, its columns still standing tall among the ancient ruins.

Must-see sights at Hermopolis' necropolis, modern Tuna el-Gebel, about 7 kilometres (4¼ miles) to its south-west, include the temple-like **Tomb of Petosiris**, a high priest of Thoth who lived shortly after the arrival of Alexander the Great, decorated in a hybrid Egyptian-Greek style; the **Tomb of Isadora**, belonging to a young girl who drowned in the Nile in the 2nd century AD; and the **Graeco-Roman catacombs**, once filled with mummified ibises and baboons, deposited as votive offerings to Thoth.

Image of the god Sobek, carved at Kom Ombo.

9

THE FAIYUM OASIS

~~~~~~~~~~~~~~~~~~~~~

Crocodiles and the Warrior Goddess in the Land of Sobek

ᒥ

'King Unas is Sobek, with green feathers, watchful face and raised forepart.'
From the Pyramid Texts of Unas, c. 2300 BC.

The crocodile god Sobek stands before me. He's pretty weathered, but unlike the king to his right – who has spent much of the past 2,000 years uncomfortably staring back at him – he's least kept his upper torso. Sobek's long snout is picked out in rough scratches; his wig neatly falls over his chest; and the horns and feathered plumes of his crown remain where they belong – on his head. All that remains of the unfortunate king is a pair of legs, an over-starched kilt and a flat stomach – admirable given his age, but nothing special. With no ceiling surviving above them, both carvings bask in the sunlight in a small chapel on the roof of the Temple of Qasr Qarun. Among the bare and unfinished walls, they're a rare find – the only indication as to whom the temple was dedicated. Elsewhere on the roof, sudden drops provide abrupt access to chambers below, the floor slabs having vanished long ago (be careful!), and there are steps to higher ground, which offers wonderful views over the expansive archaeological site.

Built under the Ptolemies, the Temple of Qasr Qarun rises like a bright yellow limestone box from the desert. Within, three central halls lead to a sanctuary that echoes with the sound of chirping birds, who fly around beneath black-stained ceiling slabs. The sanctuary is flanked by chambers. Stairways circle to the roof. The temple is compact and sturdy, yet complex, as if commissioned by a budget-conscious baron who wanted his own mini-castle. Outside, limestone blocks lie scattered across the earth; they might have been dropped from the sky by a careless god. Mud-brick walls and stones peek through the surface of the sand – tell-tale signs of buried structures. Somewhere in the vicinity, there had been a Roman bath and a fortress built under Emperor Diocletian. This was the site of ancient Dionysias, a thriving Roman town on the edge of the Faiyum Oasis, and an important stop on the caravan route that entered the desert and continued on to Bahariya Oasis, 190 kilometres (120 miles) to the south-west.

From my vantage point on the roof, to one side of the temple, the desert disappears over the horizon; if you set off walking in that direction, and were unlucky enough to miss the oases, you might not see green again until southern Chad, about 2,500 kilometres (1,550 miles) away. In all other directions, beyond the archaeological site, there are houses and fields. The cultivation spreads as far north as Lake Qarun (Lake Moeris to the Greeks), a great body of salt water that dominates

The Temple of Sobek at Qasr Qarun. The collapsed section above the entrance has since been reconstructed.

the Faiyum region. Fed by a Nile tributary called the Bahr Yusef, the lake is what brings life to this depression in the Western Desert. On its shore, among the swaying palm trees, you can enjoy the water glistening in the sunlight and the boats sailing in the cool breeze. You can relax, safe in the knowledge that although this idyllic piece of heaven was once famous as the domain of Sobek, these days you'll only find Egyptian crocodiles in Lake Nasser, hundreds of kilometres south. Or, it would seem, carved into the wall of Qasr Qarun's temple. In ancient times though, things were different. Crocodiles were an ever-present danger, and a god like Sobek could be a great ally in protecting you from certain death at the ends of their pointy teeth.

Sobek: Lord of Crocodilopolis

Sobek played various roles in the Egyptian pantheon. A god of fertility, water, creation, sometime associate of Seth and enemy of the sun god, sometime defender of Re, his character changed depending on the period, location and myth. At the Ptolemaic Temple of Kom Ombo in Upper Egypt, Sobek was a creator god who behaved like Shu in the Heliopolitan myth, separating land from sky. He was also associated with Re, defeating Apophis on board the sun god's boat and eating Apophis' helpers. Sometimes, he fused with Re to become Sobek-Re, a god particularly prominent in the Faiyum Oasis. The Coffin Texts shed further light on Sobek's mythology. Here, he is the 'Great Fish', feared and protected by everything in the water, and connected with the Nile flood (sometimes referred to as Sobek's sweat), fertility and vegetation. According to one spell, Sobek ate a part of Osiris' corpse, so the gods sliced off his tongue as punishment. Another says that Isis cut off Horus' hands and threw them into the Nile. Commanded by Re, Sobek went to find them, but couldn't pick them up, so he created fish traps to help – clearly, he was an inventor, too. When navigating the Duat's crocodile-filled waterways, the dead could take Sobek's form to ensure their safe passage – as long as they knew the magic words.

In art, Sobek is usually a crocodile-headed man, wearing an *atef*-crown with a solar disc, a wig and a broad collar. Sometimes, he takes fully crocodile form. The Pyramid Texts describe him as having green feathers – certainly an interesting way of describing a crocodile's skin (perhaps the writer didn't want to get too close). Less frequently, Sobek manifested in the form of a lion, a ram or a bull, and could be identified with Horus when searching for the dead Osiris. Sobek's mother was Neith, goddess of the city of Sais (more about her below), and his father was Senwy, a name that translates as 'Two Brothers'. His wife was Hathor, and their child was Khonsu, a god more commonly described as the offspring of Amun and Mut (see Chapter 3). Temples and chapels to Sobek were built across Egypt, often in places where crocodiles lurked in dangerous parts of the Nile. One of Sobek's most important temples was at Shedet, the ancient capital of the Faiyum Oasis, known as Crocodilopolis to the Greeks and later as Arsinoe. But undoubtedly the best preserved is the temple at Kom Ombo. Sobek shares this latter temple with Horus the Elder (it's basically split down the middle, with Horus getting the northern half and Sobek the southern). A stone-lined pit, dug into the ground close to one of its chapels, may have been home to a sacred crocodile – the temple's manifestation of Sobek.

Sacred crocodiles and votive offerings

Why keep sacred crocodiles? Wasn't that a little...dangerous? Perhaps, yes. But because the Egyptians identified certain crocodiles as avatars of Sobek, inheritors of his divine spirit, they treated them royally (and, frankly, as a bit of a tourist attraction). The Greek writer Strabo, who visited Crocodilopolis in the 20s BC, wrote that the city kept a tame crocodile in a lake. This crocodile was called Suchus, and visitors would feed him grain, wine and pieces of meat. During Strabo's tour, the priests opened Suchus' mouth and fed him cake, meat and wine mixed with honey. The crocodile then waddled off into the lake, only to be fed again soon after for another tourist. The Roman senator L. Mummius visited the same location in 112 BC, and saw the same show. According to Herodotus, some sacred crocodiles were decorated with bracelets and earrings. This statement has been confirmed by archaeologists working at Thebes, who discovered crocodile mummies with holes bored into their skulls from which earrings could be hung.

As well as the pampered sacred crocodiles, the Egyptians bred less fortunate crocodiles across the country to be killed (often when young), mummified and left by pilgrims as votive offerings at Sobek's temples. Around 2,000 crocodile mummies were buried at the southern Faiyum city of Tebtunis alone. At Dahamsha, south of Armant, crocodiles were

A crocodile mummy dated to the Graeco-Roman Period.

kept at the bottom of a temple shaft; this was sealed by a sandstone slab that could be opened at feeding time using two bronze wheels.

The 1st- to 2nd-century AD Roman writer and teacher Claudius Aelianus rather unbelievably wrote in his *On the Characteristics of Animals* that at Kom Ombo, because crocodiles were worshipped as gods, people were filled with joy when their children were taken away by them – their mothers were happy to have fed a god. But despite the Egyptians regarding all crocodiles as manifestations of Sobek, not all were treated well. Plutarch says that the people of Dendera hated crocodiles and that those of Edfu captured, killed and ate them – this was perhaps due to the reptiles' association with Seth in that city.

Neith: warrior goddess and creator

Protector of the king, goddess of hunting and warfare, mother of Sobek (and sometimes Re), Neith is one of the earliest attested Egyptian deities. Her cult symbol – two crossed arrows – makes its first appearance during the Predynastic Period, and her name is an element of the names of some of Egypt's earliest queens, including Merneith, wife of King Djet (r. *c.* 3000 BC), and Neithhotep, mother of King Aha (r. *c.* 3000 BC). Her major cult centre was at Sais in the Delta (modern Sa el-Hagar). She is the first known Egyptian divinity to be depicted in human form – on a 2nd Dynasty vase from Saqqara – and continued to be shown in this way for the rest of Egyptian history, normally with a symbol representing two unstrung bows, back to back, on her head. Sometimes, she wears the Red Crown of Lower Egypt, an association with kingship that was highlighted during the coronation ceremony, when Neith suckled the new king. In addition to her protective and royal associations, Neith was a goddess of weaving, who created mummy shrouds, and in this capacity was one of the goddesses that protected Osiris in the afterlife, along with Isis, Nephthys and Serket.

Neith also manifested as the heavenly cow, Mehet-weret (meaning 'The Great Flood'), and in this form was a creator

A bronze statuette of the goddess Neith, made during the Late Period.

goddess. Her role as creator is explained in two inscriptions at the Temple of Esna in Upper Egypt, a temple dedicated to the ram god Khnum, but at which Neith received worship too. The first of these inscriptions is a hymn that describes Neith as existing since the beginning of time and as the one who began everything. She brings about the inundation each year, enables vegetation to sprout, and is described as two parts masculine and one part feminine. She is a divine serpent who existed before everything, who gave birth to the stars and is mother of Re. (The 27th Dynasty inscription of Wedjahorresnet even goes as far as to say that birth didn't exist until Neith gave birth to Re.) She made the Duat, the god Tatenen (the first land) and Nun (the infinite waters). And she is a brave warrior in combat, who shoots arrows and defeats the enemies of Egypt, while protecting the king and his army.

The second inscription at Esna provides a detailed account of creation by Neith. In a time when there was no land or plants, the goddess Neith sprang into existence in the dark waters of Nun. At first, she materialized as a cow, but soon after became a Nile perch – the sacred fish of Esna. Light came from her eyes, and everything became clear. Then, the goddess spoke: 'Make land appear in the waters, so that I have a place to rest!' The land rose from the waters, just as she commanded, and Esna and Sais appeared on it. Everything that the goddess imagined came into existence, including Egypt. Neith then created thirty gods. She announced each of their names one by one. She was pleased with them, and they regarded her as their mother. 'Tell us what hasn't yet come into being. What will you create next?' they asked, speaking in unison. 'A god will be born today,' Neith said. 'When he opens his eye, it will be daytime. When he closes his eye, it will be night. I will strengthen him with my own strength. His children will rebel against him, but they will be defeated. He will rule forever. Thanks to my protection, nothing bad will happen to him. This god will be Khepri in the morning, Atum in the evening, and will be known as Re.'

The Ogdoad of Hermopolis now came into existence, and Re hatched from an egg, fertilized by an excretion from Neith's flesh. Neith called to Re, and he came to her. This marked the first day of the year. When Re couldn't see his mother, he cried, and his tears created the first humans. And when she returned, he salivated. The saliva that fell from his lips created the gods. The gods welcomed Re as their king forever.

Some spittle that Neith had spat out transformed into Apophis, a 120-cubit-long (63 metres or 207 feet) chaos snake, who immediately planned a rebellion against Re. The snake was helped by followers that came out from his eye. Re became bitter, and in that moment,

Thoth emerged from his heart. Re sent Thoth to deal with the rebels. Meanwhile, Neith and Re left for Esna, where she would suckle the young sun god until he was strong enough to massacre his enemies. Neith took the form of the Ahet-cow, and placed Re between her horns, ready for the journey. Before departing, she uttered seven words that created seven divine beings, who would protect them. Neith fought her enemies in southern Egypt for four months and then travelled north to Sais, where a great celebration was held in honour of her bringing Re there safely. Re told the people to light torches for Neith, and to celebrate until dawn.

Overall, this creation myth explained the meaning of a celebration at Esna, held during the third month of the summer season, when an image of Neith as a cow was taken from the temple to the quay and back again, symbolizing her defeat of Apophis. It also explains the meaning of the Feast of the Lamps at Sais, when, according to Herodotus, the Egyptians burned torches outside their homes throughout the night in honour of Athena (Neith).

Local myths: the Book of the Faiyum

The Book of the Faiyum is a collection of local myths from the Faiyum region. Its first part is dedicated to the Faiyum's entrance, where an area called the 'Southern Sand of the Wetlands' is said to be the place where the sun god's enemies breached the Faiyum to stir rebellion. Luckily, the sun god had already taken refuge in the wetlands, which were a manifestation of the celestial cow – the sun god's mother. The 'Northern Sand of the Wetlands' belonged to Osiris until Seth betrayed him, while a place called 'Battlefield' was where Horus fought Seth, and at which the sun god (of whom Horus is sometimes regarded as a manifestation) repelled his enemies. This all seems to represent the ongoing battle between fertility and the desert – certainly an ever-present problem in the Faiyum Oasis.

The Book's focus on local geography demanded some changes to traditional Egyptian mythology. Normally in Egyptian belief, the sun rose in the mountainous region to the east of the Nile Valley, and set in the mountains to the west. The Faiyum Oasis lies beyond the western mountains, creating a problem for Egyptian thinkers: why can we still see the sun moving over the Faiyum? Their answer was to adapt the mythology for their local audience. Lake Qarun is rather large, so, depending on your vantage point, it can seem that the sun is rising from or setting in the lake. Noticing this phenomenon, the Faiyum's theologians explained that the sun god rose from the lake in the morning, crossed the sky, and at dusk, entered a watery underworld beneath the lake. The sun then travelled from west to east as a crocodile, rejuvenating as it swam along the bottom of the water. As dawn neared, the god boarded his day boat in the presence of members of the Ogdoad at the lake's eastern shore, ready to rise again. Osiris provided the lake's regenerative qualities, and in the form of the annual floodwaters, he travelled from Elephantine to the Faiyum each year, guided by Isis.

All of Lake Qarun was a Temple of Sobek, the Book says. The Ogdoad built this lake-temple, taking measuring rods and laying out its perimeter. They excavated its foundation trench with their own hands, but dug so deep that groundwater – believed to be the waters of Nun emerging from beneath the land – flowed into the trench and created the lake. Crocodilopolis then came into existence. (Herodotus tells a similar story of the Faiyum being dug by hand.) The gods' true secret names were kept in this lake, which protected them. Egypt's most important deities lived in the lake as crocodiles. They ate offerings and helped to battle the country's enemies, which were represented by fish.

As we saw above, the Egyptians regarded the Faiyum's wetlands as a manifestation of Mehet-weret, 'The Great Flood' – the celestial cow goddess who gave birth to the sun god. As a result, the Book includes a local variation of the Book of the Heavenly Cow (see Chapter 5). Re defeated his enemies and travelled to the Faiyum, where he met his mother and was – without it being explicitly stated – carried into the sky. In another scene in the Book, the god Shu holds up this celestial cow, while the sun god sits beneath her udders, drinking her rejuvenating milk. At dawn, the celestial cow, as white mist, raised the sun god into the sky.

The Western Desert:
the Cave of the Beasts and the Cave of the Swimmers

We now make a brief excursion from the Faiyum Oasis to travel further into the Western Desert. Some scholars have argued that the earliest seeds of Egyptian religion and mythology can be found at the Gilf Kebir, 800 kilometres (500 miles) south-west of the Faiyum, in an area that is today practically devoid of life, but thousands of years ago was a thriving savannah. There, in the Cave of the Beasts and the Cave of the Swimmers, explorers discovered rock art painted between 6000 and 3300 BC. One painting within the Cave of the Beasts depicts an individual holding a mace, while a person in front of him is upside down, a symbol meaning death in Pharaonic times. Though there is no evidence to suggest that the mace-holding man is a king, the image of the smiting pharaoh holding a weapon over defeated enemies is found throughout ancient Egyptian history, and even back into the Predynastic Period – for example in Tomb 100 at Hierakonpolis, dated to around 3500 BC. Another scene in the Cave of the Beasts is reminiscent of later imagery of the goddess Nut as the sky arching her body over the earth. A figure below her could perhaps be an early representation of the god Geb as the land; this individual stands below the arched figure, seemingly supporting her with one arm, while leaning on his other. People walk on his legs, just as they walk on the earth. Figures in both caves, painted on their sides, were first interpreted as swimmers, but may in fact represent the dead.

The Cave of the Beasts includes paintings of headless creatures eating people. These beasts have arms and legs, but their heads have been replaced with mouths flanked by lumps. They could perhaps be early versions of the fearsome demons that the Egyptians believed inhabited the land of the dead. Some of these beasts are cut with grooves, which may have been an attempt to neutralize the dangers of depicting them. In the Pharaonic Period, because paintings were believed to have magical powers that could cause harm, dangerous creatures shown in tombs (even as hieroglyphs) were sometimes drawn with knives stabbed through them to nullify their negative influence.

The Faiyum Oasis in history and today

According to the Greek historian Diodorus, one day, when Menes, Egypt's mythical first king, was out hunting in the Faiyum, he was chased by his own dogs. He fled to Lake Qarun, where a friendly crocodile let him stand on its back and carried him to safety on the other side of the lake. In gratitude, Menes founded a new settlement: the City of Crocodiles – Crocodilopolis to the Greeks, Shedet to the Egyptians. He dedicated the lake to its crocodiles, and in an act of reckless endangerment to his subjects, commanded the people living there to worship them. This is how the region's crocodile cult came into being. There does seem to be some validity to this myth; Shedet was founded in the early days of Egyptian history, perhaps around the time of the unification under Egypt's first kings. During this time, the oasis's habitable space was much smaller than in later years because the Faiyum basin was filled by Lake Qarun, its water topped up each year via the Bahr Yusef whenever the Nile flooded.

By the Middle Kingdom, the lake had begun to shrink; so, the Egyptians manipulated the Bahr Yusef tributary, digging canals to

Ruins originally identified as the famous labyrinth of Hawara, though actually of later date, and the Pyramid of King Amenemhat III.

expand the available agricultural land in the space once covered by the lake. The Faiyum became a favourite location of the Middle Kingdom kings, who built pyramids at Lahun and Hawara, and even located their as yet undiscovered capital city, Itj-Tawy, nearby. From the Middle Kingdom onwards, the region became a popular hunting ground for royals, and the New Kingdom pharaohs built a harem palace at Gurob, close to the Faiyum's entrance. Later, Egypt's Ptolemaic rulers diverted waterways, dug new canals and built dams, tripling the available agricultural land; as a result, many Greeks settled in the region, including in newly founded towns such as Dionysias and Karanis.

When the Romans arrived, they unclogged the Faiyum's canals and fixed the dykes, which had been neglected in the later years of the

THE FAIYUM OASIS

Key dates and remains

c. 3150 BC	Probable founding of Shedet, later known as Crocodilopolis and then Arsinoe.
c. 2500 BC	King Sneferu builds a pyramid just outside the Faiyum at Meidum.
c. 1990 BC	Canals dug to expand agricultural land. Kings start to build pyramids in Faiyum region. New royal city of Itj-Tawy established, probably near modern Lisht.
c. 1840 BC	Temple of Renenutet built at Medinet Maadi by King Amenemhat III. The same king also built a temple of Sobek at Shedet. Temple at Qasr es-Sagha, perhaps dedicated to Sobek, also probably built at this time.
c. 1470 BC	Harem palace founded at Gurob.
c. 1270 BC	King Ramesses II repairs and expands the Temple of Sobek at Shedet.
c. 280 BC	New towns start to be founded, including Karanis and Dionysias (Qasr Qarun), where a temple to Sobek is built. Canals dug and dams established.
c. 170 BC	The canals become clogged and the Faiyum begins to decline.
112 BC	Roman senator L. Mummius sees the sacred crocodiles at Crocodilopolis.
c. 30 BC	Romans begin unclogging the canals and repairing the dykes.
c. 20 BC	Strabo visits Crocodilopolis and watches the feeding of the sacred crocodile.
c. AD 250	Faiyum falls into decline, towns start being abandoned.

Ptolemies. The Faiyum, like other parts of Egypt, was now tasked with producing huge amounts of grain to feed the Roman empire. But the land was overexploited, and with a falling yield, the Roman towns declined and were eventually abandoned. Later, Christians built monasteries in the region, many of which remained active into the Islamic Period. Nonetheless, suffering from neglect, the Faiyum continued its decline over successive centuries. It was only from the time of Mohammed Ali Pasha, in the early 19th century, that the oasis began to prosper once more. Today, the Faiyum continues to be a major agricultural centre, but tourism is increasingly important, with visitors drawn to its ancient sites and areas of natural beauty and wildlife, as well as the surrounding desert.

▲

Given the area's natural beauty, the Faiyum Oasis is today a popular holiday destination for Cairenes, the bustling mega metropolis of Cairo being a mere 90 kilometres (56 miles) to the north. If you decide to join them on an excursion from the city, the first stop along the highway is usually the Graeco-Roman town of **Karanis** (modern Kom Aushim), where you can visit a temple dedicated to the crocodile gods Pnepheros and Petesouchos, complete with a hidden chamber in the sanctuary, perhaps used by oracles. When arriving in the Faiyum itself, popular archaeological sites include the **Pyramid of King Senwosret II** (r. c. 1900–1880 BC) at Lahun, where many papyri have been excavated that shed light on the administration of the nearby pyramid town; and the **Pyramid of King Amenemhat III** (r. c. 1842–1794 BC) at Hawara, once famous among classical authors for its labyrinth, though nothing remains of this legendary structure today. And if that's not enough pyramids for you, why not make a quick trip to the collapsed **Pyramid of King Sneferu** (r. c. 2520–2470 BC) at Meidum, just to the east of the Faiyum; this began life as a step pyramid, like that of King Djoser at Saqqara, but was later transformed into a true, smooth-sided pyramid (before falling down... the upgrade may have been a bad move in retrospect).

Various temple sites are spread across the Faiyum region. The **ruins of the Temple of Sobek of Shedet**, the region's main cult centre, once stood just north-west of the Faiyum's capital, Medinet el-Faiyum, at Kiman Faris. Sadly, virtually nothing survives today and much lies hidden or destroyed beneath the modern city. Objects from the site can, however, be seen in the open-air museum at Karanis. Better preserved is the **Temple of Sobek at Qasr Qarun** (ancient Dionysias), built under the Ptolemies and later neighbour to a Roman fortress; and, south of Lake Qarun, the isolated ancient town at **Medinet Maadi**, where a Middle Kingdom temple is dedicated to Renenutet, Sobek and Horus. North of Lake Qarun, there's also the Middle Kingdom temple at **Qasr es-Sagha**. This is un-inscribed and unfinished, but the construction of its walls, using irregularly-shaped limestone blocks, is particularly impressive. Bored of ruins? Nature lovers can head out from the Faiyum to visit **Wadi Rayan**, a recently created nature reserve with a pretty waterfall, and beyond (if you have a four-wheel drive), a further 50 kilometres (30 miles), to the **Valley of the Whales** (Wadi el-Hitan), where you can see the fossilized remains of amphibious mammals from when the region was a prehistoric sea.

The Great Sphinx, carved under King Khafre of the 4th Dynasty, that guards the pyramids on the Giza plateau.

10

MEMPHIS AND ITS NECROPOLIS

~~~~~~~~~~

Pyramids, Legends and Ptah the Creator

 و

'See, my heart has gone out, seized. It rushes to a place that it recognizes.
It sails south so it can see the Temple of Ptah [in Memphis].... I sit and
I wait for my heart, so it can speak to me about the state of Memphis.
No business happens by my hand while my heart is removed from its place.
Come to me Ptah, take me to Memphis. Let me see you freely.'

'Longing For Memphis', from Papyrus Anastasi IV, c. 1200 BC.

The north side of the Great Pyramid at Giza rises up above me, row after row of eroded limestone blocks, stacked one on top of the other in ever decreasing layers, glowing yellow in the sunlight. It's as if they're holding up the sky itself. Or perhaps they're piercing it? In the world ranking of epic pointy buildings, the Great Pyramid definitely comes out on top. It is grand ambition realized. Awesome in its age and survival. The seemingly impossible made reality. An engineering marvel of the Bronze Age. Okay. Enough. Excuse the hyperbole – across the millennia, the Great Pyramid has already had more words spilled over it than it has blocks – but there's a reason people travel from across the world to see it. The Great Pyramid is the sole remaining wonder of the ancient world. And it doesn't disappoint.

There's no monument in the world that has so grabbed the attention, so fired the imagination, and generated so many theories surrounding its purpose as the Great Pyramid. Everyone has their own take, and many ignore the detailed and forensic work of archaeologists in favour of the more outlandish explanations. For the Great Pyramid, anything goes. Built by Atlanteans? Sure. Aliens? Okay. A focal point of mystical energy? Fine. It's a granary? Whatever. Today, the tourists around me don't seem to be thinking too deeply about it all. Re's rays are pounding down from a bright blue sky. They're sweating. I hear variations of 'it's hot' in every language under the sun.

People arrive by the coachload, in mini-buses and in horse-drawn carriages. Whether King Khufu (r. *c.* 2470–2447 BC), who raised the pyramid 4,500 years ago, ever expected to receive so much attention, we'll probably never know. Then again, if you build a tomb as monumentally over-the-top as the Great Pyramid, you probably aren't the type to shrink from the limelight. Tourist police in white uniforms mill around. Men in galabeyyas sell statuettes of Egyptian gods, postcards and cold drinks, their wares carefully arranged on small carpets laid on the ground. Above me, among the blocks, a group of tourists disappear into a roughly cut hole in the pyramid's side. This is the robbers' tunnel that intersects with the still-sealed original entrance. Within, after a sweaty descent and climb, they'll find the burial chamber of Khufu: a man for whom size clearly did matter.

In ancient times, this complex of mysterious monuments was part of a grand necropolis that stretched from Giza in the north to Dahshur in the south. It was in this long strip of desert that the Egyptians buried

Plan of the Giza plateau made by the Napoleonic mission, showing the pyramids of Khufu (the Great Pyramid, top), Khafre (middle) and Menkaure (bottom).

many of their kings beneath pyramids, and their nobles in elaborate tombs, each surmounted by decorated mud-brick chapels called *mastabas* (the Arabic word for 'bench'). These tombs formed streets of the dead that you can still explore today. The reason for this vast and famous necropolis was the great city of Memphis, just to its east. This was one of the ancient world's most important cities, built on the spot where the Delta and the Nile Valley meet. Here, merchants rubbed shoulders with scribes and nobility. Kings received their crowns and ruled from palaces overlooking the Nile. And its grandest temple was dedicated to the god Ptah, the most creative of creators.

Ptah: cosmic master craftsman

Ever felt a flash of inspiration? The sudden urge to do something creative? If you have, you can thank the god Ptah. Ptah was the Memphite region's most important deity, and one of the major gods of Egypt's pantheon. He's typically shown standing, wrapped like a mummy, or in the tight cloak worn by kings during the *sed*-festival – a ceremony in which the pharaoh's right to rule was reaffirmed, celebrated after thirty years on the throne. On Ptah's head, a skull cap takes the place of a crown, and he often holds a *was*-sceptre, symbolizing power. From the Middle Kingdom, Ptah was shown with a beard – not the beard of a god, which curves at its end, but the straight beard of a king. His wife was the lioness goddess Sekhmet, and his son was Nefertum, a god associated with the lotus flower. In the Late Period, when Imhotep, architect of the Step Pyramid of Djoser (r. *c.* 2584–2565 BC), had been deified, the Egyptians regarded Ptah as his father. The Ptolemaic priest Manetho wrote that Ptah (in his words, Hephaestus) was the first man in Egypt, and discovered fire. This is reflected in the Turin Canon, a king list dated to the 19th Dynasty that cites Ptah as the first of the gods to rule on earth. Ptah could also be called King of the Two Lands.

Despite Ptah's importance throughout Egyptian history – he's first attested on a calcite bowl from the 1st Dynasty – little is written about him in mythology. He's rarely mentioned in the Pyramid Texts and Coffin Texts, our major sources for early religious beliefs, probably because he doesn't have much of a funerary role, except in cases where he's invoked as part of the Opening of the Mouth ritual. Ptah's key function in the cosmos was as a force of creation, associated with craft and artisanal work (at least from the Middle Kingdom onwards). He was the spark of creativity in the mind. For this reason, the high priest of Ptah at Memphis held a special title: the greatest of the directors of craftsmen. Constructions were attributed to Ptah; so, for example, a temple of the god Wepwawet at Asyut is described as founded by Thoth, but built by Ptah's fingers. For similar reasons, Ptah was a god of the mining regions that produced the precious materials used in construction and craft. There was a temple dedicated to him at the turquoise quarry of Serabit el-Khadim in the Sinai.

Ptah's creative powers are best described on the Shabaka Stone, inscribed during the 25th Dynasty, but said to be copied from an already ancient worm-eaten manuscript. The text explains that the process of physical creation involving the god Atum, who evolved into the created world we inhabit (see Chapter 11), came about due to Ptah's heart and tongue. Ptah envisioned creation in his heart – where thoughts emerged, in Egyptian understanding – and used his tongue to speak words that brought all that he imagined into being. The Ennead (the traditional gods of Heliopolis) were Ptah's teeth and lips in this process. He created all of Egypt's divinities, and then, in the form of the god Tatenen, gave birth to them too. Ptah is often connected with Tatenen, whose name means 'The Rising Land'; this god was a manifestation of the first mound of creation, emphasizing creative power. Often, the two gods are united as Ptah-Tatenen (try saying that ten times fast).

A hymn to Ptah, dated to the 22nd Dynasty, describes Ptah's creative power, among other aspects of his divinity. Ptah is father of the gods, it says. He is self-created, without mother or father. He existed before anything else, and formed the land according to his heart. The text then associates Ptah with all natural phenomena, assigning him roles normally held by other gods. Acting as the sun disc, his eyes make light. He makes food grow, and the land green. He expels enemies and looks after the dead. He brings about the inundation, smelted the Two Lands, and his magic can control the gods.

In the Late Period, figurines of the unified Ptah-Sokar-Osiris became popular, these gods representing creation, metamorphosis and rebirth respectively. Often, the base of the figurine contains a Book of the Dead, or a grain mummy (a mixture of soil and grain in the shape of a body, wrapped like a mummy). Sokar, the god of Rostau – an ancient name for the Memphite necropolis, but particularly the area near the Great Sphinx at Giza – is typically shown as a mound-like bundle, with wings and a falcon's head. He could also be a falcon, or a man with a falcon's head. Sokar's wife is sometimes Nephthys (better known as the wife of Seth) or Seshat, goddess of writing. His son was Reswedja, though he is rarely mentioned, and his name is more often found as an epithet of other gods, meaning 'One who awakes uninjured'. Like Ptah, Sokar was a god of craft skills. Indeed, Ptah may have usurped this role from Sokar over time. In religious texts, Sokar is described as melting silver, gold, lapis lazuli and malachite with his fingers, and as a metalworker.

The sacred Apis bull

From as early as the 1st Dynasty, the Egyptians regarded the Apis bull of Memphis as a manifestation of the god Ptah. The bull was born of intercourse between Ptah and a virgin cow, and represented strength and virility – indeed, in the Pyramid Texts, the king is said to use the Apis bull's phallus to reach the sky. When the Apis bull died, priests searched Egypt for a successor, which they identified based on special markings: the bull had to be black with a white triangle on his forehead, a Horus falcon on his flanks and a vulture on the shoulders. The selected bull was crowned in the Temple of Ptah by the god's high priest during a full moon. He received his own enclosure and a harem of cows, and provided oracles to people. Strabo says that the bull was

The sarcophagus of a sacred Apis bull in the Serapeum at Saqqara.

brought out each day for tourists to see, and that bullfights were held nearby in front of the Temple of Ptah. The Apis' mother was associated with Isis, and so also received special treatment in Memphis.

After death, the Apis bull was mummified and given a burial fit for a king. From the New Kingdom, each bull was interred in his own huge sarcophagus, placed in a vast catacomb known as the Serapeum at Saqqara. Further catacombs were created during the reign of King Psamtik I (r. *c.* 664–610 BC) of the 26th Dynasty. Archaeologists discovered inscriptions within that record details about the bulls' lives, and stelae left by pilgrims as offerings. Above ground, there was a temple enclosure, reached by a sphinx-lined path. Nearby, there was also the Bubasteion and Anubeion – temple enclosures dedicated to Bastet and Anubis respectively, with temples, shrines and houses for priests. Here, cats and dogs were bred, killed, mummified and given as votive offerings to the gods, before being interred in vast catacombs.

An adventure of Setna and Si-Osire in Memphis

Because of Memphis' importance as a royal residence city throughout Egyptian history, its court was the setting of many stories featuring kings, princes and priests. One such tale concerns the Crown Prince Setna-Khaemwaset and his son Si-Osire. One day, while King Ramesses II (r. *c.* 1279–1212 BC) sat in court at Memphis, his council came to inform him that a Nubian dignitary had arrived with a sealed letter and a challenge: 'Is there anyone here skilled enough in magic to be able to read this letter without first breaking the seal and opening it? If not, it will be very embarrassing for Egypt.' Ramesses' courtiers didn't know what to do. 'Is it possible at all?' they wondered. In desperation, they summoned Prince Setna, known for his magical prowess, for advice. 'Give me ten days to think about it,' he said.

The Egyptians gave the Nubian dignitary food and lodgings while they tried to devise a plan. Any failure would humiliate Egypt. The weight bore heavy on Setna. He lay on his bed and cocooned himself in linen, depressed. He was cold to the touch. It was as if he'd mummified himself alive. Setna became so stressed that Meheweskhe, his wife, worried that he would fall ill. Si-Osire came to his father to ask what was wrong. Still lying flat on his back, Setna explained the situation, emphasizing that Egypt's reputation was at stake if they failed to find a solution. Si-Osire laughed. 'Don't worry!' he said. 'I can read the letter without breaking the seal or opening it.' Setna sat up. *Huh?* To prove himself, Si-Osire asked Setna to pick a scroll at random from a box in a room on the ground floor. 'Even standing on the floor above,

I'll tell you what it says.' Setna did as asked, and everything Si-Osire said was true. He immediately ran to Pharaoh, who was pleased to hear the news. Ramesses and Setna drank together in celebration.

The next morning, Si-Osire and the Nubian dignitary arrived at court. 'Be honest about the content of the letter,' Si-Osire said. The dignitary promised not to lie. And so, Si-Osire began to narrate a tale written on the letter, describing events that occurred many years ago. The tale went as follows: a Nubian king was travelling in the forests of Amun when he overheard three sorcerers talking amongst themselves nearby. Each wanted to punish Egypt using magic, and loudly explained what he would do if he got a chance. The king was intrigued, and later summoned the sorcerers to court. After listening to their plans, he chose the proposal of Horus-the-Son-of-the-Nubian-Woman. The sorcerer created wax figures, brought them to life, and gave them the instruction: 'Bring pharaoh to Nubia, whip him 500 times in the presence of our king and people, and then return him to Egypt within six hours.'

The wax figures did all that the sorcerer commanded.

The next morning, Egypt's highest officials were met with a confusing question in the royal bedchamber. 'How were things in the country while I was away?' the king said, shifting uncomfortably in his bed. The courtiers looked at each other, raising quizzical eyebrows. 'Umm, my lord. You've been in your private chambers all night,' one said, summoning his courage. 'You're still in bed now.' Perhaps Pharaoh was going mad? It was going to be a long day. Pharaoh sighed. A king can tell when he's losing the room, so he provided the only proof he could of his nocturnal travels: turning over, he revealed his badly beaten back to the court. He told them that the previous night, he'd been taken from Egypt and whipped. He was left in severe pain. The courtiers were astonished, and summoned the powerful sorcerer Horus-the-Son-of-the-Wolf, who swore an oath that he would help his king. 'This is Nubian magic!' he proclaimed. To prevent Pharaoh from being abducted again, the sorcerer concocted a spell with magical amulets, and visited Hermopolis to appeal to Thoth for help. That night, Thoth appeared in the sorcerer's dream. 'Find a chest within a sealed room in my temple,' Thoth said. 'Within will be a book of magic, written by myself. Copy it, and take it to the pharaoh. It will protect him.' The magician did all that Thoth told him, and returned to Pharaoh to create his spell of protection.

The next night, the king saw the Nubian wax figures coming for him, but they were repelled by the magician's spell. Thank Thoth! The Nubian sorcerer's plan had failed. It was time to turn the tables.

Horus-the-Son-of-the-Wolf crafted his own wax figures and commanded them to bring the king of Nubia to Egypt. That night, the figures did as he asked, and beat the Nubian king 500 times with a whip. Within six hours, they returned him to Nubia. The Nubian king, shaken, summoned Horus-the-Son-of-the-Nubian-Woman to complain. The sorcerer tried to create a magical protection for his king, but it was ineffective. The next night, the Nubian king was again taken to Egypt and beaten. And the next night too. 'I will have you executed if you don't stop the Egyptians from kidnapping me each night,' the king yelled at his sorcerer. 'Send me to Egypt,' the sorcerer said. 'I will battle with the Egyptian magician personally.' The king accepted the offer, and the sorcerer went home to prepare for his journey. Before leaving, he spoke with his mother, who warned him of the dangers of fighting an Egyptian magician. 'Leave a magical sign if you find yourself in trouble, so that I can be alerted and come to your aid,' she said. He agreed, and magically transported himself to Pharaoh's court.

When the two sorcerers came face to face at the Egyptian court in Memphis, they immediately recognized each other. The Egyptian magician had once saved the Nubian from drowning near Heliopolis, while the Nubian had taught the Egyptian the language of wolves. But they didn't let their personal history get in the way of their duty: to fight for their kings. Moving first, the Nubian sorcerer conjured a fire. The Egyptian made it rain, dowsing the flames. The Nubian raised a powerful fog, enveloping the room so no one could see. The Egyptian cast it away. The Nubian created a massive stone block and held it above the pharaoh and his followers. As it came crashing down, the Egyptian conjured a papyrus ship that caught the stone and gently sailed it away. Realizing that he was outmatched, the Nubian transformed into a bird and tried to flee. The Egyptian magician cast a spell, dropping the Nubian bird to the floor. He landed on his back. A hunter rushed over, and held his knife to the bird's neck.

Back in Nubia, the sorcerer's magical warning signs suddenly appeared in his mother's house. She quickly transformed into a goose and flew to Egypt. Arriving at the palace, she called out to her son, but the Egyptian magician saw that the goose was actually a Nubian in disguise. He used his magic to drop her to the floor, where she lay on her back. The hunter stood ready to end her life. The Nubian's mother transformed back into a woman, and begged for forgiveness. 'Make an oath that you will not cause us trouble again,' said the Egyptian magician. Horus-the-Son-of-the-Nubian-Woman proclaimed that he would not return to Egypt for 1,500 years. And so, the Egyptian magician released the Nubians from his spell, gave them a boat, and allowed them to return home.

Si-Osire finished reading the story. The sealed letter remained in the Nubian's hand. 'This man before us is Horus-the-Son-of-the-Nubian-Woman, returned after 1,500 years to inflict his magic on Egypt,' said Si-Osire. 'But by Osiris, I am Horus-the-Son-of-the-Wolf. In death, I learned that this Nubian enemy would return to Egypt, and that there would be no one able to fight him. I petitioned Osiris to allow me to return to the land, to prevent Egypt from being humiliated. He granted me my wish. I travelled up from the underworld, and watched Setna in the necropolis of Heliopolis and Memphis. I was then born again on earth, waiting for this moment.' Wasting no more time, Si-Osire raised a fire that engulfed and destroyed the Nubian sorcerer. The king and his court watched on. His mission complete, Si-Osire disappeared like a shadow. Setna let out a cry. Pharaoh was astonished. The court praised Horus-the-Son-of-the-Wolf. That night, Setna returned home in grief, but soon after, he and his wife conceived another son. For the rest of his life, Setna made offerings to the spirit of Horus-the-Son-of-the-Wolf.

The Pyramid Texts of Saqqara

We move now from the city of Memphis to Saqqara, part of the Memphite necropolis. Here, visitors have the opportunity to descend into the pyramids of Kings Unas (r. c. 2312–2282 BC) and Teti (r. c. 2282–2270 BC), both inscribed with the earliest detailed religious writings surviving from Egypt: the Pyramid Texts, a collection of spells designed to help the king achieve an eternal afterlife. The Pyramid of King Unas, built at the end of the 5th Dynasty, contains the first known example of these inscriptions. The composition itself might predate Unas' pyramid by about half a century; it uses grammar that was already archaic, and mentions earlier burial practices. The Pyramid Texts magically enabled the king to become an *akh*-spirit in death by connecting him with Osiris and the sun god – forces of regeneration and creation. Indeed, the spells refer to the king as 'the Osiris'. Other spells ensured that the king could leave his mummy and the pyramid each day to join with the gods, or reflect rituals performed during the royal funeral, such as the Opening of the Mouth ceremony, and the smashing of vessels, meant to magically destroy evil forces. Further spells protected the king from dangerous enemies.

Within each of the later Old Kingdom pyramids, the arrangement of chambers roughly follows a standard plan, developed at the end of the

5th Dynasty: there's a burial chamber, antechamber, serdab (tripartite chamber), corridor (later with vestibule) and an ascending corridor that leads to the surface. This sequence of rooms, starting in the burial chamber, reflects the stages of the king's rebirth in the afterlife. The burial chamber represented the realm of the Duat, and within it, the sarcophagus acted as the womb of the goddess Nut. The spells inscribed in this chamber enable the king to leave his body at dawn and to re-enter Nut's womb in the evening, reinforcing the symbolism of the architecture. Leaving the burial chamber, the king's spirit entered the pyramid's antechamber, which represented the *akhet* – the horizon, a place of transition. The tripartite room beside the antechamber is the horizon's eastern edge. Spells in the antechamber reflect the journey of the king's spirit through this region and help him to fight off evil forces, particularly those that threaten his rebirth. Subsequent spells enabled the king to leave the *akhet*. His spirit then passed through the corridor, vestibule and up the ascending corridor, symbolic of the birth canal, into the sky with the sun and other gods. The ascending corridor faced north, enabling the king to join the Imperishable Stars in the northern sky – stars that never disappeared from the night sky, and so were regarded by the Egyptians as eternal.

The adventures of Imhotep:
architect of the Step Pyramid of Djoser at Saqqara

Most people have heard the name Imhotep, perhaps from the old Boris Karloff *Mummy* movie, or its 1990s reboot. But Imhotep was a real person, not just a fictional movie monster. He served the last king of the 2nd Dynasty, Khasekhemwy (r. *c.* 2611–2584 BC), and then that king's son, Djoser, founder of the 3rd Dynasty. Imhotep was the high priest of Re at Heliopolis, but also chief architect of Djoser's royal tomb: the Step Pyramid at Saqqara. This was Egypt's first pyramid, and the first monumental stone structure anywhere on earth. Were its six steps a stairway to help the king reach his afterlife among the stars? The sun's rays frozen in stone? Did it represent the first mound of creation, and so a new beginning for the king? Or was it just an easy way to build a tall building – a huge marker for the king's burial beneath – that could be seen from a great distance? Perhaps all of the above. Or none. Whatever the case may be, given the importance of the pyramidal-shaped sacred *benben*-stone at Heliopolis (see Chapter 11), it seems likely that Imhotep's role in the sun cult influenced his design.

Djoser's burial is far more than just its pyramid; there are courts, chapels, buildings, a mortuary temple, a miniature tomb (perhaps for

The Step Pyramid of King Djoser at Saqqara.

the king's internal organs or his *ka*-spirit) and a columned entrance corridor, all surrounded by a massive niched enclosure wall. In earlier times, these would all have been made from mud bricks, reed matting and wood – materials that would rot away or disintegrate over the centuries. But under Djoser, they were carved from stone in imitation of these materials. Frozen in time for eternity, these structures magically became real and useable by the king's spirit in death. It was not just Djoser's body that had been mummified and preserved for eternity; Imhotep had mummified the entire funerary complex. Perhaps due to his innovations, Imhotep was rewarded with a rare honour: his name and titles were inscribed on a royal statue that stood within the Step Pyramid's entrance corridor. Its broken base was found during excavations at the site, and can now be seen in the Imhotep Museum at Saqqara.

The Egyptians never forgot Imhotep's importance. During the New Kingdom, 1,000 years after Imhotep's death, scribes treated him as a patron saint of their profession and credited him with authoring a book of wisdom. They even offered water in honour of the great Imhotep before beginning their day's work. The Egyptians of the Late Period worshipped Imhotep as a god – the son of Ptah – and associated him with healing and medicine more than architecture. He even had a temple, which stood at Saqqara in the vicinity of the Bubasteion and the Anubeion. Though lost today, the Temple of Imhotep is mentioned in various texts as a place where Egyptians went to be healed. Normal people felt that Imhotep – a man who had become a god – could understand their daily struggles, and appealed to him for assistance. The Greeks saw in Imhotep their god of medicine Asclepius, and spread his name beyond Egypt's borders. In the modern age, Imhotep has been honoured with his own postage stamp, and has lent his name to a museum at Saqqara. Doctors, mathematicians, architects, astronomers and engineers can all connect their professions with the ancient sage.

Due to his widespread fame, Imhotep featured as a character in various stories written during Egypt's Ptolemaic and Roman Periods. Parts of one tale can be reconstructed from 500 papyrus fragments, excavated at Tebtunis in the Faiyum, dated to the 1st or 2nd century AD. The best preserved of the episodes featured in this story is 'The Quest for the Divine Limbs'. It goes as follows: the dastardly Assyrians had stolen the forty-two divine limbs of Osiris, so Imhotep and King Djoser led the Egyptians on a quest to recover the sacred relics and defeat their enemies. When the two sides eventually faced each other in battle, the fighting lasted for days and many perished. Though safe in his tent, the Assyrian king was nervous. He feared defeat. So he summoned a sorceress for advice. 'Can you do something to help our situation?' he said. The sorceress decided that the time had come for the Assyrians to use magic. Drawing on her powers, she formed an image of the god Geb and brought it to life. Then, she sent it out to fight for the Assyrians. When Imhotep saw the god striding towards the Egyptian troops across the battlefield, he quickly moulded an image of the goddess Nut to face him. The creation of these two divinities sparked a new phase of magical combat. The sorceress conjured many more magical creations, including fearsome magical flames and a 100-cubit-long (50 metres or 165 feet) divine snake that killed many Egyptians. Each time, Imhotep defeated the Assyrian's creations with his own magic.

After a break in the text, we learn that the Egyptian army defeated the Assyrians and marched east to Nineveh, receiving tribute along the way. Their journey led them to the fortress of Ain-Bel, where at long last, they found the forty-two divine limbs of Osiris. There was jubilation among the troops. Other Egyptians set to work crafting golden shrines to contain the sacred limbs. That night, while King Djoser slept in his tent, the sun god appeared in his dream. 'The divine limbs must remain in Assyria for the time being,' the god said, 'and you must construct a temple here to house them.' Djoser did as the god instructed. When the king and his army arrived back in Egypt, they celebrated.

The story's other episodes are harder to reconstruct, but we can get some understanding of their content. The episode after 'The Quest for the Divine Limbs', for example, focused on Imhotep's younger sister, Renpetneferet (who may also be his wife). While visiting a temple in Memphis, King Djoser heard Renpetneferet's voice. This intrigued him, so he asked that she attend a celebration at his palace. There, a magician named Osirsobk, disguised as a priest, approached her. He held her hand as they strolled past the palace shrines. 'Where are we going?' she said. 'To visit your father, the god Ptah,' replied Osirsobk. Renpetneferet began to cry. She was afraid that the priest was a ghost. Damage to the text makes it difficult to reconstruct what happened next, but it can't have been good for Renpetneferet. She tells Osirsobk that Imhotep will kill him. When the story picks up, Renpetneferet is dead. It seems that Ptah is told of her death, and there follow various escapades involving a baboon, a ghost and the king. Further fragmentary episodes in the Imhotep story are similarly intriguing. There's the tale of a murdered man's spirit, summoned to the palace by singing and a harp, and one about a stolen golden necklace (perhaps taken by Osirsobk). Others revolve around Imhotep curing the pharaoh's blindness; a royal tomb; a Libyan camp; the conception and birth of King Djoser; and a ten-month pregnancy, though of whom it's unclear.

Legends of the Giza pyramids in classical and Arab literature
Although the pyramids rarely appear in ancient Egyptian literature and mythology, classical writers did record stories about them, particularly about their construction and purpose. The 1st-century AD historian Josephus wrote that the Hebrews were forced to build the pyramids, a claim often repeated to this day; while the Roman writer Julius Honorius and the historian Rufinus of Aquileia both say that the pyramids were the granaries of the biblical Joseph, an association popular among early Christians for centuries. Nonetheless, the majority of classical writers understood the pyramids to be royal tombs. Herodotus, who visited Egypt during the 5th century BC, heard tales about the construction of the pyramids of Giza (part of the Memphite necropolis). According to one priest, King Khufu, builder of the Great Pyramid, closed all the temples and forced everyone to labour for him as slaves. Then, when he was low on resources, he sent his daughter to work as a prostitute to bring in extra money. With the payment, she asked each customer to provide a stone block for herself. Herodotus writes that the Egyptians built the middle pyramid at Giza – the Pyramid of King Khafre (r. c. 2437– 2414 BC) – using these stones. The 1st-century BC Greek historian Diodorus Siculus, meanwhile, says that the owners of the two largest Giza pyramids were never buried in them. These kings had caused such

The Giza plateau.

hardships and performed so many cruel acts, he writes, that the people of Egypt threatened to destroy their bodies. Consequently, both of them were buried in a secret location.

Strabo records a tale about the Pyramid of King Menkaure (r. *c.* 2414–2396 BC) at Giza, a pyramid that he calls the Tomb of the Courtesan. One day, while a woman named Rhodopis was bathing, an eagle swooped down and grabbed one of her sandals. The eagle then flew all the way to Memphis, where it dropped the sandal onto the king's lap. The sandal's beauty mesmerized him, and he was so struck by the oddness of the situation that he ordered his men to search Egypt for the shoe's owner. The king's men found Rhodopis in Naukratis, a city in the Delta, and brought her to Memphis. Soon after, she married the king, and the smallest pyramid at Giza was built for her. This is perhaps the earliest version of the famous Cinderella story. The 1st-century AD Roman author Pliny the Elder also says that the third pyramid at Giza was built for Rhodopis, and expresses amazement that a courtesan could accumulate such wealth. Herodotus, however, dismisses any association between the pyramid and Rhodopis. Writing centuries before Strabo and Pliny (so they should have known better), he points out that although some Greeks say Rhodopis built the pyramid, she actually lived under King Ahmose II (r. *c.* 570–526 BC), many years after its construction by King Menkaure, and that she had been a freed slave from Thrace who moved to Egypt. She became wealthy, he writes, but not wealthy enough to build such a pyramid.

According to other classical writers, the small pyramid at Giza was built for Queen Nitocris.

Legends of the pyramids were also popular among the medieval Copts (Egyptian Christians) and Arabs. The Egyptian historian al-Maqrizi compiled many of these stories in his history of Egypt, written in the 14th or 15th century. One popular legend says that King Surid built the pyramids 300 years before the Great Flood. Surid dreamed that a cataclysm would upturn the world and that the stars would fall, so he built the two large Giza pyramids – in just six months – as repositories of ancient knowledge. He filled each with treasures, statues and the bodies of priests and kings (including himself, after finishing his 190-year reign), and covered their walls with scientific, astronomical, mathematical and medical writings. Guardian statues protected the tombs. Other medieval legends relate that the two largest Giza pyramids were built as tombs for Aristotle and Alexander the Great, or for the gods Hermes and Agathos Daimon.

In Arab tradition, the 9th-century Caliph al-Mamun forced his way into the Great Pyramid, re-opening the original robbers' tunnel that tourists still use today. Compiling different reports on this event, the 13th-century Egyptian historian al-Idrisi says that al-Mamun did this to discover the secrets hidden within. This story is repeated in *The Thousand and One Nights*, which says that al-Mamun wanted to tear down the pyramids to discover what lay within, but managed to access only one corridor. There, he found a treasure, amounting to the exact sum that he'd spent on forcing open the pyramid – lucky! The same tale is recounted by al-Maqrizi. Al-Idrisi also tells the story of a gang of 12th-century treasure hunters who broke into a pyramid, and soon after lost a member of their group. They found him three days later, his red face emerging from a wall, shouting that anyone violating the royal tombs would meet the same fate as him. Other Arab stories describe the pyramids as protected by a female guardian, or by spirits that take the forms of a naked devil, a naked woman – both with long, pointy teeth – and an old man.

The Great Sphinx at Giza

Carved during the 4th Dynasty for King Khafre, the Great Sphinx stands on the edge of the Giza plateau, staring eastward as its eternal guardian. This fusion of a lion's body and a king's head was perhaps intended as a solar symbol reflecting power, but no document contemporary to its construction spells out its function. Whatever the case may be, by the New Kingdom, the Great Sphinx had become identified as the solar deity Horemakhet, 'Horus in the Horizon'.

The Great Sphinx has been restored many times during its lifetime, first under King Tuthmosis IV (r. *c.* 1398–1388 BC) of the 18th Dynasty, when it was already over 1,000 years old. Tuthmosis erected a large stele between the Sphinx's paws to explain the reason for his restoration work and to commemorate how the Sphinx changed his life. When only a prince, Tuthmosis went hunting in the desert near Giza, the text says. He rode around in his chariot, chasing lions and game, and shot arrows at copper targets. When midday arrived, he stopped to rest in the shadow of the Sphinx. He quickly fell asleep, and the Sphinx appeared in his dream as the god Horemakhet-Khepri-Re-Atum – the sun god in all of his major daylight phases. He told Tuthmosis that if he cleared the sand from around his limbs, he would become king of Egypt. This was a significant divine proclamation, because Tuthmosis wasn't next in line for the throne. When Tuthmosis awoke, he immediately arranged for offerings to be made to the Sphinx – he didn't want to miss his opportunity to become pharaoh. From this text, it seems that the Sphinx enclosure – the pit in which the Sphinx sits – had filled with sand by Tuthmosis' reign, probably leaving only its head protruding. Further repairs to the Great Sphinx occurred during Egypt's Late Period, then under the Graeco-Roman kings, and again in the 20th century AD.

Setna and Si-Osire in the Duat

In one of the tales of Setna-Khaemwaset, the young Si-Osire (actually, as has been revealed, the reincarnation of an ancient sorcerer) and his father, the Crown Prince Setna-Khaemwaset, visit the underworld realm of the Duat via the Memphite necropolis. It goes as follows: one day, Setna and Si-Osire were at home in Memphis, when they heard a loud wailing from below. They looked out of the window to see the coffin of a wealthy man being carried in procession to the necropolis for burial. Moments later, they saw another body being carried to the necropolis. This time it was a poor man, wrapped in a mat; no one walked with his body, and there was no mournful wailing. 'By Ptah,' said Setna, 'it is much better for the rich man, carried to the sound of wailing, than for the poor man.' Si-Osire turned to his father. 'I hope you receive the same fate as the poor man when you reach the afterlife,' he said. Setna was astonished. Why would his own son wish such a pitiful afterlife on him, he wondered. 'If you let me, I will show you what happened to each man in the afterlife,' Si-Osire said. Together, they set off for the desert of the Memphite necropolis.

After a fragmentary portion of the papyrus, the story resumes with Setna and Si-Osire in the afterlife, exploring its different halls. They entered the fourth hall to find a group of people plaiting ropes. But donkeys chewed on the ropes as quickly as they were being plaited, leaving the job forever unfinished. Another group of people were jumping up and down to reach bags of bread and water hung over their heads. Each time they leapt into the air, other spirits dug holes beneath their feet. Setna and Si-Osire found noble spirits in the fifth hall. People accused of violence stood pleading beside a door, its pivot fitted into a man's eye socket. The man screamed in agony and begged for mercy. In the sixth hall, Setna and Si-Osire saw the gods and the magistrates of the people of the underworld. Their servants were making reports. Then, in the seventh hall, Osiris sat in judgment. Anubis stood to Osiris' left, offering advice, and Thoth was to his right, writing down his verdict. A set of scales was set up before them, ready to weigh a person's heart against the feather of *maat*. Spirits found to have committed more evil deeds than good deeds were destroyed by Ammit, the devourer, while those who had done more good deeds than bad joined the magistrates of the Lord of the Underworld. Those whose good and bad deeds balanced served Sokar-Osiris as excellent spirits.

A man in royal linen stood close to Osiris – a position of importance. 'Father,' said Si-Osire, 'this spirit wearing royal linen is the poor man we watched being carried from Memphis to the necropolis, wrapped only in a mat. When he was judged, his good deeds outnumbered his evil deeds. So Osiris commanded that the rich man's burial equipment be given to this poor man, who now serves Sokar-Osiris. The wealthy man was judged too, and his evil deeds outweighed his good deeds. He's now the man whose eye socket is the pivot of the fifth hall's doorway. This is why I said that I hoped you would receive the same fate as the poor man in the afterlife.' Setna wanted to know more: what had happened to the other people he'd seen in the halls of the afterlife? 'The men plaiting ropes chewed on by donkeys were cursed by a god in life,' Si-Osire said. 'They worked all hours to make a living, but women robbed them without them realizing. So they never had food to eat. And those people who jumped for provisions while spirits dug holes beneath them? They each had a life before them, but a god stopped them from seeing it.' The afterlife is kind to those who live good lives on earth, Si-Osire explained to his father, and it brings evil to those who are evil. With nothing left to learn, Setna and Si-Osire ascended back to the Memphite necropolis, walking hand in hand. What Setna had witnessed in the underworld stuck in his mind for the rest of his life, but he could never tell another person about his experiences.

Memphis in history and today

Built on the west bank of the Nile – unusual for an ancient Egyptian city – Memphis remained one of Egypt's most important cities for thousands of years. It was an administrative capital, filled with temples and palaces, a place of coronations, of scribal learning, a royal treasury, garrisons and an important dockyard. And its necropolis is one of the most famous archaeological sites on earth, known for its elite tombs and royal pyramids, including the Step Pyramid of Djoser at Saqqara – the world's first monumental stone building – and the Great Pyramid at Giza, the tallest building on earth until the construction of the Eiffel Tower.

According to the Ptolemaic priest Manetho, Memphis was founded by King Menes, Egypt's mythological first king (whose reign came to an end when he was killed by a hippo). Archaeological evidence has shown that the city's origins do stretch back as far as the beginning of the Pharaonic Period, to around 3100 BC. At this early time, Memphis was called Ineb-Hedj, the 'White Walls', seemingly after the walls that surrounded the original settlement or temple. It also received the epithet 'The Balance of the Two Lands', because it stood at the point where the Nile Valley and Delta meet – the perfect location at which to oversee Egypt's affairs. Today though, the city is best known by its Greek name, Memphis, a word derived from the Egyptian Men-Nefer, 'Established and Beautiful', name of the pyramid town of King Pepi I (r. c. 2265–2219 BC), where the priests who served his funerary cult lived.

From textual sources, we can roughly reconstruct how Memphis looked during its New Kingdom heyday. Dominating the city centre was the Temple of Ptah, a religious precinct as massive as the Temple of Amun-Re at Karnak, filled with obelisks and colossal statues. Other important cults were spread across the city, including a temple of Hathor of the Southern Sycamore and a shrine of Neith North of the Wall. The royal dockyard, 'Peru Nefer', probably stood south of the main city, while 'The Fine District of Pharaoh', where various kings built their palaces, ran along the edge of the Nile to the east of the Ptah precinct (and no doubt had great views). From papyri, we also know of a South District, divided into wards, each overseen by its own district officer. Shrines stood among the houses and streets there.

Much is also known about Memphis' Graeco-Roman phase, thanks to visits from classical writers, the inscriptions on late monuments, and surviving papyri. The city was criss-crossed with streets, lined with mud-brick houses of different sizes and standards, and each ethnicity had their own walled sector, creating Carian, Jewish and Greek

MEMPHIS AND ITS NECROPOLIS

Key dates and remains

c. 3100 BC	Probable founding of Memphis and the Temple of Ptah. Cult of the Apis bull begins. Local elite buried at Saqqara. Soon after, Saqqara becomes a place of royal burial.
c. 2580 BC	The Step Pyramid of King Djoser is built at Saqqara.
c. 2470 BC	The Great Pyramid of King Khufu is under construction at Giza.
c. 2430 BC	The Great Sphinx is carved at Giza under King Khafre.
c. 2300 BC	Kings start building pyramids at Saqqara again. First Pyramid Texts inscribed in the Pyramid of King Unas at Saqqara.
c. 1398 BC	King Tuthmosis IV erects his 'Dream Stele' between the paws of the Great Sphinx at Giza and undertakes restoration work on the monument.
c. 1330 BC	Elite start building 'temple-tombs' at Saqqara.
c. 1224 BC	Use of the Lesser Vaults for the burial of the sacred Apis bulls at Saqqara begins.
c. 612 BC	Greater Vaults for the burial of the sacred Apis bulls begin to be used at the Serapeum. Animal cults grow in popularity.
c. 585 BC	Palace of King Apries built at Memphis.
c. 450 BC	Herodotus visits Memphis.
c. 300 BC	Alexandria begins to replace Memphis as Egypt's major administrative centre.
c. 20 BC	Strabo visits Memphis.
c. AD 700	Memphis abandoned.

quarters, among others. These quarters gave their names to portions of the dykes that protected their part of the city from flooding. When the Greek writer Strabo visited Memphis in the late 1st century BC, he saw the sacred Apis bull enclosure and various temples, including that of Ptah (the Hephaestieion), a temple of Aphrodite and the Serapeum at Saqqara, where the Apis bulls were buried. He notes the ruins of ancient palaces, crumbling beside lakes, and describes Memphis as a melting pot, home to people from all over the known world.

After losing its status as the country's administrative capital to Alexandria, Memphis entered a period of decline. It was finally abandoned around the 8th century AD, shortly after the foundation of the new Egyptian capital of Fustat. But the city continued to be mentioned by medieval writers: the Armenian geographer and historian al-Yaqubi reports seeing Memphis' ruins during the 9th century; and the 12th-century Iraqi scientist Abd el-Latif describes the city as a place of wonders, of idols and half-buried lion statues, where pedestals stood on huge bases and stones from fallen buildings littered the ground beside still-standing walls. At Saqqara, part of the Anubeion's ruins was equated with the biblical Prison of Joseph, and it became an important place of Muslim pilgrimage.

Little survives of ancient Memphis today. Much of its stonework was reused during the construction of nearby Cairo, while other parts were periodically flooded when the dams that protected the city broke. Most of Memphis now lies under cultivation or has been built upon, and is spread across various areas, including Mit Rahina, Kom el-Fakhry and Kom el-Arbain, among others. The Memphite necropolis is better preserved. Divided into protected zones, spread between Giza and Dahshur, it is famous for its archaeological monuments, and is visited by tourists from across the world.

▲

The ruins of part of ancient Memphis can be visited at **Mit Rahina**, just south of Cairo near Saqqara. There, an open-air museum stands in the south-east corner of the Temple of Ptah's enclosure (of which little survives beyond the remains of a hypostyle hall and the embalming house of the sacred Apis bull). A fallen **colossus of King Ramesses II** (r. *c.* 1279–1212 BC) lies in its own building, surrounded by smaller sculptures, such as broken sphinxes. Outside, you'll find various statues, including ones of the **divine triad of Memphis**: Ptah, Sekhmet and Nefertum. There's also a **colossal sphinx**, inscribed architectural fragments, large stelae and a **mummification table** among the many other pieces on display. The rest of the archaeological site is inaccessible, fenced off, among the tall grass and palm trees beyond.

A guide to the ancient **Memphite necropolis** would require a whole book of its own, so here I'll just take you through the highlights. At Giza, you'll find the **Great Pyramid of King Khufu** (r. *c.* 2470–2447 BC), the largest pyramid ever constructed. Beside it is the **Solar Boat Museum**, containing a reconstructed boat, originally found disassembled beside the pyramid. It was perhaps meant to magically provide transport for the king in death. Nearby is the **Pyramid of King Khafre** (r. *c.* 2437–2414 BC), which still retains some of its original white limestone cladding at its peak. Walk along the pyramid's causeway to see Khafre's well-preserved **Valley Temple**, and next to it, the **Great Sphinx**. (If you want to hear the Sphinx speak, return at night for the **Sound and Light Show**). You can also visit the **Pyramid of King Menkaure** (r. *c.* 2414–2396 BC) and the ruins of his **Mortuary Temple**. Certain private tombs are also open at Giza, including the **Tomb of Princess Mersyankh III**, granddaughter of King Khufu, in the eastern cemetery beside the Great Pyramid, and the **Tomb of Seshemnefer IV**, south of the Great Pyramid.

Further pyramids can be explored at **Abu Sir**, on the way south from Giza to Saqqara. At **Saqqara**, there's the **Pyramid of King Djoser** (r. *c.* 2584–2565 BC), the world's first pyramid, while within the **Pyramid of King Unas** (r. *c.* 2312–2282 BC) and the **Pyramid of King Teti** (r. *c.* 2282–2270 BC) you can see some of the earliest religious writings so far discovered – the Pyramid Texts. The **Serapeum**, final resting place of the sacred Apis bulls, whose massive sarcophagi can still be seen within, was the most famous of the necropolis's animal catacombs. Open tombs include the double **Tomb of Akhethotep and Ptahhotep**, the **Tomb of Mereruka** (a vizier who married into the royal family), and the **Tomb of Ti**. Further south, at **Dahshur**, there's the **Red Pyramid** and **Bent Pyramid of King Sneferu** (r. *c.* 2520–2470 BC), Khufu's father, both important architectural steps on the way to designing the Great Pyramid.

The obelisk of King Senwosret I at Heliopolis.

11

HELIOPOLIS

~~~~~~~~~~~~~~~~

Rebellion and Astronomy
at the City of the Sun

'Hail to you, perfect Re of every day, who rises at dawn without ceasing.
Khepri who grows weary with works. Your rays are in the face, without one
knowing it. Electrum is not like your brilliance. You create yourself, you gild
your body, a creator, who was not created.... When you sail across the sky,
every face sees you. When you go, you are hidden from their faces. You place
yourself at dawn daily. You sail strong under Your Majesty. Over one short day,
you travel a path, millions and hundreds of thousands of lengths.
Every day is an instant under you. When you set, it is gone.'

The Stele of Suti and Hor, c. 1360 BC.

A tall obelisk points towards the sky, each side carved with a single
vertical row of hieroglyphs. It stands on a modern plinth, itself
inscribed with details about the ancient monument in various languages. Acting like the gnomon of a giant sundial, the obelisk's shadow
stretches across the ground, adapting its shape to the terrain as it
creeps along the floor. It's as if the sun god is casting a single dark
finger to point at the assorted broken remains nearby: a colossal head;
an arm; a sarcophagus; a seated statue; inscribed fragments of stone.
Passing from one to the next over the course of a day, the shadow
highlights them in slow, unstoppable motion. Perhaps Re wants me
to take a closer look at the shattered glories of his illustrious past?
Whatever the case, his golden orb watches from above as I wander
between the artefacts.

I am in a small open-air museum in Cairo's Matareya district.
A barrier of trees and a fence cut me off from the wider archaeological
site and the city beyond. There's nobody else around. This isn't

unexpected – a working-class neighbourhood, away from Cairo's main sights, Matareya isn't at the top of most tourist itineraries. Beyond the trees, cars and tuc-tucs rattle along a dusty road. A minaret rises from a nearby mosque. Half-finished apartment buildings wear concrete pillars as crowns.

In ancient times, I'd be standing inside the temple precinct of Atum and Re-Horakhty (two guises of the sun god), at the heart of Egypt's most important centre of sun worship, Heliopolis, 'City of the Sun'. The two temples stood beside one another – the Atum temple facing west, the Re-Horakhty temple east – surrounded by the same double enclosure wall. The open-air museum and adjoining archaeo-logical zone, plus the modern apartment buildings, would all have been encompassed by this massive barrier. The area just beyond the obelisk was perhaps the Atum temple's centre, where a huge circular sanctuary stood on a platform that the Egyptians called the 'High Sand of Heliopolis'.

Today, there's nothing left to see beyond the obelisk, erected under the 12th Dynasty King Senwosret I (r. c. 1974–1929 BC). The vast remains of this once great ancient city are now spread beneath the Cairo dis-tricts of Matareya and Ain Shams. It's a sad situation for poor old Re, the most powerful of ancient Egypt's gods. Luckily for him, and us, there are plenty of surviving myths and legends that preserve a flavour of what the sun worshippers of Heliopolis once believed.

The sun god: deity of many forms

Anyone who's spent more than five minutes in Egypt understands the power of the sun. The heat can be intense. There's rarely a cloud to provide respite. You dream of air conditioning and a cold drink. It should come as no surprise then that the sun god Re was the focus of a great deal of mythology, and appeared in many forms. In art, Re is typically a hawk-headed man, with a sun disc, encircled by a cobra, on top of his head. A text called the Litany of Re, known from the reign of King Tuthmosis III (r. c. 1479–1424 BC), lists seventy-four (later versions give seventy-five) manifestations of the sun god. This includes familiar deities, such as Atum, Shu, Horus, Isis and Tefnut, and more obscure forms, such as the Decomposed One, the Weeper, the Great Cat and the Traveller. The sun could be called Re-Atum, combining the two gods that represented his most powerful and ancient forms respec-tively, or the Aten, a word referring to the sun disc itself. The sun disc could also be called the Eye of Re, often itself a manifestation of dif-ferent goddesses, particularly Hathor and Sekhmet.

King Tuthmosis III offers to the sun god Re-Horakhty, who is in the form of a hawk-headed man wearing the solar disc over his brow.

The most common forms of the sun god, found in religious texts from across Egyptian history, reflect the deity's progress as he crossed the sky, sailing on his day boat from the eastern horizon to the west. This journey was only possible because the Egyptians believed the blue sky to be water, part of the endless ocean of Nun that surrounded creation, held back by the force of the goddess Nut. At dawn, the sun god was Khepri, the scarab beetle, rolling the youthful sun disc over the horizon upwards into the sky (just as a dung beetle rolls a ball of faeces); at midday, when the sun's heat is at its most intense, he was Re, his strongest manifestation; and in the evening, when old and weary, the sun god became the ram-headed creator Atum, reflecting his position as one of the oldest divinities in creation. As can be seen, the sun god aged over the course of the day. A scene at the Temple of Edfu represents this process by showing twelve images of the sun god, each standing on his own boat – one per daylight hour – and each a little older than the one before. When darkness fell, in a death-like state, the sun god boarded his night boat to sail through the afterlife realm of the Duat, where he was rejuvenated in the middle of the night, ready to be born again at the eastern horizon (see Chapter 4).

Apophis: enemy of Re

The chaos snake Apophis – less often a tortoise, crocodile or scorpion – had one aim in life: to disrupt the sun god's cycle each and every day, and thereby bring about the end of creation. Unsurprisingly, the Egyptians sometimes called him 'The Evil One'. Apophis lacked eyes, a nose and ears. He lived on shouting and breathed screaming. Given all the racket, he could appropriately be called the Roarer, and the Egyptians believed that they could locate him because of his noise. Apophis challenged Re each hour of the day, but the sun god, aided by other deities, was always victorious. The most dangerous times were dawn, when the sun god was still a child; noon, when the sun boat paused at its zenith, leaving it vulnerable to attack; and sunset, when the sun god was weakened and elderly. The night hours that Re spent navigating the Duat in a death-like state were also a hazardous phase, as was the beginning and end of the solar year.

Apophis came into being from the spittle of Re, which transformed into a 120-cubit-long (63 metres or 207 feet) snake. He immediately rebelled against the sun god, aided by his associates, but the goddess Neith defeated him (see Chapter 9). This set in motion the daily war against chaos. The Book of Overthrowing the Serpent Apophis bears spells recited by priests each day at the Temple of Amun-Re at Karnak to protect the sun god from the chaos snake. These spells speak of spearing Apophis, spitting on him, binding him, trampling him, stabbing him with a knife and setting fire to him. (That ought'a do it.) Similar rituals for overthrowing Apophis are inscribed on the walls of various Ptolemaic Period temples, including Edfu, Dendera, Esna and Kom Ombo. Still, no matter how many times Apophis was destroyed, he always returned.

The creation of the universe

The priests of Heliopolis developed one of Egypt's most influential creation myths, featuring Re-Atum as ultimate creator. There's no single text that tells this myth from beginning to end, but it can be reconstructed from various sources spread across Egyptian history.

Before creation, the universe was an endless ocean, a manifestation of the god Nun (see Chapter 1). It was perfectly still and utterly dark. Crucially, in this infinite space, there was no differentiation. According to Egyptian thought, a fundamental aspect of creation is separation and limits. Time moves, even though cyclically. We all live in a defined space. There is a separation between life and death; between you and me; between the different gods. Before creation, no such separation existed. Nevertheless, the waters of Nun still contained potential. Something can arise from nothingness. This something – this potential – took the form of a seed floating in the darkness, the origin of the god Atum. Once self-aware, the seed Atum removed the waters from around him. This created the first separation, a void in the waters, kick-starting creation. Atum would now create the world according to his heart – the seat of thought, rather than the brain, in the ancient Egyptian worldview.

Depending on the variation of the myth, because all divine fluids were imbued with creative power, Atum spat, sneezed or masturbated the deities Shu and Tefnut into existence. The god Shu represented dryness and the atmosphere. He separated earth from sky, serving as the space in which all events could occur and in which all beings could live (once they'd been created). The goddess Tefnut is harder to define. Some scholars have linked her with moisture, but she may have represented the atmosphere of the Duat – the afterlife realm. Atum placed his arms around Shu and Tefnut, and in doing so, passed his *ka* – his life force – into them. This act, along with his gift of the breath of life, enabled them to act as independent beings. Shu became associated with life, and Tefnut with order. Soon after, Shu and Tefnut went missing, so Atum sent his Sole Eye to search for them. This manifestation of his power became the sun disc, creating the first sunrise. Light now illuminated creation (making it far less likely that Shu and Tefnut would go missing again).

Shu and Tefnut were the parents of the next generation of deities: the earth god Geb, and the sky goddess Nut. According to one myth, Nut trembled because of her height above the earth – fear of heights being an unfortunate phobia for a sky goddess – so eight minor deities, called the Infinite Ones, worked in pairs to hold each of her limbs steady. Geb and Nut were the parents of Osiris, Isis, Seth and Nephthys, who appear frequently in Egyptian mythology and religion. With creation complete, the nine gods now in existence – Re-Atum, Shu, Tefnut, Geb, Nut, Osiris, Isis, Seth and Nephthys – were called the Great Ennead.

The reign of King Re on earth and the rebellion of mankind

After creation, the gods lived among the people on earth, ruled over by Re as first king of Egypt. Myths describing Re's time as king either focus on his early life as a child, or later in his reign, when he had grown old. This reflects the daily cycle of the sun, which the Egyptians believed was young in the morning and old at night. Both times were periods of danger, when the sun god was vulnerable to his enemies. As such, many myths describe rebellions against Re, led by different groups, including the children of Apophis and humans, and the actions taken to save him. Eventually, though, the sun god decided that enough was enough, and distanced himself from humanity, escaping into the sky, as in, for example, the Myth of the Heavenly Cow (see Chapter 5).

The hand of Atum or Re sometimes features in these myths of rebellion. An inscription on the statue of Djedher the Saviour, a famous priest and healer from Athribis during the 4th century BC, relates that the hand of Atum drove away a storm and tumult in Heliopolis. It protected Re during a great battle waged near the temple, when the sun god transformed into a huge ichneumon to fight the chaos snake Apophis. The Delta Mythological Manual, meanwhile, says that the divine hand of Re became pregnant with Shu and Tefnut. Its fingers transformed into snakes called the children of impotence and rebelled against Re. This is why the Egyptians held a festival of the hand, in which they created an image of a hand, and beat four of its fingers while protecting the thumb.

One short (but perhaps not so sweet) rebellion myth is recorded on the walls of the Temple of Sobek and Horus the Elder at Kom Ombo. Re and Thoth had been searching for rebels near Kom Ombo for some time, but they'd had no luck, so Re asked Thoth to send out a spy. The spy scoured the region, until, beside a great lake, he discovered 257 enemies, led by 8 officers. All of them were slandering Re. The nerve! The spy dutifully returned to Kom Ombo and reported his findings to the gods. 'Thoth,' said Re, 'can you suggest a god who will kill these enemies? One who won't allow any of them to live.' Thoth flicked through his mental list of dangerous gods. 'I suggest Horus the Elder as a lord of carnage,' he said. Re summoned the hawk-headed Horus the Elder, gave him strength, and armed him with weapons. The god set out for the lake in a rage. His feathered face crimson with anger, he unsheathed his knives and stabbed each rebel to death.

The reigns of Kings Shu and Geb

A shrine from el-Arish, along the north Sinai coast, provides us with the most detailed mythology of the reigns of Shu and Geb. After Re had departed for the sky, Shu reigned over Egypt as a good king, and defeated the enemies of his father, including the children of Apophis. When the air became dry, Shu created irrigation for the cities and villages in the nomes. He rebuilt temples in the north and south, and restored walls that had been destroyed. But just as under his father, rebellion was never far away. One night, the children of Apophis regrouped and attacked Egypt, destroying every place they passed through. Cities and villages were left devastated in their wake. Shu defended the area of el-Arish, and the gods took up positions on nearby mounds. Here, the text breaks.

When the action picks up again, another rebellion is under way. Perhaps in a panic, Shu flew into the sky with his followers, abandoning his wife Tefnut on earth. She fled to Shu's palace, where she was imprisoned and raped by her son Geb. A rainstorm erupted. The land fell dark for nine days. When the downpour ended and the light returned, Geb and his entourage visited the shrine of Shu to take the royal uraeus – a rearing cobra, symbol and protector of royalty. The snake, enraged, spat fire at the god and his followers. Geb's entourage crumbled into burnt flakes of flesh. Geb managed to escape with severe burns, which he healed with the power of the wig of Re. (I wish I could give you more information about this intriguing magical relic.) As king, Geb ensured that the Egyptians rebuilt all places that had existed under Re and Shu, destroyed in the upheavals.

Further sources shed light on the reign of Geb, particularly on his violent treatment of his parents. The Tebtunis Mythological Manual says that Geb committed an offence against Shu in the Slaughtering Place of Hermopolis; during a rebellion, Geb raped his mother Tefnut and hurt his father, Shu. To recover from his pain, Shu submerged himself in a sacred well at Heliopolis. The goddess Unut then killed Geb with a spear as punishment for further sexual assaults, and received a festival in her honour. To re-enact Geb's punishment, the Egyptians killed a goose and flayed a dog during the Festival of Thoth at Hermopolis. Another section relates that Geb took Tefnut to bed and threw her in jail. A court judgment then ruled against the god, forcing him to give up his magical protective girdle or bracelet. According to the Delta Mythological Manual, a spear was thrust into Geb's thigh because he slept with his mother. On another occasion, Geb transformed into a pig and mutilated the Eye of Re, swallowing its efflux. When the gods questioned Geb about his actions, he denied all responsibility. As Geb spoke, the efflux emerged from his skin like a disease. Thoth took the Eye of Re back to the horizon, and Geb was forced to swallow urine as punishment for what he'd done to Shu. The Magical Papyrus of London and Leiden, dated to the 3rd century AD and found at Thebes, says that Geb transformed into a bull to rape his mother, causing Shu's heart to curse his son's face.

Maat: goddess of cosmic order and balance

Maat – a word that encapsulates truth, balance, harmony, order and justice – is one of the key principles of ancient Egyptian thought. As a goddess, Maat was shown in human form wearing a feather on her head. She was the daughter of Re, and sometimes the wife of Thoth. She could also manifest as the Eye of Re. But *maat* was a concept too, symbolized by this same feather. The rules of *maat* underpinned the operation of the cosmos, set at the beginning of time. Everything happens in a state of eternal recurrence, like clockwork, from the rising

The goddess Maat, with outstretched wings and wearing the feather of *maat* on her head. From the tomb of King Seti I in the Valley of the Kings.

and setting of the sun to the annual Nile inundation. This is a form of cyclical time that the Egyptians called *neheh*. In the Heliopolitan creation myth, Tefnut – first-born daughter of Re-Atum – is equated with Maat, perhaps marking the point when cosmic order came into existence. Despite her importance in Egyptian culture, few temples to Maat are known. One stood beside the fifth pylon-gateway of the Temple of Amun-Re at Karnak, while others existed at Memphis and Deir el-Medina.

One of the king's key roles was to ensure *maat*. If it became unbalanced, it was his job to restore it. Consequently, kings are often shown offering *maat* to gods, and stress their obedience to it. Some emphasized their association with *maat* by including the word in their royal names (at his coronation, a king received four extra names in addition to his birth name). Courtiers also performed and spoke *maat*, because it was what the king loved. Viziers, who played an important role in Egypt's justice system, wore a symbol of Maat around their necks. According to court-produced wisdom texts, those who broke *maat* were punished. Indeed, all ethics and morality were informed by *maat*, from the way you treated your family and friends to high-level judgments in legal cases. Balance was always advised. Excess, whether partying too hard or working too hard, was frowned upon. And when you died, the gods weighed your actions in life against the feather of Maat to judge whether you deserved an afterlife (see Chapter 6).

Watching the skies: Egyptian astronomy at Heliopolis

The high priest of Re at Heliopolis held the title Greatest of Seers. This isn't due to him having particularly excellent eyesight, but rather because Heliopolis was an important centre for observing the sky and the movements of all the heavenly bodies. Beyond the sun and the moon, which feature prominently in Egyptian mythology, the Egyptians were aware of five planets, each sailing across the night sky in its own boat. Jupiter had various names; it was 'Horus who Limits the Two Lands', 'Horus who Enlightens the Two Lands', 'Horus the Secret One of the Two Lands', 'Horus who Opens the Secret', or 'Horus the Trader'. Saturn was called 'Horus the Bull (of the Sky)', and Mars was 'Horus the Red' or 'Horus of the Horizon'. Each of these planets was shown as a hawk-headed man. Mercury was called Sebegu and associated with Seth, while Venus was 'The One who Crosses' or the 'Morning God' and shown as a *benu*-bird (often a heron). The ecliptic – the path along which the sun, moon and planets move through the sky over the course of a year – was called the Winding Waterway. The Milky Way was seen as a manifestation of Nut. The best-preserved images of the Egyptian conception of the night sky can be found in the tomb of Seti I in the Valley of the Kings, and in one of the tombs of the courtier Senenmut, also at Thebes. There was also a representation of the zodiac at Dendera (see Chapter 5).

The decans were also important to Egyptian astronomy. The Egyptians called these thirty-six star groups, or sometimes just a single star, 'workers', and visualized them as lion-headed humans, winged snakes or female deities wearing star crowns. Every ten days, a decan disappeared beneath the horizon into the underworld, and remained out of sight for seventy days, a time during which it was regarded as 'dead' or 'resting'. At the same time, every ten days, one decan reappeared on the eastern horizon, rising just before the sun – a phase known as its heliacal rising. Though most decans can't be associated with modern star groups, some have been identified: Sopdet (Sothis in Greek and Sirius today) was originally part of a decan of three stars, but eventually came to be regarded as its own decan. Like other decans, Sopdet disappeared for seventy days each year, but its heliacal rising held particular importance to the Egyptians because it heralded the coming Nile inundation and the start of the new year. Other important decans included the foreleg of Seth, *meskhetiu*, better known today as the Plough or the Big Dipper (part of the larger constellation of Ursa Major). Isis, in the form of a hippopotamus called Ipet, guarded and kept this leg in place, ensuring that it didn't sink into the Duat. Another important set of stars was the Imperishables, called the northern circumpolar stars today.

The 'Mansion of the Benben', obelisks and the *benu*-bird

The 'Mansion of the Benben' at the Temple of Re-Horakhty in Heliopolis housed a solar symbol called the *benben*-stone. Conical or pyramidal in shape, it symbolized the first hill or mound of earth at the beginning of time. Indeed, according to the Pyramid Texts, Atum rose from the waters of creation as the *benben*-stone inside the Mansion of the Benben at Heliopolis. The *benben* also probably represented rays of light descending from the sun, itself a symbol of rebirth. The pyramid shape of Old and Middle Kingdom royal tombs may have been an attempt to replicate the *benben*-stone on a large scale – the word *benbenet* was certainly used in reference to the pyramids' capstones. The pyramidion-shaped peak of obelisks was also called a *benbenet*; and indeed, obelisks in general had a solar meaning. The earliest known obelisk was erected at Heliopolis, and many more were produced for the city's temples throughout Egyptian history.

The sacred *benu*-bird (derived from the same *ben*), normally shown as a heron, but perhaps earlier a wagtail, was a manifestation of the god Re, representing resurrection. Herodotus called the *benu*-bird a phoenix, saying that although he hadn't seen one himself, he had seen paintings of them. According to the people of Heliopolis, he writes, its plumage is part golden and part red, and it looks like an eagle. The phoenix returns every 500 years, when its father dies. At this time, the bird shapes a lump of myrrh into an egg, hollows it out, and shoves its dead father into the hole, before sealing the outside with yet more myrrh. The bird then carries this myrrh-egg-coffin all the way from Arabia to Heliopolis for burial.

Tales of the priests of Heliopolis

The priests of Heliopolis were the subject of many tales from *c.* 600 BC onwards. Many are quite fragmentary. One story, for example, features an argument between the chief scribe of the Temple of Re and his son Hareus. Hareus deeply wished to marry a woman named Tatinebethetepet, and said that if the marriage didn't happen he would kill himself. Eventually, the wedding went ahead, and that night, Tatinebethetepet became pregnant. She then went for a walk, and met a woman who appeared as a statue, holding a golden cup. The statue-woman told Tatinebethetepet that she would die, but due to the fragmentary nature of the text, it's unclear what happened next. There is mention of Psais, a deity of fate, and of Wennefer, an afterlife god, but little else is clear.

One priest of Atum at Heliopolis that appears in various late tales is Petese, son of Petetum. He was credited with a number of achievements, including deciphering a work written by Imhotep on astrology, and instructing Plato in astrology at Heliopolis. The most complete story revolves around Petese being told about his forthcoming death. At the start of this fragmentary tale, Petese is in the presence of a ghost. 'How long do I have to live?' Petese asked. The ghost refused to answer. Have it your way, Petese thought. He summoned his power and recited a spell, compelling the ghost to cooperate. 'You only have forty days left to live,' the ghost said. 'There's a list of people who are about to die, and your name's on it.' Petese returned home. He kept what had happened a secret from his wife, Sakhminofret, and dedicated himself to enjoying his remaining time on earth. One day, Petese asked the priests of Heliopolis to give him 500 silver pieces from the sun god's treasury. This would be his payment for interpreting the content of hidden books in the temple – an important job. One of the priests, a man named Hareus, refused Petese's wish. Not one to give up easily, Petese used his magic (involving a wax falcon and cat) to compel Hareus to make the payment. Hareus duly gave the 500 silver pieces to Petese, and as a bonus, said that he'd bring 500 more.

Nearing the end of his forty days, Petese prepared for his funeral. He moulded assistants out of wax and used a spell to make them perform the rites. He then brought two wax baboons to life. 'I want you to compile and write down seventy stories for me,' he told the baboons, giving them their scribal equipment. 'There should be thirty-five stories about women's vices, and thirty-five about women's virtues.' He hoped that this collection of tales would be discovered with him, and serve as his legacy after his death (despite the wax baboons having done all the real work). Petese spent his final days 'making holiday' with Sakhminofret and doing whatever he chose. After Petese's death, Sakhminofret made an offering to Re. To her surprise, the god appeared and spoke with the voice of Petese. What follows is fragmentary, but it appears that the magical baboons recited to Sakhminofret the various tales they'd collected, some of which can be reconstructed.

One of the baboons' tales, sadly missing its introduction, revolves around a blind pharaoh. The king was searching for someone to cure his blindness. In return, whoever helped him could take anything they wanted from his treasury. One person suggested that the king sleep in a temple, in the hope that a god would appear while he dreamed and provide a solution. The king, desperate, did as suggested. He was in luck. That night, as he slept, a god spoke to him. 'Your blindness will end if you cleanse your eyes with a virtuous woman's tears,' the god said. The king awoke. 'Bring all the noble women to me,' he commanded. The ladies of the court arrived, and though each cried for their king, their tears failed to heal him. Disappointed, he summoned forty harem women. Their tears failed to heal him too, so he had them executed. Before the king could kill anyone else, his son, Prince Necho, interrupted with a suggestion: 'There's a woman from Herakleopolis who is virtuous; we should bring her to court.' The king agreed, and when the woman arrived, her tears cured his blindness. Both Herodotus and Diodorus Siculus tell similar stories. In Herodotus' version, the blinded King Pheros is told by an oracle that he will regain his sight if he washes his eyes in a woman's urine. And to make things more difficult, the woman must only ever have slept with her husband. First, Pheros used his wife's urine. No result. Next, he summoned all the women he could find. None cured his blindness, so he had them burned, along with his wife. Eventually, when he finally found a woman able to help him, he married her.

The other tales told by the baboons are harder to reconstruct. One involved a son seeing his mother having sex with a soldier; the mother was then afraid that the son would tell his father. Another featured a crocodile grasping a beautiful woman in its mouth and taking her back to its lair. A very fragmentary tale describes a woman waking up locked in a coffin. Slightly better preserved is the 'The Rape of Hatmehit', in which a priest of Horus-of-Pe is either about to rape or has raped a woman named Hatmehit. The priest then challenges Hatmehit's husband, the servant Psemmut. The nature of the challenge is unclear, but it must be completed before a falcon can return. By the end of the tale, Psemmut is in prison, and Hatmehit is trying to rescue him.

Heliopolis in history and today

Heliopolis, a Greek word meaning 'City of the Sun', was the most important centre dedicated to the sun god in Egypt. Known as Iunu, 'The Pillar', to the ancient Egyptians, it stood about 30 kilometres (20 miles) north-east of Memphis, on the eastern side of the Nile. As it was some distance from the Nile, a canal connected the city to the river. Hardly anything is known about the appearance of the temples of Atum and Re-Horakhty, although their precinct seemingly sat atop an artificial mound in the southern part of the city, raising the temples up high. This was known as the 'High Sand' and represented the first land to emerge from the waters during creation. Excavations have shown that the temple precinct was surrounded by two great walls, which perhaps had only two entrances. Other major finds at Heliopolis include a stone shrine from the reign of King Djoser (c. 2584–2565 BC), decorated with images of the Ennead; subterranean tombs of 6th Dynasty high priests of Re; and an obelisk of the 6th Dynasty King Teti (r. c. 2282–2270 BC). Archaeologists have also discovered some of the tombs of the sacred Mnevis bulls of Heliopolis. Known as Menwer to the Egyptians and regarded as a herald of Re, each incarnation of the Mnevis bull had to be entirely black.

Other references to Heliopolis and its temples are found in inscriptions and the writings of classical authors. The Kushite king Piye (r. c. 752–721 BC), who campaigned in Egypt during the Third Intermediate Period, visited various shrines in the temples of Heliopolis and describes making offerings on the High Sand. Centuries later, Strabo visited its ruins. He describes the city as deserted and standing on a large mound, and mentions nearby lakes connected to a canal. The temple had been mutilated and burned by the Persian king Cambyses II (r. c. 525–522 BC), he writes, but there was still a row of sphinxes and a building filled

HELIOPOLIS

Key dates and remains

c. 2580 BC	Stone shrine of King Djoser erected at Heliopolis.
c. 2280 BC	Tombs of the high priests of Re built at Heliopolis. Obelisk of King Teti erected. Pyramid Texts of King Teti (at Saqqara) make first reference to the 'Bull of Heliopolis' – the Mnevis bull.
c. 1971 BC	King Senwosret I erects obelisks in front of the Temple of Atum. He also builds a new temple to Re-Horakhty.
c. 1450 BC	King Tuthmosis III erects two obelisks.
c. 1360 BC	King Akhenaten builds a temple to the Aten.
c. 732 BC	King Piye visits Heliopolis during his military campaign in Egypt.
525 BC	The Persian army sacks Heliopolis.
c. 20 BC	Strabo visits Heliopolis and sees a deserted city.
c. 13 BC	The two obelisks of Tuthmosis III are moved to Alexandria.

with columns. Though priests no longer served, their homes remained at the temple precinct. People performed sacred rites and explained the meaning of the temples to visitors.

Today, little remains above ground of Heliopolis' once fabulous grandeur. The city was sacked by the Persians in 525 BC, and later, under the Ptolemies and Romans, some of its obelisks were taken to Alexandria and Rome. Two obelisks moved from Heliopolis to Alexandria ultimately ended up in New York and London during the 19th century. Heliopolis' stonework was reused for building projects under the Fatimids, who ruled Egypt from AD 969 to 1171, and then for the construction of Cairo, particularly under Saladin. Due to Cairo's expansion over the centuries, ancient Heliopolis now lies beneath the city's districts of Matareya and Ain Shams. Excavations continue to reveal glimpses of the ancient city, but the only significant monument that visitors can still see is an obelisk of King Senwosret I (r. *c.* 1974–1929 BC), standing in the open-air museum in Matareya. Meanwhile, the Cairo district today named Heliopolis is a well-off part of town, which you pass through on the way to or from the airport.

▲

When visiting Cairo, you can see the 12th Dynasty **obelisk of King Senwosret I** (r. *c.* 1974–1929 BC), and other surrounding objects from ancient Heliopolis, in a small open-air museum in the Matareya district. This can be reached by taxi, or you can walk from Matareya metro station.

The ruins of the Temple of Bastet at Bubastis. The temple was
destroyed during an earthquake in ancient times.

12

BUBASTIS

~~~~~~~~~~~~~~~~~~~~

City of the Cat Goddess

⊸

'Don't mock a cat.'
The Instructions of Ankhsheshonqi, c. 1st century BC.

The worn blocks of the goddess Bastet's temple at Bubastis lie scattered in a muddy depression. Clumps of grass spring up in patches between them. All around, hieroglyphs and carved figures catch my eyes. Chunks of columns lie on their sides. And is that a leg? Beside some corrugated containers and lamp posts are the remains of a mud-brick construction. Nearby, other artefacts are displayed in much tidier conditions, carefully arranged on plinths in a modern open-air museum. The highlight is a colossal statue of a queen, her heavy wig enveloping her shoulders, one foot powerfully striding forward. With its well-kept open-air museum and separate zone of scattered blocks, the ancient site is part impeccable, part ruin. It's hard to imagine that in ancient times, hundreds of thousands of revellers descended on this city every year for a festival dedicated to the cat goddess Bastet, partying their days away in state-sanctioned drunken oblivion. Beyond the gentle scrape of an archaeologist's trowel, it's hard to imagine anything going on here at all.

Yet once, long ago, the air was filled with the meowing of adorable kittens (admittedly bred to be killed and mummified as divine offerings). There was the shaking of sistra – rattles topped with carvings of relaxing cats – and the murmur of pilgrims. People came from far and wide to this part of the south-east Delta, determined to pick up a few good cat statues and a mummified moggy to offer to the goddess Bastet. They would have oohed and aahed at her colourful cat-headed images, carved on the temple's gateway and walls, and returned home feeling blessed. For fans of our feline friends, Bubastis would be *the* place to visit in Egypt if circumstances were different. Sadly, geography and time have conspired against this once fabulous ancient city.

Like Bubastis, many ancient cities once stood among the pleasant fields of Egypt's Delta, but little remains today to mark their presence. Unlike the south of Egypt, where the inhospitable desert is never too far away and quality stone can be found in abundance, the north is wet and marshy, a great fan-shaped culmination to the Nile's journey to the Mediterranean. Farming over centuries has ploughed archaeological sites into nothingness, ancient mud bricks have been sought out as quality fertilizer, and Pharaonic stonework reused in modern constructions. What remains of the historic sites is often deep beneath the surface, in waterlogged soil that can be expensive and difficult to excavate. Nonetheless, over recent decades, ground-penetrating radar and satellite imagery have revealed the ghostly blueprints of ancient worlds, and the work of an increasing number of excavation teams has vastly improved our knowledge of this once ignored region. Bubastis (Tell Basta) is one such city, and its patron goddess, Bastet, has a long history, as does the mythological importance of the felines she represents.

Bastet: cat goddess, royal guardian and mother
Bastet is one of Egypt's earliest attested goddesses. Her name is first found on a stone vessel from c. 2700 BC, later interred beneath the Step Pyramid of King Djoser (r. c. 2584–2565 BC) at Saqqara, and was inscribed on one of the doorways leading into the Valley Temple of King Khafre (r. c. 2437–2414 BC) at Giza, built during the 4th Dynasty. Her name in ancient Egyptian is derived from the word for a particular type of ointment jar, called a *bas*. The Egyptians regarded ointment as having protective qualities, and it was also a sign of elite status. Bastet thus became a royal guardian, and was shown in this capacity as a lioness – an animal regarded as powerful enough to protect the king – or as a lioness-headed woman. (In fact, only a single image of Bastet in fully human form has ever been identified.) The semi-precious stone turquoise was regarded as the blood of Bastet, and in Spell 125 of the Book of the Dead, Bastet is one of the deities that the deceased must approach when making the negative confession, stating 'sins' that they had not committed in life: 'O Bastet, who comes out from the secret place, I have not winked.' (Yes, you read that correctly. Winking could bar you from the afterlife.)

Like most goddesses, Bastet was a daughter of Re (or Re-Atum) and could manifest as his fearsome Eye, destroyer of the king's enemies.

A statuette of the goddess Bastet enthroned. Here she is shown as a lioness-headed woman. Made during the Third Intermediate Period.

Indeed, there is the possibility that all cat- or lioness-headed goddesses were connected – the same power taking different forms depending on the situation. When the sun god's Eye – a female being – was angry, she became Sekhmet, but when calmed, she transformed into Bastet. During the Old Kingdom, these two goddesses were almost always presented together as Sekhmet-Bastet. Bastet was mother to the lion-headed god Mahes (Mihos in Greek), her child with Re-Atum (who, as mentioned above, could also be her father).

Despite traditionally being envisioned as a lioness, by *c.* 900 BC, Bastet started to be associated more with housecats, emphasizing her nurturing, childbearing and motherly qualities. She was now frequently shown as a cat, or cat-headed, was a mother to the king, and could be carved surrounded by kittens. Shortly afterwards, during the Late Period, the Egyptians produced many bronze statues of Bastet, and offered cat mummies to her in their thousands at her temples across Egypt. None of her temples was more popular than her cult centre at Bubastis.

The Festival of Bastet at Bubastis

The main annual celebration at Bubastis was the Festival of Bastet. Herodotus says that this was the principal celebration in Egypt, even more important than that of Isis at Busiris and the festivals held at Sais, Heliopolis and Buto. In his words, it was also the most enthusiastically celebrated. Men and women sailed to Bubastis from across Egypt, he writes – 700,000 of them, but children weren't allowed. Along the way, women shook rattles and played flutes. People clapped their hands and sang. And whenever their boats neared any towns, the women danced, or mocked the townswomen, perhaps to make them less appealing to the Evil Eye (and so actually helping them). Others lifted their skirts to reveal their genitals, a practice probably meant to send fertility to the village women and their fields. Similar practices were conducted in front of divine statues – for example, in front of Hathor at Esna and the Apis Bull at Memphis – in the hope of receiving fertility from the deity. Upon arriving at Bubastis, the Egyptians made animal sacrifices, and everyone drank more wine than they would normally do across the whole year. This wasn't simply to ensure that everyone had a good time; heavy drinking was an expected part of Egyptian festivals because alcohol helped to blur the lines of reality, promoting a closer feeling to the gods and the dead. Perhaps it was drunkenness (or a hangover) rather than reverence for Bastet that led King Ramesses IV (r. c. 1153–1146 BC) to declare that he didn't hunt lions during the Festival of Bastet.

Cats and cat mummies

Everyone loves cats. The ancient Egyptians were no different. The name Cat was popular among ancient Egyptian men and women – there was even a king called Pamiu, 'The Tomcat'. The serene statues of seated cats they produced are timeless pieces of art, still attractive to cat-lovers. And ancient artists doodled pictures of cats on broken pieces of limestone or papyrus to pass the time. Some show cats serving mice masters, bringing them offerings or fanning them; another drawing shows cats defending a fortress from mice. One royal prince had a sarcophagus made for his pet cat. It wouldn't be unusual for us to create similar objects and artworks in honour of our beloved pets today. But there's a point where we draw the line, and that's the ancient Egyptian practice of killing and mummifying innocent kitties. If you told a friend that you'd killed and stuffed your cat as an offering to the gods, you'd get a visit from the police.

Contrary to popular belief, the Egyptians didn't regard cats as gods, but they certainly dedicated cat mummies to goddesses depicted in feline form as votive offerings – physical prayers. The idea was that if you offered a symbol of the goddess at her temple, she might do something for you. This practice became particularly popular in the

Late Period, when catacombs (no pun intended), particularly at Bubastis and Saqqara, were stuffed with cat mummies. At Bubastis, cat mummies were interred by their thousands in large brick- or clay-lined pits, but few of them remain today. Excavated in the 19th century, the mummies were used as ballast in ships and afterwards as fertilizer. The cat cemetery itself fared little better, and is now lost beneath modern buildings. (Each apartment no doubt haunted by the incessant sound of ghostly mewing, the scratching of doors, and the mysterious phenomenon of anything placed on shelves and tables falling to the ground within minutes.)

Cat mummies came in two different forms: either with the animal's legs and tail tucked up tight against its body, creating a bowling-pin-like appearance, or with its legs and tail extended and wrapped independently, producing a more recognizable cat shape. Sometimes, the embalmers painted extra details on the wrappings, such as the cat's eyes. The mummy was then placed in a wooden coffin, carved to appear as a seated cat, or in a box, sometimes with a statuette of a cat on top. To match pilgrims' high demand for cat mummies, the Egyptians mass-produced them, breeding cats especially for the purpose of mummification at, or close to, temples. These cats were typically less than a year old when killed, usually by having their necks broken or by a blow to the head. Of those discovered at the Bubasteion (the Temple of Bastet) at Saqqara, two out of three cats suffered a violent

Cat mummies were often placed in cat-shaped wooden coffins.

end, and only one in three reached adulthood. Some of the mummies even turned out to be 'fake' cats, indicating that sometimes demand outstripped supply and corners had to be cut. Pilgrims could also buy bronze or faience cats at the temples to offer to the goddess; the priests catered for all budgets.

Despite such treatment, classical writers do suggest that the Egyptians had a particular fondness for cats. Herodotus writes that when a cat died in a house, the people of the household shaved their eyebrows in mourning (and relates an odd story about cats leaping over lines of men into burning houses). Diodorus Siculus, visiting Egypt at the end of the Ptolemaic Period, says that anyone who killed a cat, accidentally or not, was put to death, a rule that led people to swerve around dead cats in the street, announcing loudly 'it was already dead!', just in case any onlookers suspected them and decided to take matters into their own hands. This form of mob justice wasn't just something he'd been told about; he saw it with his own eyes. During his visit to Egypt, a Roman accidentally killed a cat, and the local Egyptians chased him into his house to punish him. They refused to let him go free even when royal officials arrived and the threat of Roman reprisal was raised. Diodorus goes on to say that the Egyptians called cats with clucking sounds and fed them with bread in milk. And whenever Egyptians were on military expeditions abroad, they paid a ransom for any captured cats and returned them to Egypt (even if they were low on money).

Another classical tale of Egyptians and cats is reported by the 2nd-century Macedonian rhetorician Polyaenus. When King Cambyses II invaded Egypt in 525 BC, the Egyptians resisted at the eastern Delta city of Pelusium, using catapults (okay, this time pun intended!) to hurl stones and fire at the Persian army. To stop the barrage, Cambyses gathered as many sacred animals as he could find, including cats, and forced them to march ahead of his troops. The Egyptians, afraid that they might kill one of the animals, stopped their assault, enabling Cambyses to take the city. Anyone who's ever tried to get a cat to do anything knows this story can't be true.

Further feline deities

Bastet was far from the only feline goddess in Egypt's pantheon. Among the most popular were Sekhmet, Mafdet and Pakhet. Throughout Egyptian history, Sekhmet ('The Powerful One'), the wife of Ptah and mother of the lotus god Nefertum, was a dangerous force, worshipped primarily at Memphis. She was a goddess of illness and plague (regarded as the breath of Sekhmet's messengers), and was shown as a lioness-headed woman wearing a solar disc. She spread illness through the Seven Arrows of Sekhmet and through her messengers, known as 'slaughterers', particularly during the five epagomenal days – a dangerous transitional phase between the year ending and the new year beginning that also marked the birthdays of Osiris, Horus the Elder, Seth, Isis and Nephthys (see Chapter 8). The Egyptians performed rituals to repel Sekhmet's diseases, or called on healers, skilled in magical practice and known as priests of Sekhmet, for help. Her image often adorned amulets, worn as a way of magically repelling the illnesses brought by her 'slaughterers'. Sekhmet was also a goddess of fire and the dangerous heat of the sun. The hot wind of the desert was her breath, and she breathed fire on her enemies. On the plus side, she was believed to use her fearsome powers to protect her father, the sun god Re, and when she became calm she transformed into a more peaceful goddess, such as Bastet, Hathor or Mut.

The cat-headed goddess Mafdet hunted and killed the enemies of Re. Her name translates as 'The Runner', and early images suggest that the Egyptians regarded her as a leopard or cheetah. The name of the lioness goddess Pakhet means 'She Who Scratches' (or more simply 'The Scratcher'). She had sharp claws, and equally sharp eyes, that helped her to catch prey while she protected the sun god during his nightly journey through the Duat. In the Book of the Dead, she makes an appearance in a spell to be recited over a three-headed figure of Mut: one head is Pakhet, the next is a human, and the third is a vulture. (The figure should also have a penis, wings and claws, just in case you're planning on performing the ritual.) Hatshepsut dedicated a rock-cut chapel to Pakhet at Speos Artemidos in Middle Egypt (in a valley said to have been carved from the mountain by the goddess herself). The cult of Pakhet was strong in this region. Among her priesthood, we know of Pedekem, a man buried at Tuna el-Gebel in the 4th century BC, who held the title of priest of the living cat of the Temple of Pakhet. (I imagine that most people sharing their homes with cats can empathize with a man who spent his life serving a feline deity.)

Male cats tended to be associated with the sun god and his journey through the Duat each night; consequently, they appear frequently in netherworld books. The Coffin Texts refer to a Great Tomcat who turns out to actually be Re. In the Book of the Dead, a cat manifestation of the sun god kills a snake representing Apophis, and the netherworld's twelfth gate is guarded by a demon called 'Cat'. In the Amduat, a cat-headed demon beheads bound enemies, while in the Book of Caverns and the Book of Gates, Miuty, another cat-headed demon, keeps an eye on bound enemies and protects one of the gates through which the sun god passes on his nightly journey. Both the Great Tomcat and Miuty are presented as manifestations of the sun god himself in the Litany of Re.

The 'Tale of the Herdsman'

The 'Tale of the Herdsman' is a fragmentary story dated to the Middle Kingdom. Notoriously difficult to translate, there's a lot of debate around the details of the plot and its meaning. Following the work of Egyptologist Thomas Schneider, it begins with a herdsman descending to a marsh, where he finds a rough-skinned woman covered in bristles. Her non-human appearance makes the hairs on his body rise. What the woman says to the herdsman is not recorded, but he responds that he'll never do as she asks, because he's afraid. Afterwards, the herdsman and his companions decide to take their bulls to a nearby safe spot for the night. There, they make a water incantation, meant to protect their livestock from dangerous animals, such as crocodiles. The next morning, the goddess returns to the herdsman, her hair disordered and her body stripped of clothing. The preserved text ends there. The tale seems to feature a goddess who can change form: one a scary, hairy manifestation, and the other a woman. Discounting the possibility of ancient werewolves, it's possible that this is a reference to the Wandering Goddess, who manifests as a dangerous lioness when angry (see Chapter 5).

Bubastis in history and today

The ruins of Bubastis stand on the edge of the modern city of Zagazig in the south-east Delta, a governorate capital and centre of industry, particularly known for its factories that process cotton grown in local farms. The earliest tomb excavated at Bubastis dates to the 1st Dynasty (*c.* 3100 BC), and the earliest settlement to the Old Kingdom, but the city may have been much older. Labels found in Tomb U-j at Abydos, from *c.* 3200 BC, mention a place called Bast, most probably Bubastis. The city's cemeteries were in use throughout the Pharaonic Period and into the Roman Era, and include the burials of Middle Kingdom governors. Other early excavated remains include *ka*-chapels of the 6th Dynasty kings Teti (r. *c.* 2282–2270 BC) and Pepi I (r. *c.* 2265–2219 BC), a palace of 12th Dynasty date, and a hoard of treasure, dated to the 19th Dynasty, that appears to have been buried and then forgotten. Further buildings, including probable housing, have been identified using ground-penetrating radar.

Although Bubastis' temple to Bastet certainly existed at an early date in the city's history, little can be said about its initial phases.

BUBASTIS

Key dates and remains

c. 3200 BC	First potential reference to Bubastis on a label found in Tomb U-j at Abydos.
c. 3100 BC	Earliest tomb at Bubastis.
c. 2550 BC	First archaeological evidence for settlement at Bubastis.
c. 2470 BC	Earliest evidence for construction of the Temple of Bastet.
c. 2280 BC	*Ka*-chapel of King Teti built.
c. 2260 BC	*Ka*-chapel of King Pepi I built.
c. 1990 BC	12th Dynasty palace built at Bubastis.
c. 1900 BC	Local governors buried at Bubastis.
c. 1880 BC	King Senwosret III perhaps rebuilds the Temple of Bastet.
c. 1200 BC	Bubastis treasure buried.
c. 948 BC	Bubastis becomes major royal city of the 22nd Dynasty kings.
c. 925 BC	King Osorkon I starts to rebuild the Temple of Bastet. Work continues intermittently until the reign of King Nectanebo II of the 30th Dynasty.
c. 875 BC	King Osorkon II builds a temple to Mahes.
c. 664 BC	Catacombs built for the burial of mummified cats, deposited by pilgrims as votive offerings.
c. 450 BC	Herodotus visits Bubastis.
342 BC	Bubastis is sacked by the Persian army under King Artaxerxes III.
c. 300 BC	During the early Ptolemaic Period, Bubastis becomes a wealthy city due to its position on trade routes connected with Alexandria.

Excavations have revealed Middle Kingdom architectural remains and statues of 19th Dynasty date that once probably stood in the temple's central court. Most of the temple's scattered ruins date to the Third Intermediate Period, when for a short time, under the 22nd Dynasty (c. 948–715 BC), Bubastis became Egypt's most important royal city. During this period, the Temple of Bastet was rebuilt, particularly under kings Osorkon I (r. c. 927–892 BC) and Osorkon II (r. c. 877–838 BC), with renovations of different kinds continuing through to the reign of King Nectanebo II (r. c. 360–342 BC) of the 30th Dynasty, around 550 years later. Osorkon II also built a small temple to Mahes, Bastet's son, at the north-west side of the main temple. Chapels to other deities, including Atum, stood nearby. A canal, connected to the nearby Pelusiac branch of the Nile, ran around the Temple of Bastet, creating the impression that it sat on an island surrounded by an *isheru*, a form of horseshoe-shaped sacred lake used during rituals particularly connected with feline deities (see, for example, the Mut Temple at Thebes in Chapter 3).

The priesthood of Bastet sometimes appears in fictional tales, reflecting the temple's importance among Egypt's wider population. In the tale of Setna's search for the scroll of Thoth, Tabubu is a daughter of a priest of Bastet (see Chapter 8). And in the Prophecies of Neferty, a tale set in the court of King Sneferu (r. c. 2520–2470 BC) of the Old Kingdom, Neferty is a lector priest of Bastet, who predicts the chaos of the First Intermediate Period and the arrival of King Amenemhat I (r. c. 1994–1964 BC) to restore order.

Herodotus visited Bubastis in the 5th century BC, and regarded its Temple of Bastet – whom he equated with the Greek goddess Artemis – as the most pleasing to look at in Egypt, despite it not being as large or as expensive as others in the country. He describes the temple as standing on an island, surrounded by a stone wall covered in carvings, and with a large outer court decorated with tall figures. The temple stood at a lower level than the city, he notes. He also mentions a grove of trees, which would have had a protective role connected with Bastet, and a road that led from the temple's entrance through the city's marketplace and eastwards to a temple of Hermes (Thoth) – this was no doubt a processional way. A small temple has indeed been found near the main temple, but this was dedicated to Bastet, Amun and Hekenu, rather than Thoth.

▲

Because of its lack of impressive monuments, few visitors explore the Delta, perhaps beyond a short trip to Alexandria on the coast (see Chapter 14), or the **Coptic monasteries of Wadi Natrun**. Like the rest of Egypt, the Delta's cities and regions were once home to great temples – the cult centres of prominent gods and goddesses. Of these, **Bubastis** (modern Tell Basta, ancient Per Bast) has recently been redeveloped. When visiting the site, you can walk among carefully placed artefacts in the **open-air museum**, including stone blocks inscribed with hieroglyphs, seated statues with eroded faces, and a **colossal carving of a 19th Dynasty queen**. Beyond are the ruins of the **Temple of Bastet**, destroyed during an earthquake around 2,000 years ago. Its stonework lies spread across a field like a giant jigsaw puzzle. Bubastis is rarely visited, providing a quite different experience from the often overcrowded tombs and pyramids to the south.

The base of a colossal statue of King Ramesses II at Pi-Ramesses (modern Qantir), all that remains of the royal city above ground at the site.

13

PI-RAMESSES

〰〰〰〰〰〰〰

Legends of Ramesses
and a Home for Seth

〗

'His Majesty – life, prosperity, health! – has built a mansion.
Its name is "Great-of-Victories". It is between Djahy [southern Levant]
and Egypt, and is filled with food and provisions. Its condition is like southern
Heliopolis [Thebes], and its lifespan is like the Temple of Ptah [in Memphis].
The sunlight rises on its horizon, and it rests within it. Everyone has abandoned
their towns and they have established [themselves] in its districts.'

Papyrus Anastasi II, c.1200 BC.

I'm visiting Pi-Ramesses, royal city of King Ramesses II (r. *c.* 1279–1212 BC)
and one of the greatest metropolises on earth in the late Bronze Age.
Yet there's no visitor's centre, no museum, and no ticket to enter the
area. This is probably because the only thing left to see is a pair of stone
feet in a field. Today, the farming village of Qantir marks the spot where
once stood grand palaces, garrisons, villas and temples. Beneath pleasant white clouds, I walk along a palm-lined canal, overlooking fields
of rice, corn, wheat, onions and garlic. Then down a dusty street of
concrete apartment blocks, where small shops sell ice cream, crisps,
washing powder and phone accessories. A road following the canal
connects the village to the nearby city of Faqus. Tuc-tucs and mini-
vans – the local buses – rush up and down, competing with an inordinate
number of 1960s Mercedes-Benzes that offer private rides in classic,
red-leather-lined splendour. Qantir is a charming village, much like
many others in this part of Egypt, but it's perhaps no longer fit for a
king. The passing of 3,000 years can change a place.

When Ramesses built Pi-Ramesses – 'The House of Ramesses' – on
top of his ancestral home in the eastern Delta, it was Egypt's latest

mega-city, strategically located as the perfect launching point for military campaigns into the Levant. As in any self-respecting Egyptian city, there were various temples, including, quite unusually, two dedicated to the god Seth. Son of Geb and Nut, brother of Osiris, Isis and Nephthys (who was also his wife), uncle to Horus, murderer of Osiris; to some, Seth looms large in the Egyptian pantheon as a devilish figure – a force of evil only outdone by the chaos snake Apophis. While it's true that Seth killed his brother and stole the throne of Egypt, the Egyptians didn't regard him as a solely negative force in the cosmos. Ramesses II's family had a particular devotion to Seth; his father was even called Seti, meaning 'The Man of Seth'. This isn't because the royal family weren't aware of Seth's negative aspects – throughout Seti's royal tomb in the Valley of the Kings, the word Seth is replaced with Osiris, because any mention of Seth would have upset *maat*, causing danger to the dead king. It's because Seth had long been worshipped in the north-east Delta. Even bad gods – or should I say, misunderstood gods – need a home.

The god Seth: evil, or misunderstood?

Evidence for Seth dates back to the Early Dynastic Period, centuries before the first mention of Osiris, making him one of the earliest known Egyptian gods. He's referred to as 'Lord of Naqada', a town in Upper Egypt, from as early as the 3rd Dynasty, and King Peribsen (r. *c.* 2650 BC) of the 2nd Dynasty had an image of Seth shown above his name in place of the traditional image of Horus. This depiction shows the 'Seth animal' already in the form that we find for the next 3,000 years: donkey-like, with an upright tail, squared ears and a long snout. Seth bears this animal's head when shown with a human body too. Much ink has been spent trying to determine the inspiration for the 'Seth animal', but the general consensus is that it's an invented creature. Seth can also be shown as a pig, crocodile, donkey or hippopotamus, and like the mythological beasts that the Egyptians envisioned living in the desert – winged snakes, for example – he could be described or shown with wings. Sometimes crocodiles are said to be Seth's messengers or his followers (particularly at Edfu), while other times they're his children, such as the crocodile god Maga, possibly his son with the goddess Nephthys.

Seth's relationship with Nephthys, his sister and wife, was tumultuous to say the least. She abandoned him to protect and help regenerate the body of Osiris – their brother, with whom she had committed adultery, leading to the birth of Anubis. Nephthys was a protector of the

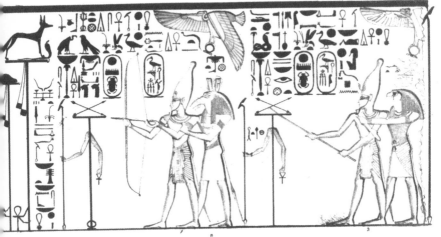

THE GODS INSTRUCTING THE KING IN THE USE OF THE BOW. KARNAK

Carving of the god Seth teaching King Tuthmosis III to shoot an arrow.
From the Temple of Karnak, Thebes.

pharaoh and represented the sun god's night barque. Plutarch saw her as a form of Nike, the Greek incarnation of victory. The Levantine goddess Anat is also sometimes said to be Seth's wife. She, along with the similarly foreign Astarte, are both offered to Seth as wives in the tale known as 'The Contendings of Horus and Seth' (see Chapter 2) – more on these goddesses below.

In myth, Seth is a force of aggression. He is testosterone-led violence, strength, a trickster, and yet a little bit dim. He was a god of thunder and storms, and while Horus ruled Egypt as king, Seth represented the lands beyond – the harsh deserts, oases and foreign countries. He even caused nightmares (for which the solution was to pray to Horus – give it a go next time you have a bad dream). Violence was part of Seth's nature from the start of his life. His birth was the beginning of turmoil, according to one spell. In the Pyramid Texts, Seth tore himself from his mother Nut, while according to Plutarch, Seth burst from Nut's side. The culmination of Seth's aggression was his murder of Osiris, his usurpation of Egypt's throne, his imprisonment of Isis and Nephthys in the spinning house of Sais, his attempts to kill Horus, and his rape of Isis – an event known from the Delta Mythological Manual, in which Isis tightly grasps Seth's penis with her vaginal muscles until she is freed. According to the Turin Papyrus, Seth ruled

Egypt for 100 years from Osiris' death to the reign of Horus. Other sources describe this as a time of misery, violence and chaos.

To the Egyptians, such aggressive behaviour was a necessary aspect of the cosmos; violence *was* sometimes the answer. Seth used his violent nature to protect the sun god on his travels, just as the king used violence to defend Egypt's borders. Kings likened themselves to Seth in war texts, prayed to him, and during the Ramesside Period, one of the army divisions was named after Seth. A relief at Karnak shows Seth teaching King Tuthmosis III (r. *c.* 1479–1424 BC) to shoot arrows, like a father with his child. Peace and violence, order and chaos, disturbance and calm – each required the other to exist. Order – *maat* – required balance. The *sema-tawy* motif found in Egyptian art, representing the unification of Egypt, includes both Horus and Seth as symbols of the united country – an acceptance of the importance of both elements for balance. This is why Seth was a deity worthy of worship. Horus might be the brains, but Seth was the muscle. Egypt needed both.

The demonization of Seth only really became fashionable from the Third Intermediate Period onwards, when texts began to present him as an evil character. The 'Revelations of the Mysteries of the Four Balls', for example, describes Seth as losing his job as protector of the sun god on his boat. Seth was driven from Re's boat because of his deeds, it explains. He associated with rebels and cut the boat's rope when it was stuck on a sandbank.

If you're going to antagonize a god, you need some powerful magic to repel him. To defeat Seth and his followers, priests across Egypt performed rituals recorded in the 'Rite of Overthrowing Seth and his Confederates'. To ensure that everyone understood the hatred for Seth, the text provides some mythological background. Seth fought in the womb, it says, and is one who acts violently and violates the law. He robs, causes disputes, and is a lord of *isfet* (disorder). He attacked temples and screamed in their sanctuaries. Seth's crimes led him to be brought before Re and judged by Thoth. But though his punishment was for him to be given to the devourer, he ended up exiled in Asia. While people across Egypt celebrated Seth's removal, cities loyal to him fell into a sorry state: Aphroditopolis became deserted; Ombos was flattened, its houses and inhabitants destroyed; the people of Oxyrhynchus cried. But this wasn't the end. Some time later, Seth returned to Egypt to cause chaos. Among his violent acts, he incited rebellion in Ankh-Tawy, stole wood from Sais, shouted in Busiris, and even ate a sacred *abdu*-fish! (How dare he!) Seth's return was an offence to the sun god, who had banished and cursed him, but Re was unaware of his arrival until Isis shouted to the sky. Isis now used her magic to repel Seth. She invoked various gods to help protect Egypt at its borders in all directions, and forced Seth to remain in foreign lands until his death.

The secret name of Seth

Despite Horus and Seth's often strained relationship, the two gods did occasionally enjoy one another's company. On one occasion Horus and Seth went sailing together in a golden boat. During the voyage, Seth was bitten by a creature, leaving Horus with no choice but to use his magic to cure his uncle. 'For my magic to work, I need to know your true, divine name,' Horus said. Now, it must be remembered that the names we know for Egyptian gods are not their true names; they kept these hidden in their bellies, for if their true names became known, they could be used to control them. Seth was understandably reluctant – after all, he and Horus hadn't always been on the best of terms. He blurted out various names, but Horus knew full well that none of these was Seth's true name. Each time, he simply questioned Seth again. Eventually, Seth gave up. 'My true name is "Evil Day",' he said. Finally, Horus could cure his uncle.

Temples to Seth and offerings of fossils

Temples to Seth weren't exclusive to Pi-Ramesses. King Tuthmosis I (r. c. 1503–1491 BC) built one at Naqada, Ramesses II one at Matmar, and the Wilbour Papyrus refers to a Temple of Seth at a place called Sepermeru, where there was a temple to Nephthys too. Because of Seth's connection with the desert, his temples tended to be built at the starting point of caravan routes, which explains the god's popularity at the Dakhla Oasis. This was a major trading centre for goods entering Egypt from the south-west, where Seth was called 'Lord of the Oasis'. A temple of Seth stood at the city of Mut in Dakhla from the 18th Dynasty through to the Roman Period. Stelae from this city record that Seth made an oracular announcement during the reign of King Shoshenk I (r. c. 948–927 BC), while under King Piye (r. c. 752–721 BC), a priest of Amun and Seth dedicated land to the Temple of Seth at Mut. Other Seth priests at Mut include Khay, who carved his autobiography on a stele, and the high priest of Seth Penbast, known from a votive statue.

Unusually (and intriguingly), the Egyptians seemingly offered fossils to Seth at Qau el-Kebir and Matmar, both sites in Middle Egypt. At Qau el-Kebir, archaeologists found two large groups of fossils in reused tombs. These had apparently been thrown into the tombs during the early 19th Dynasty. The fossils were primarily hippopotamus, but there were also boars and crocodiles, among other animals (and some human bones too). They were intermingled with artefacts of hippopotamus ivory, the majority for cosmetic use. One of the groups contained up to a few thousand kilograms of fossilized bones, while in the other, some of the bones had been wrapped in linen. At nearby Matmar's Temple of Seth, archaeologists excavated a pit containing similar fossilized bones and ivory artefacts, specially dug to receive the items. Though the pit had been recently robbed, the team still managed to recover around 500 kilograms (1,100 pounds) of bones. Linen fragments and reports from locals suggested that these had again been wrapped. Another pit may have existed within the enclosure of the Temple of Seth, for fragments of bones were found in three areas there, each disturbed and so removed from their original location.

Many of the fossilized bones discovered at Qau el-Kebir and Matmar were black in colour, heavy, and polished from spending millennia underwater. They represent animals that had lived from 5,000,000 years ago to as recently as 12,000 years ago. As to why the Egyptians offered these fossils to Seth, we can only guess. The original excavators speculated that because Seth was sacred in that part of Egypt, and because hippopotami received veneration under the 19th Dynasty and were associated with Seth, local people gathered the fossilized bones and buried them as relics. They perhaps regarded them as the bones of Seth – gods being larger than humans and their bones made of iron.

Anat and Astarte: foreign deities in Egypt

As already mentioned, one of Seth's wives was the Levantine goddess Anat. Ramesses II had a particular liking for Anat. He built a temple to her at Pi-Ramesses, described himself as beloved of the goddess, and named one of his dogs 'Anat Protects'. He even called one of his daughters Bintanath and a son Mahiranat, each referencing the goddess. Ramesses' love of Anat is probably due to her protection and power in war. She was a Levantine warrior goddess, who carried a spear, and is described as a woman who acts like a man. She wore the *atef*-crown of Osiris, and was a daughter of Re.

The relationship between Seth and Anat inspired a New Kingdom tale, revealing Seth to be hardly a model husband. A seed goddess – the Egyptian word for seed here, *metut*, having the double meaning of poison – was washing herself on the river shore, purifying her body. When Seth wandered by, he spotted the goddess and particularly admired her buttocks. He immediately mounted her like a ram. But the seed gave him a headache, making him so sick that he had to go home and lie down. Anat, Seth's wife, went to visit Re. 'I've set for the day,' Re said, exhausted after a long shift shining in the sky. 'But I know that you want Seth to be freed from the seed. Perhaps his foolishness will teach him something. The seed is married to a moon god, who can only have sex with her with fire.' As Re spoke, Isis manifested in the form of a Nubian woman. She removed the seed from her suffering brother and returned him to health.

The Levantine goddess Astarte was also prominent in Egypt during the New Kingdom and had a temple at Pi-Ramesses. Like Anat, she was a warrior, worshipped for her martial qualities, and a daughter of Re offered to Seth as a wife. She stars in a New Kingdom tale with similarities to a myth known from Ugarit in modern Syria. The harvest goddess Renenutet brought offerings of silver, gold and lapis lazuli as tribute to the Sea, ruler of the earth and sky. She then sent birds to the goddess Astarte – who, like most deities, lived in the sky – with a message: 'If you're asleep, wake up! The divine Ennead must offer tribute to the Sea.' After hearing the news, Astarte descended to the earth, and stood on the shore to speak with the Sea. The Sea now changed his demand: he wanted the Ennead to give Astarte to him in marriage. Surprised, Astarte returned to the Ennead in the sky. They gave her the Sea's tribute and added their own jewelry, perhaps in the hope of appeasing the Sea and halting the marriage. In the broken fragments that follow, Seth is mentioned. We don't know how the story ended, but with the Sea's demands becoming increasingly ridiculous, the Ennead may have called on Seth to do battle for them, in the same manner that Baal fights the Sea in the version of the tale from Ugarit.

The presence of foreign gods in Egypt was not unusual during the New Kingdom, a period when Egypt's interactions with other countries expanded significantly and there was an increasing foreign population. Baal, the Levantine god of fertility and weather, was among those that grew in popularity. From the Second Intermediate Period, Baal was associated with Seth, perhaps because both were gods of thunderstorms, though in Egypt he became more of a warrior and protector, representing the king's bravery. Other foreign gods also changed their original function during their assimilation into the Egyptian pantheon: Reshef, a god of war, plague and fire in his Levantine homeland, became a god of healing; while the god Hauron, associated with deserts, magic and illness in the Levant, became a royal guardian, and protected ordinary people from demons. He was particularly popular at Giza, where he was connected with Horemakhet – the Great Sphinx. Ramesses II commissioned a statue of himself as a child, protected by the falcon

Hauron. This once stood at Pi-Ramesses and was later found at Tanis. It is now in the Egyptian Museum, Cairo.

Legends of the Egyptian kings Sesostris and Rhampsinitus

Seth, Astarte and Anat weren't the only deities worshipped at Pi-Ramesses. There were also temples to the goddess Wadjet and the rather all-encompassing Amun-Re-Horakhty-Atum, among others. And we shouldn't forget that Ramesses II himself wanted to be remembered as a divinity. He is a living god in the sanctuary of his temple at Abu Simbel in Nubia, where his image is carved alongside Ptah, Amun-Re and Re-Horakhty. The four sit together in a row, as if waiting for a ride at a bus stop. Elsewhere, he was carved worshipping and offering to himself. Thanks to such efforts, it should come as no surprise that Ramesses entered the realm of legend. By the time of Herodotus' journey around Egypt in the 5th century BC, many stories had grown around famous pharaohs of the past, their deeds lumped together and attributed mainly to the legendary kings Sesostris and Rhampsinitus. As he travelled, Herodotus spoke with the people he met and wrote down their stories, providing insight into how the

The deified King Ramesses II (third from the left) seated beside the gods Ptah, Amun-Re and Re-Horakhty at Abu Simbel.

Egyptians of his time viewed their past. And as he wrote, he filtered their words through his Greek understanding of the world, providing a view into his own mind too.

Herodotus' Sesostris seems to be a fusion of the various king Senwosrets of the 12th Dynasty (plus perhaps a couple of later kings with different names, including Ramesses II). But where these kings campaigned in Nubia and the Levant, expanding Egypt's influence, the legendary Sesostris managed to conquer the known world. The story, told to Herodotus by Egyptian priests, goes as follows: after conquering the people of the Red Sea, Sesostris marched across the land as far as Europe, defeating various nations and tribes along the way, including the Scythians and Thracians. In each conquered territory, he erected a pillar inscribed with the details of how he beat them (with the addition of carved vaginas for those peoples he regarded as cowardly, apparently). Upon Sesostris' return to Egypt, his brother – who had been ruling the country in his absence – invited him and his wife and sons to a banquet at his home. While the royal family stood inside, patiently waiting for the event to begin and wondering what delights might be served up, the brother piled wood against the house and set fire to it. The house began to burn down around the family. As orange flames soared, and the ceiling began to fall, Sesostris' wife made a surprising suggestion: two of their six sons should lie down on the fire – their bodies would create a bridge for the others to walk over. The two sons that volunteered burned to death, while the rest of the family fled to safety.

After killing his treasonous brother, Sesostris put his foreign captives to work. They were forced to drag stone blocks to the Temple of Ptah and to dig canals that would provide water to towns far from the Nile. He then assigned each Egyptian an equal piece of land, and taxed their produce each year. If the Nile encroached on any person's fields, the king's men investigated and reduced the tax accordingly. Afterwards, to commemorate his rule of Nubia, Sesostris erected two colossal statues of himself and his wife in front of the Temple of Ptah. There were smaller statues of his sons too. Later, when the Persian King Darius (r. *c.* 521–486 BC) wanted to erect a statue of himself on the same spot, the priests of Ptah stopped him. They argued that although Sesostris had conquered as much land as the Persian ruler, he had also defeated the Scythians, something that Darius had failed to do. It seems probable that the Egyptians developed much of this legend to ensure that Sesostris always outdid the great deeds of the unpopular Persian kings.

After telling the story of Sesostris, Herodotus relates the tales of King Rhampsinitus, a fusion of the eleven Ramesses of the 19th and

20th Dynasties. Rhampsinitus owned so much silver – more than even his successors would ever accrue – that he hired a builder to construct a stone treasure chamber in his palace to store it. Although skilled, the builder wasn't entirely trustworthy. He designed the treasury so that one of its walls faced the street outside, and ensured that one stone there could be removed, giving him easy access to the royal treasure. The project took years to complete, and the builder grew old. Reaching the end of his life, he summoned his two sons. He told them of the treasury's secret entrance, where to find the stone, and how to remove it. Once their father had died, the two sons put his plan into action: they visited the palace, removed the stone, and stole some of the king's beloved silver.

The next morning, the king visited his treasury. When he found a portion of his silver missing, he was confused. The chamber's seals were intact. How could a thief have broken in? But with each passing day, a little more silver disappeared from the treasury. The king had to act, so he set a trap for the thieves. That night, the brothers sneaked into the chamber again. They moved stealthily in the darkness. But as one of them approached a pot filled with silver, he accidentally sprung the trap. He couldn't move. 'Quickly, come to me,' he said to his brother. 'If you cut off my head, no one will recognize me. The king won't be able to connect me to you.' The brother – we must assume with sadness and hesitancy – did as suggested. He ran from the treasury, carrying the severed head. The next morning, the king entered the chamber to find his silver depleted once more. And to make matters worse, there was a decapitated corpse on the floor. 'Hang the body from the palace walls,' he yelled. 'If you see anyone crying in front of it, arrest them!'

That day, the thief's mother was out walking beside the palace, when she spotted her son's body hanging from its walls. She ran to confront her surviving son. 'If you don't find a way to get your brother's body down, I will go to the king and tell him everything I know about the treasure,' she said. The thief tried to convince his mother that it was too late. That nothing could be done. But he eventually gave up and set about retrieving his brother's corpse. Luckily, he had a plan. He loaded his asses with skins of wine, and when nearing his brother's body, released the skins, so that the wine flowed to the ground. He pretended to panic. The palace guards ran towards him – not to help, but to catch the wine in their cups. He pretended to be angry with the guards, and allowed them to convince him that all was well. He offered them another skin of wine, and they drank together and laughed. Eventually, the guards passed out asleep. This was the thief's chance: he cut down his brother's body, placed it on the asses' backs, and fled home.

Rhampsinitus was furious. The thief had outsmarted him. But he had one more plan. The king asked his daughter to offer to have sex with any man who told her the greatest crime he had ever committed and his cleverest trick. If she heard the thief's story, she was to grab him and stop him from escaping. The thief learned of the king's scheme, and decided to have some fun. He cut an arm from a fresh corpse (not that of his brother), and with the arm hidden under his cloak, visited the princess. 'What is the greatest crime you've ever committed?' she asked. 'Cutting off my own brother's head when he was trapped in the king's treasury,' the thief said. 'And your cleverest trick?' 'Getting the royal guards drunk, and cutting down my brother's body.' The princess leapt forward and grabbed the thief. He turned and ran, escaping through the door. She was left alone, holding only the severed arm. The king wasn't angry when he learned what had happened. Quite the opposite: he was impressed by the thief's ingenuity. He sent messengers across the land, telling his people that the thief had been pardoned and would be given a great reward. Trusting Rhampsinitus, the thief returned to the palace, where he was given the princess in marriage.

Pi-Ramesses in the Bible

One of the reasons that Pi-Ramesses continues to be widely known today is due to its appearance in the biblical Exodus narrative, in which Moses leads the Israelites out of Egypt. Pi-Ramesses isn't explicitly named in the text in this manner, but there is mention of a store or treasure city called Raamses in Exodus 1:11, which is said to have been built by the Israelites. This city appears again in Exodus 12:37, as the location from which the Israelites begin their escape from Egypt. These references have led many people (and particularly movie-makers) to date the Exodus to the reign of Ramesses II, despite this king not being mentioned by name in the text (in fact, Egypt's king is not named at all). No evidence for either the Exodus or the ten plagues has been discovered at the site. If you pass through Qantir, site of ancient Pi-Ramesses, you won't find any piles of dead frogs or locusts, or rivers filled with blood, just a lively village and perhaps some friendly archaeologists.

Pi-Ramesses in history and today

Before Pi-Ramesses' development under the 19th Dynasty, the area experienced a period of significance as Avaris (modern Tell el-Daba), capital of the Hyksos – Egypt's foreign rulers during the Second

Intermediate Period. In this time, a temple to Seth (with its own vine-yards) stood close to the city centre. This continued in use into the time of Pi-Ramesses, when this new city enveloped it. A stele, today called the 400 Year Stele, dated to the reign of Ramesses II, once probably stood at this temple. It shows Seth wearing a high crown with a streamer, copying the style of Near Eastern deities. The Hyksos had associated Seth with Baal, the Near Eastern god of weather and fertility, a connec-tion that continued after their removal from Egypt.

During the early 19th Dynasty, King Seti I (r. c. 1296–1279 BC) built a palace at Qantir. Nonetheless, it was Ramesses II who transformed this location into Pi-Ramesses ('The House of Ramesses'), a major royal city of the ancient world, with its centre just north of Avaris. Ramesses knew that this city, built on his family's home territory, would be the perfect strategic location for launching military expeditions into the Levant. One ode to Pi-Ramesses describes the city as full of food. The sun rose and set there, and everyone was leaving their own towns to go and live there, either because it was such an attractive place to be, or because the city needed workers. There was a temple of Amun, a temple of Seth (the same as the earlier one at Avaris), a temple of Astarte, and a temple of the goddess Wadjet. Another text describes Pi-Ramesses

The ruins of Tanis. Much of the stonework from Pi-Ramesses was reused at Tanis, and can still be seen there today.

Key dates and remains

c. 1950 BC	Settlement founded at Avaris (Tell el-Daba).
c. 1650 BC	Region around Avaris becomes an independent kingdom, ruled by the Hyksos.
c. 1540 BC	The Hyksos are expelled from Egypt by King Ahmose I. The Temple of Seth continues to operate at Avaris.
c. 1460 BC	King Tuthmosis III builds a palace with Minoan frescoes at Avaris.
c. 1296 BC	King Seti I builds a palace at Qantir.
c. 1279 BC	King Ramesses II starts building the city of Pi-Ramesses at Qantir. It boasts temples to various gods, palaces, housing, chariot workshops and royal stables. The earlier Temple of Seth at Avaris is enveloped by this new city.
c. 1050 BC	Pi-Ramesses is abandoned. Its stonework is transported to Tanis.

as such a wonderful place that no other existed like it. It was laid out like Thebes and founded by Re himself. There was plenty of food, pools with birds, and ponds filled with fish. A final ode says that the city had beautiful balconies and radiant halls of lapis lazuli and turquoise, and mentions its impressive chariotry, army and ships.

Today, the only physical evidence that the ancient city ever existed at Qantir is hidden beneath the village and its fields. Excavations have unearthed stables, training grounds, chariot workshops, part of a monumental building that may have been a temple or a palace, a well, part of a royal archive, and even the door post of a house belonging to a chief of Sidon (a city in Lebanon). Caesium magnetometry scans, peering beneath the ground, have revealed the tantalizing impressions of houses, villas, administrative buildings, a cemetery and perhaps even palaces, all spread over a vast area. This was a city of planned and organic sectors, with tree-lined streets and housing for the country's elite – charioteers, architects and viziers – and for the poor. So far, only a cemetery of mostly simple pit graves has been uncovered, though other burials no doubt existed close to the city too. Textual sources tell us that the Egyptians worshipped many gods at Pi-Ramesses, but identifying the various temples is difficult. A structure in a part of the site called Tell Abu el-Shaf'ei may have been the Temple of Wadjet, described as being located in the north of Pi-Ramesses, and the location of the Temple of Seth is known, but the others haven't yet been discovered. Of these lost temples, the city's most important was dedicated to Amun-Re-Horakhty-Atum, which stood at its centre. A second temple to Seth was dedicated to 'Seth of Ramesses of Pi-Ramesses'. There's much left to discover, and archaeological investigations continue.

Don't lose heart, Ramesses fans. If you still want to get a feel for Pi-Ramesses' once majestic appearance, you can travel to Tanis, 35 kilometres (22 miles) north of Qantir. Here, you'll find one of Egypt's largest archaeological mounds (and the site where Indiana Jones discovered the Ark of the Covenant in the 1981 movie *Raiders of the Lost Ark*). Tanis' excavator in the 1940s, the Egyptologist Pierre Montet, believed this to be Pi-Ramesses, and with good reason: many of the impressive architectural remains bore the name of Ramesses II. It was only decades later that archaeologists realized Montet's mistake: these remains indeed were the shattered visage of Pi-Ramesses, but they weren't in their original location. After the Nile tributary that flowed around Pi-Ramesses silted up at the end of the New Kingdom, the Egyptians dragged its stonework to Tanis, creating a new city on a spot still suitable for shipping. It's an ancient example of smart recycling. This new, yet simultaneously old, settlement then became a major city during the Third Intermediate Period, and a place of royal burial.

▲

There really isn't much to see at Pi-Ramesses (Qantir) beyond a **pair of stone feet in a field**, so if you want to surround yourself with some of the ancient city's remains, you'll need to travel to nearby **Tanis**, where much of Pi-Ramesses' stonework was dragged. Walking among the ruins at Tanis, you'll see scattered stone fragments, weathered statues of kings, column capitals, fallen obelisks, and the **tombs of six 21st and 22nd Dynasty pharaohs**, once filled with treasures (now in the **Egyptian Museum in Cairo**). Certain columns and obelisks have been re-erected. The city also had its own temple of Amun-Re – a northern counterpart to the more famous temple at Thebes – that flourished during the Third Intermediate Period, and remained significant into Roman times. Obelisks, originally from Pi-Ramesses and moved to Tanis, can be seen re-erected at Tahrir Square in Cairo and in New Alamein City.

Pompey's Pillar, one of the few remaining standing
monuments of ancient Alexandria.

14

ALEXANDRIA

~~~~~~~~~~~~~~~~~~~~

Serapis, Cleopatra
and Alexander's Lost Tomb

ß

'[Alexander] intended to build a great city.... He directed the overseers of this
work to build it between the marshes and the sea, and measured out the ground
himself, and marked out the streets, and called it Alexandria, after his own
name.... By many it is reported to be one of the greatest and most noble cities in
the world; for beauty, rich revenues, and plentiful provision of all things for the
comfortable support of man's life, far excelling all others.'

Diodorus Siculus, *The Historical Library*, Book 17, c. 1st century BC.

It is sunset in Alexandria. Below an eroded sea wall, waves splash against
rocks and slide along sand. The harbour curves like a crescent moon,
stretching from the Citadel of Qaitbay at its west end to the Bibliotheca
Alexandria to the east. Young couples sit on the wall, admiring the
view, chatting among themselves. Palm trees sway. Silhouettes of ships
hover on the horizon. Behind me, cars beep and dance along 26 July
Road, overtaking trotting horse-drawn carriages. Beyond, modern
apartment blocks mingle with buildings constructed a century ago,
during a period of renewal. From the curving Corniche, to the road
and the buildings overlooking it, this is a 19th- and 20th-century vision
of an Alexandria reborn; so that, despite its antiquity, the city feels
young. This modernity has come at a price: much of ancient Alexandria
has now vanished, lost beneath the city and the waves, leaving little for
visitors to see of its once renowned splendours.

Still, thanks to the writings of classical authors and the work of
archaeologists, the original plan of ancient Alexandria can be reconstructed. From my vantage point on the Corniche, the Citadel of Qaitbay
stands on the spot where the Pharos Lighthouse, one of the seven

wonders of the ancient world, guided ships to port. The Bibliotheca Alexandria was built in the ancient Royal Quarter, the city sector that covered part of central Alexandria and the Silsileh promontory sticking out into the sea. Here, grand palaces, the Great Library and the Soma – the mausoleum of the Ptolemies and final resting place of Alexander the Great – once wowed ancient visitors. Behind me, Al Nabi Daniel Street has replaced the ancient Street of the Soma, which passed south from the Mediterranean to Lake Mariout. After a short distance, it crosses el-Horeya Road, formerly the Canopic Way, which connected the Moon Gate at the city's west to the Sun Gate in the east. Wherever you go, the ghost of the ancient city is never too far away.

It is here, in Alexandria, that we reach the end of our journey, at the point where Egypt meets the Mediterranean, to explore a time when Greek and Egyptian culture merged to form a curious hybrid, when the new god Serapis entered the pantheon, and where famous personalities, from Alexander the Great to Cleopatra, became legends.

Alexandria's founder myths

When Alexander the Great (r. *c.* 332–323 BC) arrived in Egypt in 332 BC, Egypt was enduring its second, and rather more brutal, phase of Persian rule. It probably isn't simple propaganda when Greek sources say that Alexander met no resistance from the Egyptians; they apparently saw him as a liberator. Even the Persians knew their time was up. Quintus Curtius Rufus, a 1st-century Roman historian, wrote that Mazaces, the Persian satrap of Egypt, crossed the river from Memphis to give Alexander 800 talents and all the royal furniture (I'm assuming that he left the furniture at the palace, though); no support from Persia was coming. It was best to leave with his life. And so began a new era – the Macedonian-Greek rule of Egypt.

Alexander became fascinated by Egypt. He offered a sacrifice to the Apis bull in Memphis, and visited the famous oracle of Zeus Amun at Siwa Oasis. Before leaving the country to continue his empire-building campaigns, he stopped at the sleepy fishing village of Ra-kedet, on the Mediterranean coast, and decided that this was the perfect location for a new port city. He had big plans: this would be a settlement 5 kilometres (3 miles) long and 1.5 kilometres (1 mile) wide, built on a grid system, divided into five sectors with three main districts for Egyptians, Jews and Greeks. The Egyptian sector, named Rakhotis, would stand where Ra-kedet had stood. Alexander decided where temples would be located, and to which deities they would be dedicated. The 1st–2nd-century Greek historian Arrian says that Alexander wanted to

Alexandria's harbour with the Citadel of Qaitbay, original location of the Pharos Lighthouse, visible in the distance.

personally lay out the plan of the city's outer defensive wall on the ground, but lacked any means to do it. Luckily, one of his soldiers devised a plan: he took barley meal from the soldiers' bags and sprinkled it behind Alexander as he walked, leaving a trail. Both Plutarch and Quintus Curtius Rufus tell the same story, but add that birds swooped down to eat all the barley; after some debate, this was regarded as a good omen. The official day of foundation was 7 April 331 BC.

Another tale of Alexandria's founding is given in the *Alexander Romance*, a Hellenistic text that survives in many editions and provides an often fantastical account of the life of Alexander. It goes as follows: during the city's construction, a serpent kept slithering around and scaring the workmen, so much so that they couldn't work. Alexander commanded that the serpent be killed, and the next day, on the spot where the *stoa* (portico) would one day stand, the workmen caught the snake. As ordered, they killed it. Afterwards, Alexander announced that it had been the Agathos Daimon – a good spirit that brought luck, equated by the ancient Egyptians with their god of fate, Shay. He commanded that it be honoured and receive a proper burial. Later, when the workmen were putting down Alexandria's foundations, many snakes appeared and slithered into four houses. These too were recognized as Agathoi Daimones, and because they scared away venomous snakes, Alexander decreed that people should feed them. This became an annual custom.

Alexander at Siwa Oasis: becoming a god

Perhaps the most famous event during Alexander's time in Egypt was his trip to Siwa Oasis to visit the oracle of Zeus Amun, referred to as Zeus Ammon in the classical sources. Arrian provides an account of this desert journey, saying that Alexander wanted to go to Siwa because of the oracle's reputation for always being correct, and to know if he was descended from Amun. (Also, Perseus and Herakles had gone there, and Alexander wanted to equal them.) As Alexander and his troops crossed the desert to the oasis, the track became obscured by wind-blown sand and his guides could no longer lead them. Luckily, Alexander spotted two snakes and suggested that they follow them to the oasis. Arrian notes that in another version of the story, Alexander and his army followed two crows. Whatever the case, it worked, and Alexander safely arrived at the temple. In Diodorus' account, Alexander's army were suffering from thirst in the desert; a rainstorm enabled them to fill up their water skins, but sand dunes now blocked their trail. The guide pointed to a murder of crows in the distance and suggested that these signalled the correct path to the temple. Quintus Curtius Rufus and Plutarch give similar accounts.

When Alexander approached the Temple of Amun in Siwa, he was greeted by eighty priests carrying the statue of Zeus Amun on a golden boat. The statue's body was encrusted with emeralds and precious stones. The god directed the priests' movements, and women sang hymns. Plutarch says that Alexander asked the high priest of Amun whether any of his father's murderers had escaped. The priest was concerned, and asked Alexander to be careful, for his father was not a mortal. Alexander changed his approach, and instead asked if Philip's murderers had been punished, and if he, Alexander, would be lord of mankind. The oracle of the god replied positively, and Alexander celebrated by making offerings to Zeus Amun, and giving money to the priests. Plutarch goes on to ponder whether Alexander believed himself to be a god after his visit to Siwa because of the Siwan priest's bad pronunciation of 'O paidion', meaning 'O my son'. as perhaps 'O pai Dios' – 'O Son of Zeus'.

The ruins of the Temple of Amun still stand at Siwa. It was originally built under King Ahmose II (r. c. 570–526 BC) of the 26th Dynasty, shortly after Siwa became an important stop along the trade route from the recently founded Greek city of Cyrene in Libya. Amun offered oracles in the traditional Egyptian manner: priests carried a divine barque bearing the god's statue, and tipped it backwards or forwards to signal 'yes' or 'no' to questions posed, or towards one of various written answers placed on the floor. The oracle was already famous among the Greeks before Alexander's journey, thanks to the visitations of ambassadors from Cyrene. Athenians visited the temple at Siwa in the 4th century BC, while in the 5th century BC a Persian army, sent by Cambyses II to destroy the oracle, was lost in a sandstorm during their journey through the desert.

The lost tomb of Alexander the Great

When Alexander died unexpectedly in Babylon in June 323 BC, his body was mummified and kept in that city while his followers decided where to bury him. Alexander himself had wanted to be buried at Siwa Oasis, a location that would eternally place him close to his true father, the god Zeus Amun. Perdiccas, regent of the empire since Alexander's death, had other plans. Whoever had the body of Alexander would control a key symbol of his rule. People would flock to visit the corpse; they would offer to it; it would become a sacred cult object. Even more importantly, according to Macedonian tradition, a king buried his predecessor. Whoever buried Alexander would be legitimizing their own position as his heir, and thus their rule. It was probably with these thoughts in mind that Perdiccas commissioned an elaborate hearse, and planned to send the body to the traditional royal burial ground of Aegae in Macedon. But Perdiccas left Babylon on campaign while the hearse was still being made, and once it was ready, men loyal to General Ptolemy, satrap of Egypt, seized it and took Alexander's body to Egypt.

According to the *Alexander Romance*, Ptolemy first buried Alexander's body in Memphis, following instructions given to him by the oracle of Zeus at Babylon. It remained there while a more suitable tomb was constructed in Alexandria. We don't know when Alexander was buried in this new Alexandrian tomb, or its location, but what is clear is that within a century, he was moved again. Ptolemy IV (r. *c.* 222–205 BC) built a new mausoleum in Alexandria to house the bodies of the royal family and Alexander together. His message was clear: the Ptolemies were Alexander's true successors. This new mausoleum was called the Soma (or Sema), was probably cylindrical in shape, and stood somewhere in Alexandria's Royal Quarter. The royal bodies rested below ground, in a rock-cut space, seemingly beneath a pyramidal roof. Initially, Alexander lay there in a gold coffin, but this was later melted down and replaced with a glass one. His body became something of an attraction for the Roman emperors that visited Egypt after the fall of the Ptolemies. Julius Caesar made the journey to see it, as did Augustus, Caligula, (very probably) Hadrian, Septimius Severus and Caracalla.

The Soma was probably destroyed or severely damaged in AD 365, when an earthquake and tsunami hit Alexandria. But Alexander's body may have been saved. The 4th-century Greek rhetorician Libanius refers to it being displayed in Alexandria *c.* AD 390 (though he himself was not an eyewitness). Since then, various attempts have been made to identify the remains of Alexander's tomb in Alexandria. One possibility is the Alabaster Tomb at Chatby, in the eastern part of the city. This forms part of a 3rd-century BC Macedonian-style burial, sometimes argued to be the antechamber to Alexander's tomb. Another is the Attarine Mosque, resting place of the 'Alexander sarcophagus' (for which, see below). A final candidate is the Nabi Daniel Mosque, dedicated to the Prophet Daniel. Some believe that this was built on the site of Alexander's tomb; a connection linked to a local tradition, dated to the 9th century AD, that describes the life of the Prophet Daniel in a similar manner to the exploits of Alexander.

What happened to King Nectanebo II?

In the early 19th century, one of the most famous objects in the British Museum's collection was a sarcophagus, thought, at the time of its removal from the Attarine Mosque of Alexandria, to be the sarcophagus of Alexander the Great. Visitors to the Attarine Mosque had for centuries described a house-like chapel with an Egyptian sarcophagus in its grounds, believed to be the resting place of Alexander. When the French savants of Napoleon's expedition arrived in Egypt in 1798, they removed the sarcophagus from the mosque, only for it to fall into British hands in 1801. From that point, it found its way to the British Museum. Decades later, following the decipherment of hieroglyphs, the sarcophagus's star faded, when it turned out not to belong to Alexander the Great, but to King Nectanebo II (r. *c.* 360–342 BC), last ruler of the 30th Dynasty, who fled Egypt when faced by Persian invasion. As a result, the sarcophagus was never occupied, and today it is mostly ignored – just another sarcophagus in the British Museum's sculpture gallery.

According to the *Alexander Romance*, Nectanebo II had a rather strong connection to Alexander the Great – he, rather than Philip II of Macedon, was his father. The story goes as follows: King Nectanebo II was skilled in magic. Rather than send armies into battle, he would take a bowl of water and fill it with wax images of his enemy's ships and troops. Calling on the spirits, gods and demons, he infused these images with life, so that whenever a ship sank in his bowl, it sank in real life. One day, Nectanebo's informants told him of a great Persian army, 10,000 strong, coming to attack Egypt. Of course, Nectanebo wasn't afraid, he simply went to his palace and prepared his bowl. When he looked into it, he saw that Egypt's gods controlled the Persian ships and their armies. It was the end of Egypt, he realized. So, he did what any noble ruler would do: he took some gold, shaved off his hair and beard, and sailed to Pella in Macedonia, where he began a new life as a priest, advising people on the movement of the stars. Nectanebo didn't tell anyone where he was going, so the people of Egypt were left confused. After the Persian invasion, they asked the gods what had happened to their king. A response came from the oracle of the Serapeum: Nectanebo would return as a young man, not as an old man, and he would defeat the Persians. This just confused the Egyptians even more, but to ensure that everybody remembered the prophecy, they wrote down its words on the pedestal of a statue of Nectanebo. Then, they waited.

In Macedon, Nectanebo became so famous for his prophecies and magic that he came to the attention of Queen Olympias, wife of King Philip II. Philip had left for war, but before departing had told Olympias that upon his return, she must bear him a son or never feel his embrace again. Fearing rejection, she summoned Nectanebo, hoping that he could see the future and advise her on the best course of action. When Nectanebo arrived at the palace, he immediately desired the queen for himself. Using his powers of prophecy, Nectanebo discovered that the only way that she could avoid being rejected by Philip was to become pregnant from sex with an incarnate god. This god would be Amun of Libya, who would take the form of a middle-aged man, with hair and a beard of gold, and golden horns on his forehead. That night, the god embraced Olympias in a dream, so the next day she asked Nectanebo to make him appear again. She wanted to sleep with him. Nectanebo requested a room adjoining her own, where he could make prayers to Amun, and instructed her that when the god arrived, she should cover her face and not look directly at him. Then, using a fleece of sheep's wool with horns, he created a disguise, to make him appear like the god. That night, he entered Olympias' chamber. They had sex, and he told her that she would become pregnant with a child who would become king of the world.

The next morning, Olympias told Nectanebo that the god had visited her that night. She wanted him to appear again. From that point, the visitations became regular, and each time, the queen believed Nectanebo to be the god Amun. As signs of Olympias' pregnancy became more obvious, she asked Nectanebo what she should say to Philip when he discovered the news. Nectanebo told her not to worry: Amun would appear to Philip and explain everything to him. She would not be in trouble. After the queen left, Nectanebo cast a spell on a sea-hawk, and made it learn all the things that he wished Philip to know. The sea-hawk then flew to Philip and spoke to him in a dream. Philip awoke, concerned. He summoned a dream-interpreter, and explained to him that in the dream, he saw a god having sex with his wife. She became pregnant, and then he saw himself sewing up Olympias' body with papyrus. The interpreter listened intently before giving his verdict: Olympias had become pregnant by an Egyptian god, Amun.

When Philip returned from war, he found Olympias anxious. She feared his reaction to her pregnancy. Philip calmed her, saying that it was the god's doing, not hers. But a few days later, he changed his tune. Philip confronted Olympias, announcing that a god had not slept with her, and that he would capture the man who had made her pregnant. Nectanebo overheard the conversation, and devised a plan. While a feast was being held at the palace, Nectanebo transformed into a snake and slithered into the dining hall, hissing at and terrifying the guests. Olympias saw that it was the god, and he slid onto her lap, kissing her with his tongue. Philip watched, at first with annoyance and then amazement, as the snake transformed into an eagle and flew away. Philip interpreted the event as a sign of divine affection, and asked his queen which god had slept with her. 'Amun of Libya,' she replied. When it came time for Olympias to give birth, Nectanebo stood beside her, interpreting the cosmic signs to determine the exact, perfect moment to deliver the child. And when the baby was finally born, Philip was happy; he was now content that the father was a god, and named the boy Alexander.

One night, twelve years later, the young Alexander asked Nectanebo if he could see the stars that the Egyptian priest had been studying. The two walked outside together, and while looking to the sky, Nectanebo explained astrology. Without warning, Alexander grabbed Nectanebo, and shoved him down a pit. The priest smashed his skull at the bottom. 'You are trying to understand heaven, when you don't understand the earth,' Alexander said. Nectanebo was dying. 'I knew this would happen one day,' he told Alexander, 'because I prophesied that I'd be killed by my own son.' How is this possible, Alexander wondered. In his dying moments, Nectanebo told his life story, and Alexander felt affection for his father. He carried the body home, and told his mother the truth about Nectanebo and Amun. She was shocked, but nonetheless, they gave Nectanebo a proper burial in Macedon.

The Serapeum and Serapis

The Serapeum is one of Alexandria's few remaining ancient sites that can be visited by tourists. It is best known today for its 30-metre-high (100-foot) column, erected under the Roman emperor Diocletian (r. *c.* AD 284–305), but popularly known as Pompey's Pillar. As its name would suggest, the Serapeum was dedicated to the god Serapis. His temple boasted a famous statue of the god, since destroyed, and underground passages, which included catacombs for jackal burials, associated with a temple of Anubis, and a subterranean offshoot of the main library of Alexandria. Though little remains at the Serapeum today, you can explore these underground passages.

Who was Serapis? Alexandria, as a newly founded city, needed a god to call its own, one that would be acceptable to both Egyptians and Greeks. Legends spread of a new god introduced into the city. According to Plutarch, King Ptolemy I (r. *c.* 310–282 BC) had a dream in which he saw a colossal statue of the god Pluto in Sinope, a Greek colony in northern Turkey, despite never having seen this statue before or recognizing the god. The statue asked Ptolemy to bring it to Alexandria as soon as possible, so when he awoke, he asked his advisors whether such a statue existed in Sinope. One well-travelled man said that it did, for he had seen it; so the king sent two men to Sinope to steal it. When the statue arrived in Alexandria, the king's advisors confirmed that it depicted Pluto, who in Egypt was known as Serapis. The city's new god had arrived. Tacitus gives a similar account of the statue of Sinope demanding to be brought to Alexandria, but adds that the statue may have been brought from Memphis or Syria instead.

Tacitus says that Serapis could be associated with Asclepius, Jupiter or Osiris, while Plutarch provides various explanations for the god's identity. Dismissing suggestions that the god was a son of Herakles, he says that most priests regarded the god as a merging of Osiris and the sacred Apis bull, the bull being a physical manifestation of Osiris' soul. This is the interpretation usually accepted today. During the Late Period, each Apis bull of Memphis, though a manifestation of Ptah in life, became Osiris in death, creating the god Osor-Hapi. The Greeks transcribed this first as Oserapis, and then as Serapis in Alexandria. Effectively, Ptolemy took a god known to the Greeks in Memphis, and repurposed him for a new, Alexandrian audience.

In Memphis, Osor-Hapi was shown as a mummified man with a bull's head, surmounted by horns, two feathers and a solar disc. But in Alexandria, images of Serapis borrow their iconography heavily from that of Pluto – god of the underworld to the Romans, Hades to the

A bust of the god Serapis, copied from an original sculpted during the late 4th century BC.

Greeks – with a splash of Dionysus. Shown as a bearded man in a Greek robe, Serapis wore a corn measure on his head (or sometimes Osiris' *atef*-crown), and often held a sceptre. As husband to Isis (who became increasingly Hellenized in this period, see Chapter 1) and father of Harpokrates (Horus the Child), his family group mimicked that of Osiris. He was a god of fertility and of the dead, of healing, the sun and royalty. In short, Serapis was a god with many roles, appealing to all, embodying the functions of various ancient Egyptian gods. As time passed, his fame spread across the Mediterranean world and beyond; images of Serapis could be found from York in Great Britain to Bagram in Afghanistan.

Serapis was unusual, in that he was a true fusion of Egyptian and Greek religious traditions, creating something new. For the most part, as we've seen earlier in this book, the Greeks simply equated the Egyptian gods with their own. The Egyptian fertility god Min, for example, typically shown with an erect penis and an upright arm, was thought to be their god Pan. Heryshef, normally depicted as a ram and described in the Coffin Texts as 'Lord of Blood and Butchery', came to be regarded as Herakles. Thoth became Hermes, Hathor and Isis could be Aphrodite, Zeus was Amun-Re, Bastet was Artemis, Neith was Athena, Horus was Apollo and Seth was Typhon.

Kom el-Shugafa: Greek and Egyptian gods in the catacombs

For visitors to Alexandria, the fusion of Greek/Roman and Egyptian mythology is most prominent at the necropolis of Kom el-Shugafa, which dates to the Roman Period and is located close to the Serapeum. After the catacombs were established in the 2nd century AD, wealthy citizens contributed to a fund to secure a proper burial within. But the presence of many smaller burials in its later phases indicates that the catacombs were eventually opened up to wider usage. Then, as now, the main entrance is down a spiral staircase that provides access to an eerie world of burial chambers and empty niches, once filled with bodies, split over three levels. On the first level, there's a banquet hall (*triclinium*), rotunda and burial chambers; the level below features the main burial chamber, built in the style of a classical temple; and the lowest level, where more burials existed, was flooded until recently.

The main burial chamber exhibits a great deal of Egyptian influence. Two statues, sculpted in Egyptian style but with classical-inspired heads, flank the steps down from the rotunda to the burial. The walls of the chamber's entrance are carved with bearded snakes, wearing the Double Crown of Upper and Lower Egypt, while on the entrance's other side (in the burial chamber itself), Anubis and Seth (or possibly another Anubis, it's hard to tell) are shown dressed as Roman soldiers. Each of the three niches in the burial chamber contains a Roman-style sarcophagus, with a carved scene above. The central niche shows Anubis tending to a mummy lying on a lion-headed funerary bier, canopic jars below to contain the internal organs. He is flanked by Horus and Thoth. Both side niches depict Isis-Maat spreading her wings in protection over the Apis bull, who receives an offering from the king.

Meanwhile, in the Hall of Caracalla (also called the Nebengrab) – a separate catacomb entered through a breach in the wall of Kom el-Shugafa's rotunda – the walls of two burial niches are decorated with Egyptian and Greek mythological themes, painted sometime between the late 1st century AD and mid-2nd century AD. In both, the upper scene shows Anubis embalming Osiris, with the Egyptian deities Isis,

Nephthys and Horus present. The scene below depicts episodes from the mythology of Persephone, including her being taken to Hades, the underworld from which she could only return to earth for six months each year – a popular scene in Roman tombs. Artemis, Athena, Aphrodite and Hades all feature in these scenes too.

The death of Cleopatra: myth and reality

Queen Cleopatra VII (r. *c.* 51–30 BC) was the last ruler of the Ptolemaic Dynasty (and apparently the only one of them to learn the Egyptian language). She attempted to revive Ptolemaic power through associations with Rome, leading to relationships with two of the empire's most powerful men, Julius Caesar and later Mark Antony. A propaganda war meant to demonize Antony, initiated by Octavian – Antony's brother-in-law and the future Augustus Caesar – transformed into a true war at the Battle of Actium in 31 BC, when the Romans defeated Antony and Cleopatra's naval fleet. The couple retreated to Egypt, where Antony committed suicide. Shortly afterwards, Cleopatra also ended her own life rather than be paraded through Rome as Octavian's captive. The story goes that under guard and sealed in her own tomb, she allowed herself to be bitten by a poisonous asp that she had smuggled into the chamber. Cleopatra's dramatic suicide-by-snake marked the start of Roman rule in Egypt, and became the stuff of legend, inspiring books, plays, paintings, sculptures, TV series and movies. Is this the way it really happened?

In fact, there's very little evidence to corroborate the story. Strabo, who lived at the time of Cleopatra, wrote that she died either by an asp bite, or by using a poisonous ointment. In his *Parallel Lives*, Plutarch describes Cleopatra testing poisons and venomous creatures on condemned prisoners, and deciding that the asp provided the most tranquil death. He then speculates on what may have happened: an asp was either brought into her chamber in a basket filled with figs or in a water jar, or she stored the poison in a hollow comb in her hair. Whatever the case, there were two slight punctures in her arm, he says. He concludes: no one knows how she died. Cassius Dio, writing in the early 3rd century AD, also says that Cleopatra tested asps and reptiles on people. He suggests that an asp may have been brought into the chamber hidden in a water jar or with some flowers, or perhaps that she kept a pin covered in poison in her hair. He mentions the prick marks on her arm, but adds that Octavian, upon finding Cleopatra dead, summoned the Psylli, experts in sucking out reptile poison from a body, in the hope of reviving her. Their attempts failed.

Modern critics argue that the accounts of Cleopatra's death by asp are all a bit far-fetched. Why use an asp (or indeed, as is more probable, an Egyptian cobra) when a poison would be far more convenient? It's also important to bear in mind that a cobra would be difficult to hide – cobras on average being at least a metre in length – and that cobra poison can lead to a very unpleasant death. A carefully chosen poison would be less painful, more predictable, and easier to carry and hide. So, if the asp (or cobra) never existed, where did the story come from? Plutarch says that Octavian held a parade in Rome after his return from Egypt, in which he exhibited a statue of Cleopatra with an asp – perhaps an Egyptian statue of Cleopatra wearing the royal uraeus on her forehead, the snake that protected pharaohs from their enemies. This could have inspired the asp story.

Alexandria in history and today

Alexandria flourished as one of the ancient world's greatest cities for around 1,000 years, from the time of Alexander the Great into the Byzantine Era. Although the city was founded by Alexander, it was his successors in the Ptolemaic Dynasty that truly brought it to its full potential, particularly Ptolemy I, II and III, with further development under the Romans. Visitors marvelled at its wide streets for horses and carriages, its marble edifices, its elaborate palaces and temples and its

The obelisks better known today as Cleopatra's Needles. The standing obelisk is the one now in New York, while the London obelisk lies buried in the ground on its side, just visible at the bottom right.

ALEXANDRIA

Key dates and remains

332 BC	Alexander the Great annexes Egypt.
331 BC	Alexander founds Alexandria.
323 BC	Alexander dies. General Ptolemy becomes satrap of Egypt.
310 BC	Ptolemy I becomes King of Egypt.
51 BC	Cleopatra VII becomes Queen of Egypt.
48 BC	Julius Caesar travels to Egypt.
41–30 BC	Mark Antony spends time in Egypt.
31 BC	The Battle of Actium.
30 BC	Death of Cleopatra. Egypt becomes part of the Roman empire.
AD 116	Jewish rebellion defeated by Trajan and destruction of Alexandria's Jewish quarter.
215	Violence during Emperor Caracalla's visit to Alexandria.
272	Ptolemaic palace complex damaged during Emperor Aurelian's recapture of the city from the Palmyrene empire.
297/8	Emperor Diocletian retakes Alexandria from rebel L. Domitius Domitianus.
365	Alexandria hit by a devastating tsunami and earthquake.
389	The burning of the Serapeum.
391	Pagans and Christians clash. Pagans hide in the Serapeum.
641	Alexandria taken by the Arab army of General Amr ibn al-As.

bustling markets. The city's harbour was split in two by the Heptastadion, an embankment connecting the Alexandrian coastline with Pharos Island. On this island, the Pharos Lighthouse guided ships to port, the busy international trade bringing great wealth to the city. Meanwhile, the Great Library and Museon were their own beacons, summoning intellectuals from across the world, leading to advances in all fields, from science, astronomy, medicine, engineering, mathematics and geography to music, literature and philosophy.

Although distinctly Greek in design and architecture, there was an ancient Egyptian influence on Alexandria too. Dotted among the Greek buildings and squares were ancient Egyptian statues, sphinxes and obelisks brought to decorate the city from across the country (but particularly Heliopolis). Religious architecture differed in style too: Egyptian temples to Isis mingled with Greek temples to Poseidon (built close to the sea, of course), Pan (apparently offering good views of the city, according to Strabo), Hephaestus, Hermes, Nemesis and Tyche, among others. Under the Romans, the main centre of emperor worship was the Caesareum, from where the two 'Cleopatra's Needles' (a pair of obelisks originally erected in Heliopolis) were sent to New York and London. The temples we know of in Alexandria are only a fraction of those that once existed; the 12th-century AD *Notitia Urbis Alexandrinae*, an inventory of the city's monuments, probably based on a 4th-century original, lists 2,478 temples in two districts of the city alone.

Alexandria was designed as a rectangular grid with five districts, in which people of Egyptian, Greek and Jewish backgrounds concentrated in three sectors. These groups, plus immigrants from across the known world, created a vibrant, cosmopolitan atmosphere. By the middle of the 1st century BC, the city had 500,000 inhabitants. To keep everyone in good spirits, Alexandria held grand celebrations, theatrical performances and festivals, including the city's own version of the Olympic Games called the Ptolemaeia. Drinking and partying were a major part of life. (Indeed, the Ptolemies were so fond of Dionysus – Greek god of wine and festivals – that Ptolemy IV (r. *c.* 222–205 BC) established a new society of drinkers in honour of the god.) But there was frequent violence too. The city was known for the aggression of the populace, which could even turn against the ruling Ptolemies. The mob killed Ptolemy XI (r. *c.* 80 BC) after he murdered the much-loved Queen Berenice III. They'd only been married for nineteen days. Extreme violence between the city's various groups, particularly the Greeks against the Jews, and later between pagans and Christians, caused widespread death and destruction.

When Egypt converted to Christianity under the Romans, some ancient sites were transformed into churches. A church of St John the Baptist was built at the Serapeum, for example, and the Caesareum became the Church of St Michael. After the Arab conquest of Egypt in AD 639, Alexandria began a decline that continued into the Ottoman Period (AD 1517–1805). Today, Alexandria is Egypt's second largest city, filled with grand 19th- and 20th-century buildings and known for its rich cultural and intellectual scene, embodied by the new Bibliotheca Alexandria. It continues to thrive as a major port and industrial centre, and attracts tourists from around the world.

▲

Over the years, construction work on roads or buildings and underwater explorations in the bay have revealed pieces of ancient Alexandria. The catacombs of **Kom el-Shugafa**, the temple remains of the **Serapeum** (location of **Pompey's Pillar**) and the Roman amphitheatre at **Kom el-Dikka** are the best preserved and most accessible parts of the ancient city. Divers can experience monuments still preserved underwater; these include sphinxes and statues, just off the coast from **Fort Qaitbey** (originally the site of the Pharos Lighthouse), and further to the east, the remains of what may have been the palaces of the **Royal Quarter**. Although the Great Library of Alexandria disappeared long ago, you can explore its modern descendant, the **Bibliotheca Alexandria**, which houses a small but excellent museum. To see where the sarcophagus of King Nectanebo II (r. *c.* 360–342 BC), now in the British Museum, once stood, you can visit the **Attarine Mosque**. From Alexandria, you can take a bus to **Siwa Oasis** (around eight hours) and visit the ruins of the **Temple of Zeus Amun** (where you can pretend that you're Alexander the Great – proclamations of divinity are not guaranteed).

FURTHER READING

The chronology of ancient Egypt used in this book follows A. Dodson and D. Hilton, *The Complete Royal Families of Ancient Egypt* (London and New York, 2004). There are many good travel guides dedicated to exploring Egypt. One that focuses specifically on travel and archaeology is W. J. Murnane's *The Penguin Guide to Ancient Egypt* (London, 1996). To delve deeper into Egyptian mythology and religion, and to learn more about the deities themselves, the books and articles below are a good starting point.

Egyptian religion and mythology

Bleeker, C. J., *Hathor and Thoth: Two Key Figures of the Ancient Egyptian Religion* (Leiden, 1973).

David, R., *Religion and Magic in Ancient Egypt* (London, 2002).

Dunand, F., 'The Religious System at Alexandria', in D. Ogden (ed.), *A Companion to Greek Religion* (Malden, 2011), pp. 253–63.

Dunand, F. and C. M. Zivie-Coche, translated by D. Lorton, *Gods and Men in Egypt: 3000 BCE to 395 CE* (Ithaca, NY, 2004).

Griffiths, J. G., *The Conflict of Horus and Seth from Egyptian and Classical Sources: A Study in Ancient Mythology* (Liverpool, 1960).

Hart, G., *Egyptian Myths* (London, 1990).

Hornung, E., translated by J. Baines, *Conceptions of God in Ancient Egypt: The One and the Many* (Ithaca, NY, 1982).

Hornung, E., translated by D. Lorton, *Akhenaten and the Religion of Light* (Ithaca and London, 1999).

Kemp, B. J., *How to Read the Egyptian Book of the Dead* (London, 2007).

Lesko, B. S., *The Great Goddesses of Egypt* (Norman, 1999).

Meeks, D. and C. Favard-Meeks, translated by G. M. Goshgarian, *Daily Life of the Egyptian Gods* (London, 1997).

Morenz, S., *Egyptian Religion* (Ithaca, NY, 1973).

Morenz, L. D., 'Apophis: On the Origin, Name, and Nature of an Ancient Egyptian Anti-God', *The Journal of Near Eastern Studies* 63 (2004), pp. 201–5.

Pinch, G., *Egyptian Mythology: A Guide to the Gods, Goddesses and Traditions of Ancient Egypt* (Oxford, 2002).

Pinch, G., *Handbook of Egyptian Mythology* (Santa Barbara, Denver and Oxford, 2002).

Pinch, G., *Egyptian Mythology: A Very Short Introduction* (Oxford, 2004).

Quirke, S., *Ancient Egyptian Religion* (London, 2000).

Quirke, S., *The Cult of Ra: Sun-Worship in Ancient Egypt* (London, 2001).

Raven, M. J., *Egyptian Magic, The Quest for Thoth's Book of Secrets* (Cairo, 2012).

Redford, D. (ed.), *The Oxford Encyclopedia of Ancient Egypt* (3 vols; Oxford, 2001).

Redford, D. (ed.), *The Oxford Essential Guide to Egyptian Mythology* (Oxford, 2003).

Riggs, C., *Ancient Egyptian Magic* (London and New York, 2020).

Ritner, R. K., *The Mechanics of Ancient Egyptian Magical Practice* (Chicago, 1997).

Sandman-Holmberg, M., *The God Ptah* (Lund, 1946).

Sauneron, S., *The Priests of Ancient Egypt* (Ithaca, NY, and London, 2000).

Shafer, B. E. (ed.), *Religion in Ancient Egypt: Gods, Myths, and Personal Practice* (Ithaca, NY, and London, 1991).

Shaw, G. J., *The Egyptian Myths: A Guide to the Ancient Gods and Legends* (London and New York, 2014).

Smith, M., 'The Reign of Seth', in L. Bareš *et al.* (eds) *Egypt in*

Transition: Social and Religious Development of Egypt in the First Millennium BCE (Prague, 2010), pp. 396–430.

Smith, M., *Following Osiris: Perspectives on the Osirian Afterlife from Four Millennia* (Oxford, 2017).

Stevens, A., *Private Religion at Amarna: The Material Evidence* (Oxford, 2006).

Taylor, J. H., *Journey Through the Afterlife: Ancient Egyptian Book of the Dead* (London, 2010).

Tazawa, K., *Syro-Palestinian Deities in New Kingdom Egypt: The Hermeneutics of Their Existence* (Oxford, 2009).

Te Velde, H., *Seth, God of Confusion: A Study of His Role in Egyptian Mythology and Religion* (Leiden, 1967).

Teeter, E., *Religion and Ritual in Ancient Egypt* (Cambridge, 2011).

Tower Hollis, S., *Five Egyptian Goddesses: Their Possible Beginnings, Actions, and Relationships in the Third Millennium BCE* (London, 2019).

Tyldesley, J., *The Penguin Book of Myths and Legends of Ancient Egypt* (London, 2010).

Verner, M., *Temple of the World: Sanctuaries, Cults, and Mysteries of Ancient Egypt* (Cairo and London, 2013).

Wilkinson, R. H., *The Complete Temples of Ancient Egypt* (London and New York, 2000).

Wilkinson, R. H., *The Complete Gods and Goddesses of Ancient Egypt* (London and New York, 2003).

Zecchi, M., *Sobek of Shedet: The Crocodile God in the Fayyum in the Dynastic Period* (Todi, 2010).

Select translations and sources

Allen, J. P., *The Ancient Egyptian Pyramid Texts* (2nd edition; Leiden and Boston, 2015).

Bakir, Abd el-M., *The Cairo Calendar No. 86637* (Cairo, 1966).

Beinlich, H., 'The Book of the Faiyum' in H. Beinlich *et al.* (eds), *Egypt's Mysterious Book of the Faiyum* (Dettelbach, 2013), pp. 27–77.

Borghouts, J. F., *Ancient Egyptian Magical Texts* (Leiden, 1978).

Caminos, R. A., *Late-Egyptian Miscellanies* (London, 1954).

Copenhaver, B. P., *Hermetica: The Greek Corpus Hermeticum and the Latin Asclepius in a New English Translation* (Cambridge, 1992).

De Buck, A., *The Egyptian Coffin Texts*, Vol. I (Chicago, 1935).

Diodorus Siculus, translated by C. H. Oldfather, C. L. Sherman, C. B. Welles, R. M. Geer and F. R. Walton, *Library of History, Books 1–40*, (12 vols; Cambridge, MA, 1933–67).

Faulkner, R. O., *The Ancient Egyptian Coffin Texts* (3 vols; Warminster, 1972–78).

Faulkner, R. O., edited by C. Andrews, *The Ancient Egyptian Book of the Dead* (London, 1996).

Goyon, G., 'Les travaux de Chou et les tribulations de Geb d'après Le Naos 2248 d'Ismaïlia', in *Kemi* 6 (1936), pp. 1–42.

Herodotus, translated by A. D. Godley, *The Histories* (London and New York, 1920).

Hoffmann, F. and J. F. Quack, *Anthologie der Demotischen Literatur: Zweite, neubearbeitete und erheblich erweiterte Auflage* (Berlin, 2018).

Hornung, E., translated by D. Lorton, *The Ancient Egyptian Books of the Afterlife* (Ithaca, New York, 1999).

Jasnow, R. and K.-T. Zauzich, *Conversations in the House of Life: A New Translation of the Ancient Egyptian Book of Thoth* (Wiesbaden, 2014).

Jørgensen, J. B., *Egyptian Mythological Manuals. Mythological Structures and Interpretative Techniques in the Tebtunis Mythological Manual, the Manual of the Delta and Related*

Texts (unpublished PhD thesis; Copenhagen, 2013).

Lichtheim, M., *Ancient Egyptian Literature* (3 vols; Berkeley, 1975–80).

Lloyd, A. B., *Herodotus Book II* (3 vols; London, New York, Cologne, 1975–88).

Manetho, translated by W. G. Wadell, *Aegyptiaca* (London, 1940).

McDowell, A. G., *Village Life in Ancient Egypt: Laundry Lists and Love Songs* (Oxford, 1999).

Meeks, D., *Mythes et légendes du Delta d'après le papyrus Brooklyn 47.218.84* (Cairo, 2006).

Murnane, W. J., *Texts from the Amarna Period in Egypt* (Atlanta, 1995).

Parkinson, R. B., *Voices from Ancient Egypt: An Anthology of Middle Kingdom Writings* (London, 1991).

Parkinson, R. B., *The Tale of Sinuhe and Other Ancient Egyptian Poems, 1940–1640 BC* (Oxford, 1997).

Plutarch, translated by F. C. Babbitt, *Moralia*, Vol V: *Isis and Osiris* (London, 1936).

Quack, J. F. and K. Ryholt, 'Notes on the Setne Story P. Carlsberg 207', in P. J. Frandsen and K. Ryholt (eds), *A Miscellany of Demotic Texts and Studies* (Copenhagen, 2000), pp. 141–63.

Ryholt, K., *The Story of Petese Son of Petetum and Seventy Other Good and Bad Stories (P. Petese)* (Copenhagen, 1999).

Ryholt, K., 'An Elusive Narrative Belonging to the Cycle of Stories About the Priesthood of Heliopolis', in K. Ryholt (ed.), *Acts of the Seventh International Conference of Demotic Studies, Copenhagen, 23–27 August 1999* (Copenhagen, 2002), pp. 261–367.

Ryholt, K., *The Petese Stories II* (Copenhagen, 2006).

Ryholt, K., 'The Life of Imhotep (P. Carlsberg 85)', in G. Widmer and D. Devauchelle (eds), *Actes du IXe congrès international des études démotiques. Paris, 31 août*

– *3 septembre 2005* (Cairo: 2009), pp. 305–15.

Simpson, W. K. *et al.*, *The Literature of Ancient Egypt* (Cairo, 2003).

Smith, M., *Traversing Eternity: Texts for the Afterlife from Ptolemaic and Roman Egypt* (Oxford, 2009).

Spiegelberg, W., *Der Ägyptische Mythus Vom Sonnenauge (Der Papyrus Der Tierfabeln – "Kufi") nach dem Leidener Demotischen Papyrus I 384* (Strasbourg, 1917).

Stoneman, R., *The Greek Alexander Romance* (London, 1991).

Strabo, translated by H. L. Jones, *Geography, Books 1–17* (8 vols; Cambridge, MA, 1917–67).

Vandier, J., *Le Papyrus Jumilhac* (Paris, 1961).

Van Dijk, J., 'Anat, Seth and the Seed of Pre', in H. L. J. Vantiphout *et al.* (eds), *Scripta Signa Vocis; Studies about Scripts, Scriptures, Scribes and Languages in the Near East, Presented to J. H. Hospers by His Pupils, Colleagues and Friends* (Groningen, 1986), pp. 31–51.

Vinson, S., *The Craft of a Good Scribe. History, Narrative and Meaning in the First Tale of Setne Khaemwas* (Leiden, 2018).

Ancient Egyptian archaeology

Arnold, D., translated by S. H. Gardiner and H. Strudwick, *The Encyclopedia of Ancient Egyptian Architecture* (London, 2003).

Bard, K. A. (ed.), *Encyclopedia of the Archaeology of Ancient Egypt* (London, 1999).

Barta, M. and M. Frouz, *Swimmers in the Sand: On the Neolithic Origins of Ancient Egyptian Mythology and Symbolism* (Prague, 2010).

Bietak, M. and I. Forstner-Müller, 'The Topography of New Kingdom Avaris and Per-Ramesses', in M. Collier and S. Snape (eds), *Ramesside Studies in Honour of K. A. Kitchen* (Bolton, 2011), pp. 23–50.

Cauville, S., *Le Temple de Dendera: Guide archéologique* (Cairo, 1990).

El-Daly, O., *Egyptology, The Missing Millennium: Ancient Egypt in Medieval Arabic Writings* (London, 2005).

Hewison, R. N., *The Fayoum, History and Guide* (new revised edition; Cairo, 2001).

Kemp, B. J., *The City of Akhenaten and Nefertiti* (London and New York, 2013).

Kemp, B. J., *Ancient Egypt: Anatomy of a Civilization* (3rd edition; London and New York, 2018).

Kitchen, K., 'Towards a Reconstruction of Ramesside Memphis', in E. Bleiberg and R. Freed (eds), *Fragments of a Shattered Visage, the Proceedings of the International Symposium of Ramesses the Great* (Memphis, TN, 1991), pp. 87–104.

Kurth, D., translated by A. Alcock, *The Temple of Edfu: A Guide by an Ancient Egyptian Priest* (Cairo, 2004).

Lehner, M., *The Complete Pyramids* (London and New York, 1997).

McKenzie, J., *The Architecture of Alexandria and Egypt, c. 300 BC–AD 700* (New Haven and London, 2007).

O'Connor, D., *Abydos: Egypt's First Pharaohs and the Cult of Osiris* (London and New York, 2011).

Official Guidebook of the German Institute of Archaeology, Cairo, Elephantine, The Ancient Town (Cairo, 1998).

Rosenow, D., 'The Great Temple of Bastet at Bubastis', *Egyptian Archaeology* 32 (2008), pp. 11–13.

Rosenow, D., 'Revealing New Landscape Features at Tell Basta' *Egyptian Archaeology* 37 (2010), pp. 17–18.

Shaw, I., *Exploring Ancient Egypt* (Oxford, 2003).

Snape, S. R., *The Complete Cities of Ancient Egypt* (London and New York, 2014).

Strudwick, N. and H. Strudwick, *Thebes in Egypt: A Guide to the Tombs and Temples of Ancient Luxor* (London, 1999).

Thompson, D. J., *Memphis Under the Ptolemies* (2nd edition; Princeton, 2012).

Vivian, C., *The Western Desert of Egypt: An Explorer's Handbook* (Cairo, 2000).

SOURCES OF QUOTATIONS

Translations by the author unless otherwise specified. The original Egyptian passages can be found at the sources given below.

Chapter 1: Aswan
'Isis, the great one...'
Bénédite, G., *Le Temple de Philae*, Part 1 (Paris, 1893), pp. 62–63.

Chapter 2: Edfu
'Sail northward from the south...'
Chassinat, É., *Le Temple d'Edfou*, Vol. VII (Cairo, 1932), p. 4.

Chapter 3: Thebes – East Bank
'Thebes is the pattern for every city...'
Gardiner, A. H., 'Hymns to Amon from a Leiden Papyrus', in *Zeitschrift für Ägyptische Sprache und Altertumskunde* 42 (1905), p. 20.

Chapter 4: Thebes – West Bank
'I oversaw the digging...'
Sethe, K., *Urkunden der 18. Dynastie*, Vol. I (Leipzig, 1906), p. 57.
'See, I do not wish...'
Černý, J. and Gardiner, A. H., *Hieratic Ostraca*, Vol. I (Oxford, 1957), pl. 8, 3.

Chapter 5: Dendera
'O beautiful one...'
Junker, H., 'Poesie aus der Spätzeit', *Zeitschrift für Ägyptische Sprache und Altertumskunde* 43 (1906), pp. 114–16.

Chapter 6: Abydos
'Regarding this cenotaph...'
Sethe, K., *Aegyptische Lesestücke zum Gebrauch im akademischen Unterricht*, 2nd edition (Leipzig, 1928), pp. 80–81.

Chapter 7: Tell el-Amarna
'Making a presentation of many offerings...'
Helck, W., *Urkunden der 18. Dynastie*, Book 22 (Berlin, 1958), pp. 1,983: ll. 1–4; 1,985: ll. 8–15.
'You are far, but...'
Sandman, M., *Texts from the Time of Akhenaten* (Brussels, 1938), p. 93: l. 16.
'You create the land...'
Ibid., pp. 94: l. 17; 95: l. 2.
'When you have risen...'
Ibid., p. 95: ll. 17–18.
'You stand up at dawn...'
Davies, N. de G., *The Rock Tombs of El Amarna*, Part VI (London, 1908), pl. XIV.

Chapter 8: Hermopolis and Tuna el-Gebel
'Thoth, put me in Hermopolis...'
Gardiner, A. H., *Late-Egyptian Miscellanies* (Brussels, 1937), pp. 85–86.
'Hail to you, moon, Thoth...'
Helck, W., *Urkunden der 18. Dynastie*, Book 22 (Berlin, 1958), pp. 2,091: ll. 11, 16; 2,091: l. 19–2,092: l. 4.

Chapter 9: The Faiyum Oasis
'King Unas is Sobek...'
Sethe, K., *Die Altaegyptischen Pyramidentexte*, Vol. 1 (Leipzig, 1908), p. 260 (Spell PT 317, Phrase Pyr. 507b).

Chapter 10: Memphis and its Necropolis
'See, my heart has gone out...'
Gardiner, A. H., *Late-Egyptian Miscellanies* (Brussels, 1937), p. 39.

Chapter 11: Heliopolis
'Hail to you, perfect Re...'
Helck, W., *Urkunden der 18. Dynastie*,
Book 21 (Berlin, 1958), pp. 1,943:
l. 16–1,944: 2; 1,944: ll. 7–14.

Chapter 12: Bubastis
'Don't mock a cat.'
Glanville, S. R. K., *The Instructions
of 'Onchsheshonqy (British Museum
Papyrus 10508)* (London, 1955), pl. 16.
'O Bastet, who comes...'
Naville, E., *Das Aegyptische
Todtenbuch der XVIII. bis XX. Dynastie*,
Vol. I (Berlin, 1886), pl. CXXXV.

Chapter 13: Pi-Ramesses
'His Majesty – life, prosperity,
health...'
Gardiner, A. H., *Late-Egyptian
Miscellanies* (Brussels, 1937), p. 12.

Chapter 14: Alexandria
'[Alexander] intended to build...'
Translation by Booth, G., *The
Historical Library of Diodorus the
Sicilian: In Fifteen Books*, Vol. 2
(London, 1814), pp. 201, 202.

PICTURE CREDITS

Album/Alamy Stock Photo *160*; British Library/Bridgeman Art Library *86*; DEA/ Getty Images *208*; duncan1890/iStock *78–79*; Iri-en-achti/Public Domain *220*; Library of Congress, Washington, D.C. *232*; Metropolitan Museum of Art, New York *161*, *211*; New York Public Library *2, 6, 14, 17, 23, 24, 34, 36, 47, 49, 54, 58, 60, 63, 70, 82, 92, 94, 96, 102, 125, 127, 140, 142, 152, 156, 158, 170, 172, 181, 184, 192, 195, 200, 223, 228, 236, 239, 249*; Staatliche Museen zu Berlin *122*; The Trustees of the British Museum *213*; Universal History Archive/Shutterstock *106, 107, 119*; Vatican Museums/Photo Jastrow 2003 *246*; Werner Forman Archive/Shutterstock *138*; Zu_09/iStock *175*

ACKNOWLEDGMENTS

I'd like to thank my wife Julie Patenaude for reading the early drafts of this book and for providing valuable comments and corrections. My thanks also go to Henning Franzmeier for his Thoth-like wisdom on all things Pi-Ramesses/Qantir. I am grateful to Colin Ridler for inviting me to combine my love of ancient Egypt and travel writing in a single book, and thank Sarah Vernon-Hunt for overseeing the initial phases of the project. Colin's successor, Ben Hayes, steered this book to completion, along with editor Jen Moore, who made the text shine. I thank them and everyone at Thames & Hudson for their guidance, creativity and support. This book was written over the course of a busy three years, encompassing moves from the UK to Germany and then on to France. I wrote the final words in Lille, under lockdown during the COVID-19 pandemic – not the way I'd expected to finish a Traveller's Guide.

INDEX

*To the memory of Léo-Paul Patenaude (1939–2020),
a man who had a book collection to rival the
Great Library of Alexandria.*

Frontispiece: A colossal royal statue, half-buried in front of the
Temple of Luxor.

First published in the United Kingdom in 2021 by
Thames & Hudson Ltd, 181A High Holborn, London WC1V 7QX

Egyptian Mythology: A Traveller's Guide from Aswan to Alexandria © 2021
Thames & Hudson Ltd, London

Text by Garry J. Shaw

Typeset by Mark Bracey

All Rights Reserved. No part of this publication may be reproduced
or transmitted in any form or by any means, electronic or mechanical,
including photocopy, recording or any other information storage
and retrieval system, without prior permission in writing from the
publisher.

British Library Cataloguing-in-Publication Data
A catalogue record for this book is available from
the British Library

ISBN 978-0-500-25228-4

Printed and bound in Printed in China
by Reliance Printing (Shenzhen) Co. Ltd

Be the first to know about our new releases,
exclusive content and author events by visiting
thamesandhudson.com
thamesandhudsonusa.com
thamesandhudson.com.au